THREE CHAPTERS OF

LETTERS

RELATING TO THE

SUPPRESSION OF MONASTERIES.

EDITED FROM THE ORIGINALS IN THE BRITISH MUSEUM

BY

THOMAS WRIGHT, ESQ. M.A. F.S.A. &c.

CORRESPONDING MEMBER OF THE ROYAL INSTITUTE OF FRANCE,
(ACADEMIE DES INSCRIPTIONS ET BELLES LETTRES.)

DA
20
.C17
vol. 26
1968

151786

PRINTED FOR THE CAMDEN SOCIETY,

———

1843.

Reprinted with the permission of The Royal Historical Society

JOHNSON REPRINT CORPORATION   JOHNSON REPRINT COMPANY LTD.
111 Fifth Avenue, New York, N.Y. 10003   Berkeley Square House, London, W.1

RELEASE

ST. JOSEPH'S UNIVERSITY

3 9353 00257 3614

Series No. I, 26

First reprinting, 1968, Johnson Reprint Corporation
Printed in the United States of America

COUNCIL

OF

THE CAMDEN SOCIETY,

FOR THE YEAR 1843-4.

President,

THE RIGHT HON. LORD BRAYBROOKE, F.S.A.

THOMAS AMYOT, ESQ. F.R.S. Treas. S.A. *Director.*

CHAS. FREDERICK BARNWELL, ESQ. M.A. F.R.S .F.S.A.

THE REV. PHILIP BLISS, D.C.L., F.S.A.

JOHN BRUCE, ESQ. F.S.A. *Treasurer.*

JOHN PAYNE COLLIER, ESQ. F.S.A.

C. PURTON COOPER, ESQ. Q.C., D.C.L., F.R.S., F.S.A.

T. CROFTON CROKER, ESQ. F.S.A., M.R.I.A.

SIR HENRY ELLIS, K.H., F.R.S., Sec. S.A.

THE REV. JOSEPH HUNTER, F.S.A.

SIR FREDERICK MADDEN, K.H., F.R.S., F.S.A.

THE REV. LANCELOT SHARPE, M.A., F.S.A.

THOMAS STAPLETON, ESQ. F.S.A.

WILLIAM J. THOMS, ESQ. F.S.A., *Secretary.*

ALBERT WAY, ESQ. M.A. DIR. S.A.

THOMAS WRIGHT, ESQ. M.A., F.S.A.

PREFACE.

By much the greater portion of the following letters has been printed from a volume in the Cottonian Library in the British Museum, (MS. Cotton. Cleopatra, E. IV.) composed of letters and documents, which appear to me to have been selected at some early period from the Cromwell papers, so long preserved in the Chapter House at Westminster, and now lodged partly in the Record Office at the Rolls House, and partly in the State Paper Office. I have added to these a few documents taken from other collections in our national repository, and more especially from the Scudamore Papers, lately added to the treasures of the British Museum.

I leave these letters to tell their own story. They throw light on the history of a great event, which changed entirely the face of society in our island, an event which I regard as the greatest blessing conferred by Providence upon this country since the first introduction of the Christian religion. I will not at present enter into the history of this revolution, but leave the documents for others to comment upon. I have suppressed nothing, for I believe that they contain nothing which is untrue ;

and the worst crimes laid to the charge of the monks are but too fully verified by the long chain of historical evidence reaching without interruption from the twelfth century to the sixteenth. Those who have studied in the interior history of this long period the demoralizing effects of the popish system of confession and absolution will find no difficulty in conceiving the facility with which the inmates of the monasteries, at the time of their dissolution, confessed to vices from the very name of which our imagination now recoils. These documents are of peculiar importance amid the religious disputes which at present agitate the world; and I think that even the various lists of the confessions of the monks and nuns of the several religious houses, entitled *comperta,* and preserved in manuscript, ought to be made public. The great cause of the Reformation has been but ill served by concealing the depravities of the system which it overthrew.

I will only add that I have done what I could, under circumstances, to ascertain the dates of these letters, and arrange them in chronological order. It was the custom at this period in dating letters to write the day of the month without the year, which now gives rise to considerable difficulties. In the description in the Cottonian Catalogue the dates of these letters are thrown into almost hopeless confusion.

TABLE OF CONTENTS.

THREE CHAPTERS OF LETTERS

RELATING TO THE

SUPPRESSION OF MONASTERIES.

CHAPTER I.

THE PERIOD PREVIOUS TO THE PASSING OF THE ACT FOR THE SUPPRESSION OF THE SMALLER MONASTERIES.

ALTHOUGH it is uncertain when the idea of dissolving the Monasteries was first talked of, it is certain that the axe was first laid to the tree by Cardinal Wolsey, who obtained grants for suppressing a number of the smaller monasteries in order to found a college at Oxford (now Christ's Church) and another at Ipswich. Wolsey himself (in his letter to the King, printed in Ellis, Orig. Lett. Second Series, ii. p. 18) calls them "certain exile * and small monasteries, wherein neither God is served ne religion kept." The zealous Catholics were alarmed by this measure, and justly regarded it as an example which would not fail to lead to a more general demolition of the religious houses. Some of the abbots attempted to avert the danger by offering sums of money for his scholastic foundation instead of the abbey lands, as in the present example of the abbot of York. There were even some tumultuous outbreaks of popular dissatisfaction. Grafton (Chron. p. 382, new edit.) says,—"You have heard before how the Cardinall suppressed many monasteries, of the which one was called Beggam in Sussex, the which was verie commodious to the countrey : but so befell the cause, that a riotus company, disguised and unknowne, with painted faces and visers, came to the same monasterie, and brought with them the chanons, and put them in their place againe, and promised them that whensoever they rang the bell, that they

---

* Poor, lean, endowed with small revenues, Lat. *exilis*, (not *alien priories*). It is a word of no uncommon occurrence in the writers of this age.

would come with a great power and defend them. Thys doyng came to the eare of the kings counsayle, which caused the chanons to be taken, and they confessed the capitaynes, which were imprisoned and sore punished." When Wolsey was beginning to decline in the royal favour, the suppression of these religious houses was one of the first charges brought against him.

The small monastery of Romburgh or Rumburgh in Suffolk is supposed to have been founded about the time of the Norman Conquest. It was given by Alan the Savage, fourth Earl of Richmond and Earl of Britany, about the time of Henry I. to the Abbey of St. Mary at York, which had been founded about 1078, by Alan Rufus, the first Earl. At least such is the opinion of antiquaries, who consider the statement in this letter, that Romburgh was given to the Abbey of York by Alan Niger (the second Earl), to be erroneous. The cell of Romburgh was suppressed by Wolsey, and the site and revenues granted to his college at Ipswich in 1528, the date of the present letter. Edmund Walley, or Whalley, the writer of the letter, was abbot of St. Mary's at York from 1521 to 1530.

I.

THE ABBOT OF YORKE TO CARDINAL WOLSEY.

[MS. Cott. Cleop. E. iv. fol. 46.*]

PLEASETH your grace to understaunde, that I, your pore oratour, have lately receyvid certen lettres frome our priour of Romeburgh, with other of our brethren there beinge, by whose purporte I perceyve that your graces pleasure ys to suppresse the said priory of Romeburgh, and also to unite, annex, and improper the same unto the church of Saint Peters in Ipiswiche; and for the accompleshment of the same, as they wryte unto me, your officers came to the said priory the xjth day of this present moneth; and there, after the redinge of certen lettres commissionall not onely of your grace, bot also of our holy father the pope, and of our soveraigne lorde the kynge, for the same purpose directed, intered into the same priory, and that done, toke away as well the goodes moveable of the said priory, beinge a membre of our monastery, and gyven unto us by Alen Niger, summe tyme erele of Richemound, and our secounde refounder, by whose gyfte next unto the kinges grace we have had moost benefyttes, laundes, and profettes gyven us, by reason whereof we be most notabily charged with massez, suffragies, and other almouse dedes for hys benefyttes to us most charytably exhibite, bot also certen munimentes, evidencez, and specialties, tochinge and apperteynynge unto our monastery, which we had lately sent unto our said priour and brethren there, for the tryall of certen laundes and rightus which lately did depende betwixt us and certen men of worshipp in Cambridge shyre in contraversie, and yet doith depende unde-cised, and for none other purpose. In consideracion wherefore, yf yt might please your grace, forasmuch as we have a greate parte of our laundes graunted unto us by reason of the said Alen Niger, whereby we be daly charged as doith appere by compo-sicion made betwixt us and the said Alen Niger, and also con-firmed by Boniface the iij[th] *anno sui pont. tercio* under certen cen-sures and paynes with clausis dirogatorye, as more largely by hys said graunte doith appere, that the said pryory might consiste and abyde as a membre unto oure monastery, as yt haith done this thre hundred yeres and more, with your graces favour, your grace shall not onely put me and my brether to a greate quietude, bot also take away many sundry doubties and greate perels of the residew of our laundes graunted unto us by the said erele, which be right notable, yf the same suppression or alienation no farther procede; and, besydes that, minstre unto us a more notable acte then ye had gyven us ten tymes more laundes then unto the same priory doith apperteyne and belonge; for of trueth the rentes and revenuez unto the same priory belonging doith very lytill sur-mounte the sum of xxx[li]. sterlinge, as far as I perceyve. And yet towardes your speciall, honourable, and laudable purpose concern-ynge the erection and foundacion of the said college and scole, I am right interely contentid, for your tenderinge of the premisses, to gyve unto your grace ccc. markes sterlinge, which shall be de-liverd unto your grace immediately. Most hummely desyring your grace to accepte my pore mynde towardes your most noble acte, which shuld be far better yf that my lytill pore [estate] thereunto wolde extende, protestinge ever that yf your graces pleasure be to have the said priory to the purpose above recyted, that then with all my study, diligence, and labour, I shall continually indever my self for the accompleshment of the same, accordingly as my dutie ys. Trustinge ever that your grace will se our pore monastery no farther hyndred, bot that we may in tyme commyng lyve lyke religiouse men, and serve Almighty God with our nombre determinate, and hereafter avoide both in law and good conscience all perells that thereby may ensue; and also pray for our founders, benefactours, and your good grace, accordingly to the foundacion of our monastery, as our dutie ys; and so knowith Jhesus, who preserve your most noble grace in high honour and greate prosperytie long to continew. Frome our monastery of Yourke, the xxth day of Septembre.

Your most bownden bedeman, EDMOND, abbot of Yourke.

To my lorde legates good grace.

The following letter was written in the beginning of the year 1529. The history of the small priory of black canons at Butley in Suffolk is very obscure, and the list of priors particularly imperfect. It was founded in 1171, by the celebrated lawyer Ranulf de Glanvil. Whether Wolsey designed to suppress it or not is uncertain, but this letter shows the tyranny which the haughty Cardinal exerted over the religious houses.

II.

RICHARD, BISHOP OF NORWICH, TO CARDINAL WOLSEY.

[From MS. Harl. No. 604, fol. 55.]

In moste humble maner I commende me unto your grace, doynge the same t'undrestande that I have hard youre message and credence commytted unto Maister Doctour Stewarde, your chapelain, to showe unto me, and have showed unto hym my full myende therin, the which I doubte not he wull declare unto your grace.

And where the president and convent of the howse of Butley, sone after the departynge of their late priour and maister there, prefixed and assigned a day for their election of a new priour, and

appoynted certayn of myn officers at that day to be there fully
myended and determyned to procede to their election by the way
of inspiracion, the same so prefixed for the election, after their
service said and other ceremonyes observed, whan thei were redy
and at the poynt to procede to their election, your lettres of sequestracion and inhibition to the contrarye were delyvered unto
the president and convent, the which thei obeide, as became theym
to do, and differred their election for that tyme. And whereas
nowe I understonde that the said president and convente, before
the said Maister Stewarde and other your officers, have proceded
to their election, and fully compromytted in your grace to name
and appoynt one of the brether and convente there, suche one as
your grace shall thinke moste mete and profightable for the place,
surely as I am credibly enfourmed there be dyverse of the brether
right hable and mete for that office, and specially one Sir Thomas
Sudbourne, celerar there, who had been electe and chosen *per viam
spiritus sancti* at the first day prefixed for their election by the commen consent of all the brether, if your grace is inhibicion had not
been, as myn officers than beynge there have reported unto me; wherfore your nominacion in this behalve onys made and intimate unto
the convent, my truste is your grace wulbe contented that I shall
confirme the said election and the priour so by your grace electe.
And thus Almyghty God long preserve your grace to your hertes
moste desire. At Hoxne, the xij[th] day of January, 1528, by your
oratour and chapelaine,

RI. NORVICEN.

To my lorde cardynall is grace be these lettres dd.

The following letter is one of many instances of the influence which the vacillating
measures of the court had upon men's minds at the first outbreak of the Reformation.
William Barlow was a native of Essex, and originally a canon of St. Osythe's. In
his youth he was a partizan of the church reformers. He afterwards held appointments
in different religious houses in England, was sent by Henry VIII. on an embassy to

Scotland, and in 1535 was made bishop of St. Asaph. He was in a few weeks removed to the bishopric of St. David's, and afterwards to that of Bath and Wells. He fled from England on the accession of Mary ; but on Elizabeth's return he was promoted to the bishopric of Chichester. Tanner has given the titles of such of his books as were printed. In his Dialogue he had reflected bitterly on Wolsey for the dissolution of the small monasteries with which he intended to endow his new college.

III.

WILLIAM BARLOW TO THE KING, A.D. 1533.

[From MS. Cott. Cleop. E. iv. fol. 121.]

Prayse be to God, who of hys infinyte goodnes and mercye inestimable hath brought me owt of darcknes into lyght, and from deadly ignoraunce unto the quicke knowlege of trothe, from the which through the fendes instygacyon and fals perswasyones I have greatly swerved, wrappynge my selfe in manyfolde erroures and detestable heresyes agaynst the doctryne of Chryst and determynacyon of holy churche, in so moche that I have made certayne bookes, and have suffred theym to be emprynted, as the Treatyse of the Buryall of the Masse, a Dyaloge betwene the Gentyllman and Husbandman, the Clymbynge up of Fryers and Religious Persones, portred with fygures, a descripcion of Godes worde compared to the lyght ; also a convicyous dyaloge withowt any tytle, inveynge specyally agaynst Saynt Thomas of Canterberye, which as yet was never prynted nor publysshed openly. In thes treatyses I perceyve and aknowlege my selfe grevously to have erred, namely, agaynst the blyssed sacrament of the altare, dysalowynge the masse and denyenge purgatorye, with slawnderous infamye of the pope and my lorde cardynall, and owtragious raylyng agaynst the clergye, which I have forsaken and utterly renownced. Wherfore I beynge lately informed of your hyghnes endued with so excellent learnynge and syngler jugement of the trothe, which endevored not onely to chace awaye and extyrpe all heresyes, but also to se a reformacyone of slawnderous lyvynge, for the restraynte of vyce in all estates, to the furtheraunce of

vertue and avauncement of Godes worde; also considerynge the
pyteous favour voyde of rygour, and mercye abhorrynge cruelte,
which your hyghnes hath used towarde other of your subgettes
fallen into soche lyke heresyes, as have submytted theym selves
humbly unto your grace; I have made sute by all meanes possyble
freely withowt mocyon of any man to come and present my selfe
afore your highnes fet, to submytt my selfe unto your mercyfull pleasure, besechynge your gracyous pardone. Also as ferre forthe as
I have knowlege in all thinges to acertayne your grace unfaynedly
whatsoever your hyghnes shall vouchesave to demaunde of me,
your unworthye subgett and oratour,

WILLIAM BARLO.

The next letter relates to one of the fathers of the reformation, Hugh Latimer, and his
sturdy opponent Hubberdin. Stowe gives an account of Latimer's preaching at Bristol in
1534, the date of the present letter. He was active in detecting the practices of the Maid
of Kent, and was, in the year following that in which this letter was written, made Bishop
of Worcester. At the time of his preaching at Bristol he was looked upon with some disfavour; on the 2nd October, 1533, he had been forbidden to preach at London. Foxe
describes Hubberdin as "an old divine of Oxford, a right painted Pharisey, and a great
straier abroad in al quarters of the realme to deface and impeache the springyng of Gods
holy gospell." It appears that at this time the zealous papistry of Hubberdin was as
distasteful to the government as the bold doctrines of Latimer. It would seem that
Hubberdin had touched too nearly upon the question of the King's supremacy.

The abbey of St. Augustine in Bristol appears to have been founded early in the
twelfth century; its church, dedicated to the Holy Trinity, is now the cathedral. William Burton is stated, in the Monasticon, to have been made abbot on the 9th of
September, 1534. He, with eighteen of his monks, subscribed to the King's supremacy,
and we may therefore suppose that he was one of the moderate party.

IV.

COMMISSIONERS AT BRISTOL TO SECRETARY CROMWELL.

[MS. Cotton. Cleopat. E. iv. fol. 56.]

In my moste humble wyse, with dew recommendacyons as ap-
pertaynethe, advertysynge your masterschype that I recevyd your
letter the Saterday v^{th} day of Julii, at vj. of the cloke at ny3te,

commaundynge me by vertu of the same in the kynges name to electe and chose fyve or vj. oneste men to assyste and helpe me in all cawsys consernynge the behavynge as well of Latomer as of Huberdyn, and ther prechyns, and spesyally what wordes Hyberdyn schold have consernynge the kynges hyȝe magesty. And accordynge to thys commaundmente immedyatly I electyd and chose the reverend lord abbot of Saynt Augustynes by Brystow, Johan Cabull, Thomas Broke, Richard Tunell, late mayres of the seyd towne of Brystow, and Thomas a Bowen, gentyllman. So electe and chosyn wee concludyd to sytt Sunday the vj. day of Julii at after none at a place callyd Saynte Jamys, and then and there apperyd before us as well of the spyrytuallte as of the temporalte, to whome wee declared and rede the commyssyon wherfore they wher callyd, and so gave them inyoncyon at a day to sertefy the kynges hyȝnes and hys moste honorable councell what Latomer had prechyd, wherby thys the kynges towne of Brystow rune in infamy, dyscorde, stryfe, and debate. And lyke charge we gave them to sertefy us what Huberdyne had prechyd consernynge the kynges hyȝnes, or any worde that myȝte sounde to the kynges hygh dysplesure, in any plase or places, as they at ther perell wood aunser. And apon whych inyoncyon, bothe of the spyrytualte and of the temporalty browȝte before us and sertyfyed, as by ther sertyfycattes more at large schall appere. And farder to advertyse your masterschype the very truthe, accordynge to our dewtys and your commaundment, what we do know in thys matters, we sertefy yow by the relacyons of many onest and credable persons, that the seyde Latomer came to Brystow and preched there the second Sonday in Lente laste paste ij. sermons, on in Saynte Nycholas chyrche afore none, and another yn the Blake Fryers at after none, and the Monday nexte folowynge he prechèd the thyrd sermone yn Saynte Thomas chyrche, yn the whych sermondes he prechyd dyvers sysmatyke and yronyous opinions : as yn hell to be no fyer sensyble ; the sowles that be yn purgatory to have no nede of our prayers, but rather to pray for us ; no sayntes to be honoryd ;

no pylgrymage to be usyd; our blessyd lady to be a synner; as hyt hathe ben reportyd and taken by the herers; but for my selfe I never hard hym preche yn Brystow, for I was then syk, but by reson of hys iij. sermondes dyvers of the kynges subyectes wythyn thys the kynges seyd towne, as manyfestely hathe apperyd hytherto, ys to be feryd be sore ynfectyd in the same, insomoche grete stryfe and debate ys amonge the kynges subyectes here, and that amonge all maner of sortes of pepyll from the hyeste to the loweste withyn the same towne. And so dyd contynu from the foresayde second Sonday yn Lent unto Ester nexte ensuynge, and yet dothe contynu, at which tyme of Ester Huberdyn came to Brystow and preched yn Sainte Thomas Chyrche at after none on Ester eve, and at Saynte Nycholas Chyrche before none on Ester day, and there prechyd scharply agenste Latomers artycules, provenynge them be auctorytes as well by the Olde as the New Testamentes sysmatyke and yrronyous. And whereas yt was very yll from the seyd seconde Sonday yn Lente tyll Ester then nexte ensuynge, yt hathe ben wors sens Ester; for many that favoryd Latomer and hys new maner of prechynge, and other many that favoryd Hyberdyne yn hys olde maner of prechynge, bothe the seyde partes hathe ben more ardente now sens Ester then they were before. Wherefore, as to our symple resons, wythowte the kynges moste noble grace provyde sume convenyante remedy, muche more ynconvenyens ys lyke to ensu. Also, that same Sonday on Gylberte Cogan came to the howse of the Grey Fryers* in Brystow, and sayd to the warde of the same howse that he schowlde be ware what he scholde wryte and testyfy, for there schowlde cume iiij. c. that showlde testefy the contrary, as the seyde warden shewyd hyt manyfestely before all the commyssyoners. On Fryday the xjth day of Julij, Johan Drews wyth others brow3te yn before us syttynge yn commyssyon a boke of

---

* Little is known of the history of the house of the Grey Friars (or Franciscans) in Bristol, and there is no list of priors. It was founded some time before 1234.

many names, and iij. artycles comprisyd yn the same boke, where apperyth every mans confessyon. That boke so resevyd, callyd before us on Thomas Butteler, examyned hym what he had herde Hyberdyn preche yn Saynt Thomas Chyrche; he answeryd, that a number of erytykes were yn Brystow, and from that nombre he brow3te hyt to xx^{ti} or xxx^{ti} erytykes, acordynge to the fyrste artycull. After Thomas Walker was demandyd what he had herd of Hyberdyn yn the same sayde chyrche; he confessed that the sayd Hyberdyn sayd there was xx^{ti} or xxx^{ti} erytykes, acordynge to the fyrste artycull, and he sayd he hard hym say no more, and yet hys name ys to the second and the thyrde artyculles. Also another man came before us, and sayd that Huberdyn schowlde say that all Brystow was knaves and erytykes. John Drws persevyng every man to be examyned thys by hym selfe, knewe very well ther confessyons wolde nothynge agre wyth the artycles yn ther seyde boke, wherefor he desyeryd that every man schowld brynge yn hys confessyon by wrytynge, and for as moche as yt was over longe and tedyows, as well to the commyssyoners as to the partys, we condessendyd to reseve there bylles, whych bylles and bokes, as well of the spyrytualte as of the temporalte, which your mastershype shall reseve of thys berer, wyth our dayly servys and prayer to preserve your longe lyfe and good to the plesure of God and your moste harteste desyer. And Almy3ty God preserve owre moste redouptyd soveraynge lorde moste ryall person, bothe bodely and gostely longe to endure. A.M.E.N.

     Per me, WILLIELMUM BURTON, *abbatem monasterii divi Augustini.*

     Bye me, JOHN CALLE.

     THOMAS BROKE.

     Per me, RYCHARD TENELL.

         THOMAS ABOWEN.

         By me, JOHAN BARTHOLOMEW.

The following letter must have been written before the preceding, but it will be best understood in its present position. Cromwell was inclined to shew more favour to Latimer than his opponents expected, and the ease with which the latter excused the mistaken harshness of their censures is very remarkable. Little is known of the history of the house of Dominicans, or Friars Preachers, in Bristol, and there is no list of the priors. Dr. Hylsey succeeded Fisher as bishop of Rochester, which shows that he was compliant with the spirit of the times.

V.

JOHN HYLSEY TO CROMWELL.

[From MS. Cotton. Cleopat. E. iv. fol. 140.]

Master chawnselar, I commende me unto you as hartly as I may thynke, trustynge yn Gode that you be (the which Jesu contynewe) yn good prosperyte. Ytt is nott owt off your mastershyppys remembrance, that yn the Lent I dyd wrete unto you off the grete dyvysyon that was (ye and yett ys) amonge the peple yn the towne of Brystoll, off the whyche I wrote unto yowe that hytt came by the prechynge of owne Mr. Latymar, a man nott unknowne. I wrote to you allsoe that he spake off pylgremages, worshyppyng off seyntes, wurshyppyng off ymages, off purgatory, etc. yn the whyche he dyd vehemently perswade towarde the contrary, that the peple ware nott a lytle offendyd. I wrote alsoe that some men thowht necessary to preache agenst hym, the whyche I supposyd nott best, except that he sholde be put to sylence, for fere off far dyr dyvysyon (the whyche by this cause ys nowe happenyd yn dede); and some thowht hytt metur to have hym before hys ordynarye to be examynyde, and soe the trewthe to be knowen; and yn thys thynges I desyryd you to do that you thowht metyst to reforme your peryshynge flock, to whome I wrote as to the shepparde off the sayd flocke. Nowe upon thys my byll men hathe crafftly usyd them selfe, ye and crafft was usyd to me or thys byll camme frome me, but that makythe nott nowe, the lettre ys off myne owne hande as thys ys, and nowe seynge that men hathe fownde the way to convey hytt to you otherways then they ynformyd me that they wolde, I cannott denye mye hande, nother wyll nott; wherfore puttynge asyde all thnges that sholde

seme to excuse myn actte, thes war the occasyon of my letter:
fyrst the fame that I harde of thys man, master Latymer, before
that I knewe hyme, the whyche same decevyd nott only me butt
other as well lernyd as I; seconde was the vehement perswadynge
ayenst the abuse off the thynges, as ys above wretyn, wythe more,
as off massys, off scale celi, pardons, the fyre off hell, the state off
the sowlys yn purgatory, off faythe wytheowt good wurkes, off
ower lady to be a synnar or noe synnar, etc. The whyche I and
syche other dyd suppose that he dyd preache to the yntent to
confownde thes thynges; wherapon bothe the wurshypffull men,
master Doctor Powell, master D. Goodryche, master Heberdynne,
master pryour off Seynt Jamys, and I, dyd preache agenst, approvynge purgatory, pylgremages, the wurshyppynge off seyntes
and ymages, alsoe approvynge that feyth wytheowt good wurkes
ys but deade, and that ower lady beynge full of grace ys and was
wytheowtte the spott of synne. But when we had dunne, I reken
we laboryd but yn vayne, and browht the peple yn greter dyvysyon
then they war, as they doe hytherto contynewe. I beseeke God
to helpe hytt, for ower kryynge owne agenst another ys nott frut-
ffull, nother takythe onny effecte; ffor sens I have communyd
wythe master Lattymar, and I have harde hyme preache, and
have yntytle hys sermon sentens for sentens, and I have percevyd
that hys mynd ys myche more agenst the abusynge off thynges
then agenst the thynge hytt selfe. More, the thyrde thynge that
causyd me to wrete unto you was thys dyvysyon that remanythe
and yncreasethe yett amonge us, the whyche wyll nott (by thys
way that we have begone) be ceasyd. Therfore hytt lyythe yn
you to devyse some other way, as God and your goode cownsell
shall ynforme you. Yn my jugement, by that that I knowe off
master Latymars mynde nowe, yff he myght have your lycens, he
woolde opyn hys mynde yn thys matters that the peple sholde be
content, and thys woolle plese the cownsell of the towne well, for
apone thys they be agreyde, and hopythe apone your good helpe
yn hytt. And yff I may wythe my lytle understondynge furder

thys matter, to brynge hytt unto an unytye, as God ys my jugge, I wyll doe my dylygens, and yff he *(quod absit)* shollde hereaffter sey onny thynge that sholde sowne other wyse then the catholycall determynacion off the chyrche, ther wylbe inowhe that wylbe redy to note hyt wythe more dylygens then hytherto. The forth was my coscyens, thowhe hytt ware for the tym erronyows, and decevyd for lacke off takynge hede dylygently, to marke and knowe the abuse off a thynge frome the thynge. Thy fythe cause I shall reserve secretly to my selfe, lest that I sholde seme to put other men yn gylty off my factes, that I doe nott yntent, Gode wyllynge, whoe have you yn hys proteccion. Wretyn yn Brystoll, 2ᵃ Maii,

By me, Frere JOHN HYLSEY, doctor
and pryor off the Freers Prechurs ther.

The letters which follow relate to an affair that had much influence in bringing the monks into disfavour, and hastened the great revolution which it is the object of the present volume to illustrate. Elizabeth Barton, so celebrated under the title of the Maid of Kent, was originally a servant, and being subject to strange epileptic fits, she was chosen by a violent party as an instrument of deception. She was taught to pretend to have visions and revelations, and was first brought forward by Richard Masters, parson of Aldrington. Archbishop Warham, and even Sir Thomas More and bishop Fisher, were either deceived, or gave encouragement to this pious fraud; and the former caused her to be placed as a nun in the priory of St. Sepulchre at Canterbury. She was there under the immediate surveillance of Dr. Edward Bocking, a canon of Christ's Church, who was one of the most zealous partizans of the plot; and another monk, named Richard Dering, or Deering, took down her pretended visions, and formed them into a book. This plot was allowed to go on for some time, and the fathers and nuns of Syon, the Charter House, and Sheen, with some of the friars observants of Richmond and Greenwich, participated largely in it. But at length the public violence with which the King's proceedings, in seeking a divorce from Catharine of Arragon, and his quarrel with the pope, were attacked, called down the vengeance of the Court; and the " holy maid" was seized and examined in the Star-chamber, when she confessed the conspiracy and her accomplices. Elizabeth Barton, Bocking, Dering, and others concerned in this affair, were afterwards condemned of high treason, and executed at Tyburn on the 20th of April, 1534. One of these was Hugh Rich, a friar observant. The following letter appears to have been written by one also

concerned in the conspiracy, but who had undertaken to examine the last-mentioned
person, and gives us a brief catalogue of the principal visions of the nun.

VI.

LETTER TO SECRETARY CROMWELL.

[From MS. Cotton. Cleopat. E. iv. fol. 75.]

Sir, may it please you to be advertysed that accordyng to your
comaundement I have put the artykylles of the communycacion betwene me and Mr. Ryche in wrytyng, and, as he sayth yow have
them in wrytyng before, ever as I hard thynges wurthy to be
notyd uppon the margent of my bok in the Doche and Frenshe
tong, to thentent he shuld not understond my purpose, I dyd
writ them. Yet dyd I not beleve sutche taylys (which he
cawlyth revelacions), for I have lernyd the gospell, *Attendite a
falsis prophetis.* Yf I had remembred another comaundement as
well as I dyd that, *Non concupisces rem -proximi tui,* with the
saying of Catho *cum bonis ambula,* I shuld not have fallyn into
this mysery. I have in remembraunce xxx. or xxxj. of these taylles
which ar not possible to be set forth in wrytynges, that there
intent shuld be known, and I suppose that xx. sheytes of papor
wyll not wryte them at lengh in order. Wherefore I have
written the name of the story whereuppon it dothe treate, so that
then (yf it be as he sayth) the hole story wulbe in your remembraunce.

Fyrst, of an angell that appered and bad the nun go unto the
kyng, that infydell prynce of Inglond, and say that I comaund
hym to amend his lyve, and that he leve iij. thynges which he
lovyth and purposyth uppon, that is that he tak none of the popis
right nor patrymony from hym, the second that he distroye all
these new ffolkes of opynyon and the workes of there new
lernyng, the thyrde that yf he maryed and tok An* to wyffe the

* The King was married to Anne Boleyn in the January of 1533.

vengaunce of God shuld plage hym, and (as she sayth) she shewyd this unto the kyng, etc.

2. Item, after this ii. or iij. monethis the angell apperyd and bad hur go ayen unto the kyng, and say that synce hur last beyng with his grace, that he hath more hyghlyer stodyed to bryng his purpose to passe, and that she saw in spyryt the kyng, the quene, and the yerle of Wylshere * standyng in a gardeyn together, and that the dyd devyze how to bryng the matter to passe, and by no meanys it wuld not be, but at the last a lyttell devyll stode besydes the quene, and put in hur mynd to say thus, " Yow shall send my father unto themprowre, and let hym shew the emprowre your mynd and conscience, and gyve hym these manny thowsand docates to have his good wyll, and thus it wulbe browght to passe." Go and fere not to shew the kyng this taylle and prevy tokyn, and byd hym take his owyld wyff ayen, or elles, etc. It is so nowghty a mattur that my hand shakyth to write it, and some thynges better unwritten then written. '

3. Item, that whan the kynges hyghtnesse was over at Callys, she saw the oyste takyn from the preyst with the blyssid blud, and that angelles browght it hur for to receave, saying, etc. ij. sheytes wull scant write this story.

4. Item, that she was charged to go unto the cardenall† whan he was most in his prosperyte, and shew hym of iij. swordes that he had in his hand, one of the spyrytuallty, another of the temperallty, and the other of the kynges maryage; a long mattur. The bysshop of Cant. and Bokyng to be remembred.

5. Item, another season after the angell comaundyd hur to go unto the sayd cardynall, and shew hym of his ffall, and that he had not done as she had comaundyd hym by the wyll of God, etc.

* Thomas Boleyn, Viscount Rocheford, created Earl of Wiltshire in 1529, the father of Anne Boleyn. In the year following, (1530) the Earl of Wiltshire, with Dr. Stokesley (the elect Bishop of London) and Dr. Edward Lee (the King's Almoner), was sent on an embassy to Bologna, where the Pope and Emperor were to meet, to declare to them the decision of the universities in favour of the king's new marriage.

† Wolsey.

6. Item, that syns he dyed she saw the disputacion of the devylles for his sowylle, and how she was iij. tymes lyfte up and culd not se hym nether in hevyn, hell, nor purgatory, and at the last where shew saw hym, and how by hur pennaunce he was browght unto hevyn, and what sowylles she saw ffly thorow purgatory, etc.

7. Item, more the angell warned hur that she shuld go unto a sertayn abbot, and warne hym to take iij. of his bretherne by name, for they were purposed to have them away that nyght with iij. mens wyffes, and that God wuld they shuld have bettur grace, etc.

8. Item, of another that had betyn hym zelfe so with roddes that his stamell* was blody, which he thowght to have beryed in the garden, and she by the comandement of the angell met hym, etc. a hy mattur for penance.

9. Item, of ij. other monkes which had takyn shippyng to go unto Tynldalle, which by hur prayer was torned, and the ship had no powre to depart from the haven, etc.

10. Item, that the angell comaundyd hur to go to another monke, and byd hym burne the New Testament that he had in Inglyssh, and of great vysions seen by the same in tokyn of grace, etc.

11. Item, of the warnyng that the angell gave hur of a woman that cam unto sent Thomas of Cantorbery, a mervelos mattur and a long, etc.

12. Item, the angell shewyd hur that ambassett of the pope shuld be at Cantorbery, and how she sent by hym the message of God unto the pope, how he shuld be scorged of God for ij. cawsis, etc.

13. Item, that she spok by the comaundement of God at London with oone other, and bad hym write the messag of God unto the pope, to the which she dyd set hur hand, etc.

* The *Stamel* was a coarse shirt, worn by religious persons.

14. Item, of the owild bysshop of Cantorbery, how he had pro-mysed to mary the kyng, and of the warnynges by the angell of God, etc.

15. Item, that she dyd shew unto docter Bokyng the owyr of his deth, and zence that she harde the disputacion betwene the angelles and the develles for hys sowle.

16. Item, she dyd se hym whan he went unto hevyn, with his wurdes that he spok, and how sent Thomas was there present and accompanyd hym, etc.

17. Item, of the goyng and retorne of the yerle of Wylshere into Spayn, with the receavyng of the kynges letters there, and the answere of themprowre, etc.*

18. Item, of the vyzion that she had, yf the kyng shuld have maryed at Callys, of the greate shame that the quene shuld have had, etc.†

19. Item, of sutche persons as the angell of God hath ap-poyented to be at hur deth, whan she shall receave the crowne of marterdom, and the tyme, with the place.

20. Item, how dyvers tymes the devell hath appered unto hur; oone tyme he cam in the lykenes of a goodly man, and browght with hym a lady, and beffore hur face had to do with hur uppon hur bed, with other matteres to abhomynable, etc.

21. Item, of a sertayn vysion that Goldes‡ wyffe had uppon sent Cateryns day, which the angell of God dyd shew by hur prayer, etc.

22. Item, how at Corteupstreytte,§ whan Mr. Gold went unto masse, the other Goldes wyffe desyryd hur to mak hur prayer unto God to know the state of prynces dowager, of ij. other

---

* The Earl of Wiltshire was sent on an embassy to Spain in 1531.

† Anne Boleyn attended the Court to Calais, and it would appear by this passage that it was the king's intention to marry her on that occasion.

‡ There were two persons of the name of Golde active in this affair; Thomas Golde, and Henry Golde, parson of St. Mary Aldermary, London. The "Mr. Gold" mentioned in the next article is the parson.

§ Our Lady of Court-at-Street, in the parish of Limne, was a little chapel, with an image of the Virgin, much resorted to. It was here that the nun commenced her visions.

wemen, and of ij. freers, which was Rich and Risby :* as sone as the preyste began *confiteor*, she ffyll in a traunce, and of hur wunderfull answere, etc.

23. Item, of a sertayn gentylman dwellyng abowit Cantorbery, that had long tymes ben temptyd to drown hym selfe by the spryte of a woman that he had kept by his wyffes days, which is damned, etc. a long matter and a straynge.

24. Item, of the vysions sene by hur sister, marvelous, and how she tok the blud of our Lordys sydes in a challys, and how she saw the playg for the citty of London, etc.

25. Item, of the wurdes that the nun spake unto Mr. Richardes, how the angell of God asked for his fayth, with sertayn prevy tokyns that she shewyd hym that he had in his memento, with dyvers other thynges in your howse which cawsith them all to muse, etc.

26. How the angell of God hath comaundyd hur to say that all ar but yllusions, for the tyme is not cum that God wulle put forth the wurk, etc.

27. Item, of 9 | 9 | 9 |, the rayn of the kyng how long he shall reyngne, as sayth a prophecy which agreeth with hur sayng, etc.

28. Item, of iij. letteres A. F. G., by a profycye that is in the handes of holly Richard; yf yow send to me John Gooddolphyn your servant, I can cawse hym to ffynd hym by enquere at the Temple.

29. Item, more a greate matter of a golden letter that Mary Magdalene dyd send, and how the angell comaundyd hur to cownterfayt another, by cawse the people shuld have powre upon hur boddy, etc., with monney that was hyd, etc.

30. Item, that vj. days beffore the sayd Riche was takyn, he went to a man that hath a prophesy, and with hym Nesywyck the observaunt, which shewyd unto them wunderos thyng, pennes and yncornes, letteres of prophesy, and of all ther troble at Powlys Crosse. This man dwellyth ij. mylys ffrom Bugdeane, his name is Handford, etc.

* Hugh Rich has been already mentioned : Richard Risby was one of the nun's accomplices.

The following letter, upon the same subject as the preceding, is from Thomas Goldwell, prior of Christ's Church, Canterbury, the oldest monastery in England, having been founded by St. Augustine. Thomas Goldwell was prior during the twenty-three years preceding the dissolution of the monastery. Warham was Archbishop of Canterbury from February 1503 to August 1532, and was succeeded by Cranmer.

VII.

THE PRIOR OF CHRIST'S CHURCH TO CROMWELL.

[From MS. Cotton. Cleopat. E. IV. fol. 79.]

As consernyng the knowlege of suche thynges as Elizabeth Barton, nun, hath spoken, whiche as she sayde she had knowlege of in traunces and revelaciones, thies be the thynges that I have herd and have knowlege in. At the begynnyng therof, the whiche was abowte vij. or viij. yeres past, as I thynke, my lord Warham, then being archebusshope of Caunterbury, sent his comptroller called Thomas Walle to Caunterbury, and caused me to send two of my brothern, the whiche was the selerer, Doctor Bockyng, and dompne William Hadley, bacheler of divinite, to a place called Courthopestrete, to see this woman, and to see what traunces she had. They went thider at the begynnyng, as I suppose, somewhat ageyn theire myndes, and also ageyn my mynde, except the obedience that I do owe unto my lord of Caunterbury; and he had not byn, I wold not have sent them thider. After this he caused and gave licence to the selerer to be this womannys gostely ffader, and so he hath contynued ever syns, as ferre as I knowe, and resorted unto her at tymes convenyent when he wold hym silf, and that by my lord of Caunterburies licens, and most tymes not be myne. The tyme that I have ben acquaynted with her, as I thynke it past not two yeres at the most. Fader Risby, one of the observaunt ffriers, nowe being warden of the place of ffriers in Caunterbury, he was mover and chief causer that I was acquaynted with her. I suppose, and his mocyon had not be, I had never bene acquaynted with her, for my mynde was not to be ffamelyerly acquaynted with women. He shewed unto me that as he thought

she was a persone moche in the ffavoure of God, and had speciall
knowlege of hym in mony thynges, and he thought, and so sayde
unto me, that I shuld have moche spirituall comfort in her
spekyng.   Sith that tyme she hath byne with me at dyner dyvers
seasons, as I suppose vj. or vij. tymes at the most ; and at suche
tymes as she hath ben with me she hath showed unto me that
dyvers seasons she had revelacions and speciall knowlege ffrom
God in certen thynges consernyng my lord of Caunterbury that
was, my lord cardynall, and also the kynges highnes, consernyng
his mariage, so that she sayde if he dyd mary another woman, his
grace shuld not rayne kyng past one moneth afterward ; and also
she sayde that she had byn with the kynges grace, and showed
hym therof two tymes at the lest ; and also she sayde the she had
shewed the same unto my lord of Caunterbury, that was my lord
Warham, as I suppose she dyd, for she was meny tymes with
hym, and, as the selerer shewed unto me at dyvers seasons, he
gave moche credens unto her wordes in suche thynges as she
knewe, and surmysed to knowe, that she dyd shewe unto hym.
She sayde also that if Almyghty God dyd suffer his grace to
rayne kyng, yet he shuld nott be so accepted in the reputacion of
God, as she sayde it was shewed unto her by revelacion.   Also
she hath reported that at the kynges grace being at Calice, a prist
there being at masse, the holy sacrement was taken from the awter
and brought unto her, the whiche as she sayde she dyd receyve.
Also the selerer shewed unto me that she had revelacions consernyng the popes holynes ; he sayde that it was shewed unto her
that if the pope dyd geve sentence ageyn the quene that then was,
Almyghty God wold be displeased with hym, and send plages to
hym for it ; what the plages shuld be I cannot tell.   I do not remember that he dyd shewe any unto me.   This be the thynges
that they dyd speke unto me, and my answer was unto them,
'Thies be mervelus thynges that ye speke of, if they be trewe.'   I
do not remember that I made them any other answer at any tyme,
and this thynges before rehersed I herd onely of them thre, that

is of the nun, of the selerer, and of ffader Risby; and of none
other, nether by noo other meanes, but onely by theire spekyng;
for as consernyng the bookes that the selerer dyd write, I dyd
never rede them, nor never sawe them but onely when they were
delyvered, one of them to Mr. Attorney before his last goyng to
London, and the other to John Antony, when he was sent for it,
at what tymes I dyd see them, but I dyd not rede apon them, as
they can testyfy that dyd receyve them.   Also I am suer that the
selerer will testifie for me, that he dyd never showe me the booke,
nor eny thyng els that he wrote for her, or consernyng the seid
nun, but onely one quayer,* the whiche he willed me to rede and
to loke uppon, and it was consernyng dyvers that were ded; one
of them was the selerers unkyll, called Master Benet, and one
other was a servaunt of our house called Stephen Villers.   As he
wrote in that quayer, the nun was desired to pray for them, and to
knowe what case they were in; and, as he wrote there, she had
knowlege by revelacion that they were in payne, and for what
offences they were there, and also what prayers and other goode
dedes shuld be don for them to delyver them owte of payne.   Hit
was also shewed in the same quayer howe she was meny tymes
trobeled with her gostely enmy, the whiche moved her to incon-
tynency, and to unclene levyng.   Other speciallties I do remember none that I red in the seid quayer; and moo thynges then
this that he wrote for her I never red, nor had in my kepyng at
eny tyme, and that I will depose uppon my conciens.   And as
consernyng suche traunces as she had at Courthopestrete, or els
where, I was never present at eny of them.   Howbeit as the
nunnes of her house do report of her, this vj. or vij. yere she hath
be wunt to be sykke abowte the conception(?) of our lady, and to lye
thre or iiij. dayes without mete or drynke, as they say; and the last

---

* A quire.   The monks and professed scribes wrote their manuscripts in separate
pieces, each consisting of *four* double leaves, or sixteen pages, and hence called a *qua-
ternio*, whence is derived our modern word *quire*.   These *quaternios* or "quayers,"
were afterwards bound into a volume.   The French *cahier* appears to have the same
origin.

yere when she lay so I [was] desired by the selerer and her silf
also to see her, and so I dyd; but at that tyme she was nott
r . . fformed nor spake nothyng but as a syke body is wount to do.
Other thynges then I have rehersed before I do remember none
to write unto you nowe; if any other thyng come to my mynde, I
will not ffayle to write unto you, and to sertefie you of the same,
by Goddes grace, etc.

       Per me, THOMAS *priorem Ecclesiæ Christi Cantuarie.*

The following petition to the King appears to have been written by the monks of
Christ's Church, Canterbury, who feared to be compromised in the affair of Elizabeth
Barton.

VIII.

PETITION OF THE MONKS OF CANTERBURY TO THE KING.

[From MS. Cotton. Cleopat. E. iv. fol. 81.]

After our most humble submission and subjection to your
gracis majestie, if we had not taken consolacion of the comon fame
reporting your majestie to be as full of benignitie, grace, and
mercy, as ever was cristened prince reignyng in Englonde, we had
bene not onelie dejected into intollerable sorowe and pensifenes,
but had also bene in dispaire to make any supplicacion to your
hignes, or to be harde graciouslie in the same. But now, considering your gracis most benigne nature, moche more inclyned to
mercy and pitie than to the rigour of justice, we be anymated and
set in comforte to humyliate our selfes as prostrate afore your
highnes, and to beseche the same to remytte and forget the necli-
gences and offences commytted ayenst your grace by certen persons
of our congregacion and monasterie, which causith us all most
woofullie to lamente and sorow. And where the demerites of our
miserable brother dan Edwarde Bocking, doctour of dyvynitie, be
so highe heynous, so grevous, and so displeasaunte to your
majestie, that we dare not ones open our lippes to make any
prayers or supplicacion to your highenes for hym, yet if it might

please your highnes of your most gracious benignitie and naturall
goodnes to extende your superaboundant grace uppon hym, he
should have a thousande tymes more cause to lawde, magnyfie,
observe, love, and praye for your grace, then they which never
offended, acording to the wordes of the gospell, *Cui plus dimitti-
tur, plus diligit.* Whose temeritie, furious zele, and malicious
blynde affection, went aboute, most gracious king, not onely to
compase and imagene to let, stoppe, impedite, and sclaunder your
gracis mariage and lawfull matrimonye which ye now enyoye to
Goddis pleasure, but also, as well before as after your said mariage
was concluded and consumate, hath travailed to bring us all into
gret suspicion of your highnes, so that we by infection and cor-
rupcion of hym might have bene likewise noted of untowarde
myndes contrarie to your gracis saide mariage. Of which note of
suspicion we be moche desirous to be purged and clered to your
highnes ; ffor we thinke verelye that none of us (the said doctour
Bocking onelie excepted) hath by wey of preching, teching, or by
secret or open communycacion, moved, exhorted, or excited any
persone to sey, thinke, or do any thing contrarie to your gracis
mariage, afore it was concluded or after. Nevertheles it can not
be denyed but that some of us, not many in nombre, and specially suche as were brought into our religion by doctour Bocking,
beyng of the yonger sorte, have bene enfourmed by the said
doctour of certen counterfeyted, false, and most malicious revelacions, as well concernyng your gracis said mariage, as also otherwise imagened and fayned by the most lyeng and false nonne, late
of Saynt Sepulcres in Canterburie, agenst your majestie. And
where that any of us have harde, beleved, or conceled the said
false revelacions, or any of theme, we be right pensyve and in-
wardelie sorye, most humbly beseching your grace of your remys-
cion and most mercyfull pardon therfore, promytting unto your
majestie that none of us shall never hereafter in worde or dede
openlie or pryvatelie do any thing that may sounde or be judged
prejudiciall, hurtfull, or contrarie to your gracis said mariage, or
the noble issue proceeding of the same ; but shall oblige our selffes,

our monasterie, and successours, at all tymes hereafter to be of
consonant myndes, wordes, and deades, to the mayntenaunce,
supportacion, and determynacion allredy passed by the clergie of
both the provynces of your gracis realme, and to the sentence of
our most reverend hed, spirituall father, and ordynarie, the
archebisshope of Canterburie, pronounced for the strenght, vale-
dite, and liefulnes of the said mariage, acording to the lawe of
God, as we of dutye ar bounde to doo; ffor gret folie it were,
most gracious soveraigne, to be imputed unto us, that we being
poore simple religeous men, of small lernyng and judgement,
shoulde presume to thinke or sey any thing contrarie to the determynacion of so many singuler and notable lerned men, not onlie
of your gracis said clergie of this realme, but also of the most
famous clerkes of Cristynde, or contrarie to the diffynytyve sentence of our said spirituall hedd and father, to whose judgement
we gyve full feith and credence, as membres conforme to our said
hedd, and to the body of your gracis said convocacions. Which
we holy promyse to observe, and for our powers mayntayne and
defende, and also contynuallie praye to God Almightie that his
goodnes graunte unto your grace long lyf to his pleasure and your
hertis desire, and sende your highnes in your said mariage prosperous and desiderate yssue, to succede in your realme and to
reigne in the same, as many hundreth yeres to come, in honour
and felycitie.

The next letter on this subject is from Roland Lee (afterwards bishop of Coventry
and Lichfield, and Lord President of the principality of Wales), and Thomas Bedyll,
who was afterwards a very active visitor of the monasteries. It appears that they had
been sent to Canterbury to pursue there the examinations relating to the proceedings
of the " holy maid."

IX.

ROLAND LEE AND THOMAS BEDYLL TO CROMWELL.
[From MS. Cotton. Cleopat. E. iv. fol. 83.*]

After our moost hertie commendations, theis shalbe to advertise
yow that, God willing, we entend shortly to retorne homeward, ffor

we fynd not so greate maters here as we thought we shuld have doen. The crafty nunne kept herself very secrete here, and shewed her marchaundise more openly when she war far from home; and if she had been as ware in other places as she hath been here, we suppose she had continued in her falshede lenger than she hath doen, whiche was to long. The greatest cause of demore here now, is to accomplisshe certen practises whiche we have devised with the frere observantes of Canterburie, and we trust to bring thaim to some good effect. We tarry also to examine the priour of Hortone,* whiche is detected as a participant of the nunnys revelations concernyng the kinges grace reigne and his marriage. We have wreten unto yow that we fere that in caas we shall carry the parson of Aldingtone to Londone agayne now shortly, he wol miscary by the wey, or sone after; whereupon we desire you to send us your advise. We beseche you to be good maister to John Antony, for he hath shewed as muche kyndnes unto us as a man of his behaviour myght do, and hath always beene diligent to further our causes as myche as he myght. As towching the monkes of Christes churche whiche bee detected in this mater, whiche be but v. or vj. yong men, whiche have red part of Bokkinges boke of the nunnys revelations, my lord of Cauntrebury, now being in his visitacion, wol examine thaim at his leysure, and therfore we think it shal not be nede for us to tarry upon thair examination, onles ye send us contrary word by this berer, wherin and in other the premisses we desire you to send unto us your mynd at lenght. ffrom Cauntrebury, the xth day of December.

Yower owne, ROLAND LEE. Evyr your awne, THOMAS BEDYLL.

* At Monks' Horton, five miles from Hythe, was a cell of the priory of Lewes. Richard Gloucester, *alias* Brisley, was its last prior.

X.

LIST OF THE NUN'S GOODS.

[From MS. Cotton. Cleopat. E. IV. fol. 84.]

Stoffe receyvyd the xvj. day of Februare, of dame Elysabeth Barton, by the handes of the priores of sayent Sepulcres withowt Canterbury, into the handes of John Antony of Canterbury, as her after foloeth.

ffyrst, a coschyn blade, and one old coschyn,

ij. carpettes, whereof one ys cut in to pecys.

A old matteres, vij. corsse schettes, a kyverlet and a peyer of blanckettes, with ij. pyllos, and a bolster.

ij. platers, iiij. dysches, ij. sausers, and a lyttell basen, wayyng xij^{lb}. at iiij^d a lb. wyche my laydy priores hath and payed iiij^s.

A whyet corter, wych my lady priores hath, and payed xij^d.

A lyttell old dyaper towell.

iij. pylloberes.

ij. canstyckes.

A coet, wyche dame Kateren Wyttsam hath, payed v^s.

A pece of a plancke for a tabyll.

A lyttell chyst.

Stoffe wyche remayneth in the nonnere pertaynyng unto dame Elysabeth Berton, at the request of my lady priores.

ffyrst, ij. nyew coschyns, gyven unto the churche.

A old mantell, and a kyrtell, unto the yongest nonne.

A Yrysche mantell, a colere, with ij. grett chystes, and ij. stolys, and a canstycke, to my lady priores.

A kyverlet, and a old kyrtell, to dame Alys Colman, at the request of my lady priores.

It has been already stated that Sir Thomas More and Bishop Fisher were involved in the affair of the " holy maid of Kent:" they were committed to the Tower about the time of her execution, and were both condemned to the scaffold. Fisher was be-headed on the 22nd of June, 1535, and Sir Thomas More suffered on the 6th of the following month. The following is the draught of a letter written by Cromwell to Fisher, before his imprisonment.

XI.

CROMWELL TO BISHOP FISHER.

[Cotton. MS. Cleopat. E. iv. fol. 85*.]

My lord, in my right hertie wise I commende me to your lord-ship, doing you to understand that I have receyved your lettres dated at Rochester the xviijth day of this moneth, in whiche you declare what craft and cunnyng ye have to persuade and to set a good countenaunce upon all that mater, drawing som scriptures to your purpose whiche, wel weyed acording to the places whereof they be taken, make not so muche for your purpose as ye allege thaim for. And where in the first lefe of your letters, ye write that ye doubt nothing, neither before God nor before the worlde, if nede shal that require, so to declare your self, whatsoever hath beene said of you, that ye have not deserved suche hevy wordes or terrible thretes as hath beene sent from me unto you by your brother.

How ye can declare your self affore God and the worlde when nede shal require, I can not tell; but I think verely that your declaration made by thes lettres is far insufficient to prove that ye have deserved no hevy wordes in this behalf; and to sey playnly, I sent you no hevy wordes, but wordes of great comforte, wylling your brother to shewe you how benigne and merciful the prince was, and that I thought it expedient for you to write unto his highnes and to recognise your offence and desire his pardon, whiche his grace wold not denye you now in your aige and sikkenes. Whiche my counsel I wold ye had folowed, rather than to have writen thes lettres to me, excusing your self as thoughe there were no maner of defaut in you.   But, my lord, if it were in an other mannys caas than your owne, and out of the mater whiche ye favor, I doubt not but that ye wold think him that shuld have doen as ye have doen not only worthy hevy wordes, but also hevy dedys. For wher ye labor to excuse your self of your hering, beleving, and conceling of the nunnys fals and fayned revelations, and of your manyfold sending of your chapeleyn unto her, by a certen intent whiche ye pretende your self to have had to knowe by commonyng with her, or by sending your chapellaine to her, whether her revelations were of God or no, alleging diverse scriptures that ye were bound to prove thaim, and not to receve thaim affore they were proved; my lord, whether ye have used a due meane to trie her and her revelations, or no, it appereth by the prouffe of your owne lettres; ffor wher ye write that ye had conceyved a greate opinion of the holines of this woman for many considerations rehersed in your lettres, comprised in vj. articles, whereof the first is grownde upon the brute and fame of her; The secunde upon her entering into religion after her traunces and disfiguration ; The third upon rehersall that her gostly father, being lerned and religious, shuld testifie that she was a maide of greate holines; The fourth upon the report that diverse other vertuose prestes, men of good lernyng and reputation, shuld so testifie of her, with whiche gostly father and preestes ye never spake, as ye confesse in your letters; The fyveth upon the prayses of my late lord of Canterbury, whiche shewed you (as ye write) that she had many greate visions ; The sixt upon this saing of the prophete Amos, *Non favet Dominus Deus verbum, nisi revelaverit secretum suum ad servos suos prophetas ;* by whiche considerations ye were induced to the desire to know the very certente of this mater, whether thes revelations whiche were pretended to be shewed to her from God were true revelations or nott.   Your lordship in al the sequell of your lettres shewe not that ye made no forther trial upon the trueth of her and her revelations, but only in commonyng with her, and sending your chapellaine to her with idle questians, as of the thre Mary Magdelens.

By whiche your conversing and sending, ye tried out no thing of her falshed, nouther (as it is credibly supposed) entended to do, as ye myght have doen many weyes more easely than with commonyng with her or sending to her; for litel credens was to be gyven to her affirmyng her owne fayned revelations to be frome God. ffor if credense shuld be gyven to every suche lewd person as wold affirme him self to have revelations from Good, what redyer wey wer ther to subvert al common welths and good orders in the world?

Verely, my lord, if ye had entended to trie out the trueth of her and of her revelations, ye wold have taken another wey with you. First, ye wold not have beene contented with the vayne voyces of the peple making brutes of her traunses and disfigurations, but like a wise, discrete, and circumspect prelate, ye shuld have examined (as other have) suche sad and credible persons as wer present att her traunsces and disfigurations; not one or two, but a good number, by whoes testimony ye shuld have proved whether the brutes of her traunces and disfigurations were true or not. And likwise ye shuld have tried by what craft and persuasion she was made a religious woman. And if ye had beene so desirous as ye pretende to enquire out the trueth or falshed of this woman and of her revelations, it is to be supposed ye wold have spoken with her godd, religious, and wel lerned gostly father or this tyme, and also with the vertuose and wel lerned preestes (as they were estemed), of whoes reaportes ye wer informed by thaim whiche herd thaim speke; ye wold also have beene mynded to se the booke of her revelations which was offerd you, of whiche ye myghte have had more trial of her and of her revelations than of a hundred communications with her, or of as many sendinges of your chapellen unto her. As for the late lord of Cauntreburys seyng unto you that she had many greate visions, it ought to move you never a deale to gyve credence unto her or her revelations; ffor the said lord knew no more certente of her or of her revelations than ye dyd

by her owne reaport. And as towching the saing of Amos the
prophet, I think veryly the same moved you but a litell to herkyn
unto her; for sythe the consummation and thende of tholde testament, and sythens the passion of Christ, God haithe doen many
greate and notable thinges in the worle, whereof he shewed no
thing to his prophetes that hath commen to the knowlege of men.
My lord, all thes thinges moved you not to gyve credence unto
her, but only the very mater whereupon she made her fals pro-
ficyes, to whiche mater ye were so affected (as ye be noted to be
on al maters whiche ye enter ons into), that no thing could come
amysse that made for that purpose.

And here I appelle your conscience, and instantly desire you to
answer, whether if she had shewed you as many revelations for
the confirmation of the kinges graces mariage whiche he now
enjoyeth, as she did to the contrary, ye wold have gyven as
muche credence to her as ye have doen, and wold have let the
trial of her and of her revelations to overpasse thes many yeres,
where ye dwelt not from her but xx. mylys, in the same shire,
where her traunces and disfigurances and prophecyes in her
traunces were surmised and countrefeyted. And if per caas ye wol
sey (as is not unlike but ye wol sey, mynded as ye were wont to
be) that the maters be not like, for the law of God in your opinion
standeth with the one and not with thother; suerly, my lord, I
suppose this had beene no greate cause more to reject the one
than the other, for ye know by histories of the Bible that God
may by his revelation dispense with his owne law, as with the
Israelites spoyling the Egiptians, and with Jacob to have iiij. wifes,
and suche other.

Think you, my lord, that any indifferent mann, considering the
qualite of the mater and your affection, and also the negligent
passing over of suche lawful trialles as ye myght have had of the
said nunne and her revelations, is so dull, that can not perceyve
and discerne that your commonyng and often sending to the said
nun was rather to here and know more of her revelations, than to

trie out the trueth or falshed of thes same? And in this behalfe
I suppose it wolbe hard for you to purge your selfe before God or
the worle, but that ye have beene in greate defaut herin, belevyng
and conceling suche thinges as tended to the destruction of the
prince. And that her revelations were bent and purposed to that
ende, it hath beene duely proved affore as greate assembly and
counsel of the lordes of this realme as hath beene seene many yeres
heretofore out of a parliament. And what the said lordes demed
thaim worthy to suffer, whiche herd, beleved, and conceled thees
fals revelations, be more terrible than any thretes spoken by me
to your brother.

And where ye go abought to defende that ye be not to be
blamed for conceling her revelations concernyng the kinges grace,
bicause ye thought it not necessary to reherse thaim to his highnes for vij. causes ffolowing in your lettres, affore I shewe you my
mynde concernyng thees causes, I suppose that, albeit ye percaas
thought it not necessary to be shewed to the prince by you, yet
that your thinking shal not be your triall, but the law must diffine
whether ye owghte to utter it or not.

And as to the first of said vij causes: albeit she told you that
she had shewed her revelations concernyng the kinges grace to
the king her self, yet her seyng or others discharged not you but
that ye were bound by your fidelite to shewe to the kinges grace
that thing whiche semed to concerne his grace and his reigne so
nyghly; for how knew you that she shewed thes revelations to
the kinges grace but by her owne seyng, to whiche ye shuld have
gyven no suche credence as to forbere the utterance of so greate
maters concernyng a kinges welth? And why shuld you so sinis-
terly judge the prince, that if ye had shewed thes same unto
him he wold have thought that ye had brought that tale unto him
more for the strenghing and confirmation of your opinion then
for any other thing els? Veryly, my lord, whatsoever your
judgement bee, I se dayly such benignite and excellent humanite
in his grace, that I doubt not but his highness wold have ac-

cepted it in good part, if ye had shewed the same revelations unto him, as ye were bounden to do by your fidelite.

To the secunde cause: Albeit she shewed you not that any prince or other temporal lord shuld put the kinges grace in danger of his crowne, yet there were weyes inowghe by whiche her said revelations myght have put the kinges grace in daunger, as the foresaid counsel of lordes have substancially and dewly considered. And therefor, albeit she shewed you not the meanes whereby the daynger shuld ensue to the kinge, yet ye were neverthelesse bounden to shew him of the daunger.

To the third: think you, my lord, that if any person wold come unto you and shewe you that the kinges destruction were conspired against a certen tyme, and wold ferther shewe you that he were sent from his maister to shewe the same to the king, and wol sey ferther unto you that he wold go streyct to the king, were it not yet your duety to certifie the kinges grace of this revelation, and also to inquire whether the said person had doen his foresaid message or no? Yes verely, and so were ye bound, though the nunne shewed you it was her messaige from God to be declared by her to the kinges grace.

To the iiij^the: here ye translate the temporal duety that ye owe to your prince to the spiritual duety of suche as be bounde to declare the worde of God to the peple, and to shewe unto them the perill and punisshement of syne in an other worle, the concelement whereof perteyneth to the judgement of God, but the concelement of this mater perteyneth to other judges of this realme.

To the vth: ther wuld no blame be anexed to you, if ye had shewed the nunnys revelations to the kinges grace, albeit they were afterward found fals; for no man owght to be blamed doing his duety. And if a man wold shewe you secretly that there were a greate mischief entended against the prince, were ye to be blamed if ye shewed him of it, albeit it were a fayned tale, and the said mischief were never imagined?

To the sixt, concernyng an imagination of master Pacy: it was knowen that he was beside him selfe, and therefore they were not blamed that made no report thereof. But it was not lik in this caas, ffor ye toke not this nunne for a mad woman; for, if ye had, ye wold not have gyven unto her so greate credence as ye dyd.

To the final and vij[th] cause, where ye lay unto the charge of our soveraine, that he hath unkyndly entreated yow with grevous wordes and terrible letters for shewing his grace trowthe in this greate mater, whereby ye were disafected to shewe unto him the nunnys revelations : I beleve that I know the kinges goodnes and natural gentilnes so well, that his grace wold not so unkyndly handle you as you unkyndly write of him, onles ye gave him other causes than be expressed in your letter. And whatsoever the kinges grace hath sayed or writen unto you heretofore, yet that notwithstonding ye were neverthelesse bounden to utter to him thes pernicious revelations.

Finally, where ye desire for the passion of Christ that ye be no more quykkened in this mater, for if ye be put to that straite ye wyl not lose your soule, but ye wyl speke as your conscience ledeth yow, with many moo wordes of greate curraige : my lord, if ye had taken my counsel sent unto you by your brother, and folowed the same, submitting your selfe by your letter to the kinges grace for your offensis in this behalf, I would have trusted that ye shuld never be quykkened in this mater more. But now, where ye take upon yow to defie the hole mater, as ye were in no default, I can not so far promisse you. And suerly, my lord, if the mater come to triall, your owne confession in thes lettres, besides the wittnes which ar against you, wolbe sufficient to condemne yow; wherefor, my lord, I wol eftsones advise you that, leyng apart al suche excuses as ye have alleged in your letters, whiche in my opinion be of smal effect, as I have declared, ye beseche the kinges grace by your letters to be your gracious lord, and to remitte unto you your negligence, oversight, and offence committed against his highnes in this behalf, and I dare undertake that his highnes shal beningnely accepte yow into his gracious favor, al mater of dyspleasere past affore this tyme forgoten and forgyven.

As towching the speking of your conscience, it is thought that ye have writen and have spoken as muche as ye can, and many thinges (as som right probably beleve) against your owne conscience. And men report that at the last convocation ye spake many thinges whiche ye could not wel defende, and therefor it is not greatly ferede what ye can sey or write in that mater, howsoever ye bee quykkened or strayted, and if ye had taken, etc.

It appears that other of the monks and friars concerned in these plots against the King's marriage were indulged with visions, as well as Elizabeth Barton. The two following letters are curious specimens of their strange revelations. The first is from a monk of the Charter House.

XII.

VISION OF JOHN DARLEY

[From MS. Cotton. Cleop. E. IV. fol. 129.]

M^d. That I, John Darlay, monke of the Charterhous besyde London, had in my tyme licence to say service with a ffather of our religion, named ffather Raby, a very old man, in so moch when he ffell seke and lay apon hys deth bed, and after the tyme he was anelede and had recevyd all the sacrament of the church in the presens of all the covent, and whan all they war departed, I sayde unto hym, " good ffather Raby, yff the dede man come to the qwyke, I besuch yow to com to me," and he said, " yea," and mediately he dyed the same nyghte, wich was in the clansyng days last past, *anno* xv^{c}xxxiiij. An sens that I never dede thynke apon hym to saynt Jhon day Baptist last past.

Item, the same day at v. of the cloke at after none, I beyng in contemplacion in our entre in our ssell, sodanly he appered unto me in a monkes habyt, and said to me, " whhy do ye not ffolow our ffather?"* and I sayd, " qwherffor?" He sayd, " 'for he is marter in hevyn next unto angelles." And I said, " wher be all our other fathers wich died as well [as] he?" He answer and said, " they be well, but nat so well as he." And than I said to hym, " ffather, how do ye?" And he answerd and said, " well enought." And I said, " ffather, shall I pray ffor yow?" and he said, " I am well enowght, but prayer both for yow an other doith good." And so sodanly vanyushd away.

Item, upon Saturday next after, at v. of the clocke in the mornynge, in the same place in our entre, he appered to me agayne with a lange whyte berd, and a whyte staff in his hand, lyftynge it up; wherapon I was affrayd, and than lenynge apon his staff sayd to me, " I am sory that I lived not to I had ben a marter." And I said, " I thinke ye be as well as ye war a marter." And he sayd, Nay, ffor my lord of Rochester and our ffather was next unto angelles in hevyn. And than I said, " ffather, what elles?" And than he answerd and sayd, " the angelles of pease ded lamment and murne withowt mesur;" and so vanyushed away.

Written by me, John Darly, monke of the Carterhows, the xxvijth day off June, the yere of our lord Good as afforsaid.

The date of the following letter is somewhat uncertain; but the bishops of Canterbury, Salisbury, and Worcester seem to have been Cranmer, Shaxton, and Latimer; so that it may be placed in the March of 1535 or 1536. It is placed here on account of its connection with the foregoing, by the vision story at the commencement; and it will serve as a curious description of the feelings of the King and the reformers towards the monks just before the dissolution of their houses. Latimer's sermon at St. Paul's Cross is particularly characteristic of the sudden change which had taken place since his preaching at Bristol. The bishop of Rochester, who inhibited confession at the Crutched Friars, was John Hilsey, originally a friar of Bristol, already mentioned. The bishop of London was John Stokesley, who was not one of the reforming bishops, having been appointed to the see as early as 1530.

---

* Probably he alludes to John Houghton, the prior of the Charter-house, who had been hanged and quartered at Tyburn, on the 27th of April, for refusing to acknowledge the King's supremacy.

XIII.

LETTER OF THOMAS DORSET.

[From MS. Cotton. Cleop. E. iv. fol. 110.]

To the right worshipfull Mr. Horsewell, maiour, Mr. Elyete, Mr. Hawkyns, and William Aishrygh, of Plommourthe, theire bownden and beholdyn Thomas Dorset, curate of S. Margarete in Lothbury in London, sendith gretyng and good helthe in our Lord Jesu Criste. Amen.

On the morowe after that master Hawkins departed from hens, I havyng nothyng to doo, as an idler went to Lambhethe to the byshopis place, to see what newis ; and I toke a whery at Pawlis wharffe, wherin also was allredye a doctour, namyd doctour Creukehorne, which was sent for to come to the byshope of Canterbury. And he before the iij. byshopis of Canterbury, of Worcetre, and Salesbury, confessed that he was rapte into heven, where he see the Trinite settyng in a pall, or mantell, or cope (call it what you please), of blew color, and from the midle upward they were thre bodyes, and from the midle were they closid all thre into on bodye, they were but on, havyng also but ij. feete nor but ij. legges ; and he spake with our ladye, and she toke hym bye the hande, and bad hym serve her as he had doon in tyme passed, and bad hym to preche aborde that she wold be honorid at Eppiswhiche and at Willisdon* as she hath bee in old tymes, *ne forte:* this he said he wolde abyde bye. Then my lord of Canterbury apposed hym nerre, and he made but weke aunswer, and was bade to departe and come agayne the second day aftre. So did he ; but at the laste he denyed his vision. Then he wold prove purcatory by a certayne vers in the Saulter, but when it was betin well to him he cowld nott byde bye it. The byshope

---

* At Ipswich and Willesdon there were images of the Virgin, which were objects of great reverence in Popish times. Saunderus, De Schismate Anglicano, mentions them :—" Sic et populus Christianus in Anglia ad certa loca sacra (in quibus B. Virginis aliæque sanctorum statuæ fuerunt erectæ, et operibus Dei mirandis honorabiles demonstratæ) orationis ergo ascendebat, cujusmodi tunc erant Walsinghamum, *Ipsvicus*, Vigornia, *Vilsedonum*, Cantuaria, et alia ejusmodi, quæ omnia Cromvellus disjecit et deformavit."

asked hym what shold move hym to take handefaste bye that place. " Mom," quod he, " My lord of London saide that it made well for it. What place in the Saulter it was, I can nott tell."

Then was there on Lamberte * within a vijth dayes and lesse aftre that, whiche was detecte of herysie to the iij. byshopis; his articles was this, that it was syn to pray to saintis. Then came he to his aunswer, and the thre byshopis cowld nott saye that it was necessari or nedefull, but he myght nott make syn of it; and yf he wolde agree to that, he myght have byn goon bye and bye, but he wold nott. Then was he comaunded to ward in the porter logde, and remayne there from that Monday tyll Frydaye nyght. Then he was sett at large to goo whether he wolde. He came thether backe agayne the morow to knowe the byshopes pleasure, whether he were all free or nott, and then theie apposid hym agayne, and he byde bye it, yet cowde they fynde it bye no scripture that we owght to do it. The byshope of Worcetre was most extreme agaynst hym, so was he sent to ward agayne. And on the next mornyng, which was Sondaye, they sent bothe hym and his articles to my lord chauncellour, and there he remaynyth in prison yet. My lord of Northefolk, the erle of Essex, and the cowntes of Oxfforthe, wrate to this byshopis agaynst hym, and for that cause men suppose they handelid hym so to please theym to geate favor, which thyng hathe within thys litle whyle don great hurt to the truthe, but what shall come of hym God knowith onlye.

Doctour Heyms prechithe before the kyng, as he is appoyntid, every Wedynsday this Lent, and on Wedynsday in the Ymbre he saide in his sermone that God hathe brought the truthe of his worde to light, and princis be the ministeris of it to gyve comaundement that it shold goo forward, and yet is no thynge regarded and make of hym but a Cristmas kyng. On Tewisdaye the same weke the byshope of Rochestre came to the Cruched Fryers, and inhibite a doctour and iij. or iiij. mo to hyre confessionis, and soe in Cardmaker, and oder in their placis. Then came

---

* This Lamberte was afterwards burnt in Smithfield for heresy.

the byshope of Londonis aparitor, came and raylid on thother byshope, and saide that he nor no suche as he is shall have jurisdiccion within his lordes precincte. Then was the byshope of London sent for on Thursday to make aunswer to it, but he was sike and myght nott com. Then on Fryday the clergye sate on it in the convocation howse at after-non a long tyme, and lafte of till anodre daye, and the meane tyme all men that have takyn any hurt, losse, or wrong at his hande, must bryng in their byllis and shall have recompence.

On Sondaye last the byshope of Worcetre preched at Paulis Crosse, and he saide that byshopis, abbatis, prioris, parsonis, cannonis resident, pristis, and all, were stronge thevis, ye dukis, lordis, and all; the kyng, quod he, made a marvelles good acte of parliament that certayne men sholde sowe every of theym ij. acres of hempe, but it were all to litle, were it so moche more, to hange the thevis that be in England. Byshopis, abbatis, with soche other, shold not have so many servauntes, nor so many dysshes, but to goo to their first foundacion, and kepe hospitalytie to fede the nedye people, not jolye felowis with goldyn chaynes and velvet gownys, ne let theym not onis come into the howsis of religioun for repaste; let theym call, knave byshope, knave abbat, knave prior, yet fede non of theym all, nor their horses, nor their doggis, nor ye[t] sett men at lybertye; also to ete fleshe and whit mete in Lent, so that it be don without hurtyng of weke consciences, and without sedition, and lykewise on Frydaye and all dayes. The byshope of Canterbury seythe that the kinges grace is at a full poynte for fryers and chauntry pristis, that they shall awaye all that, savyng tho that can preche. Than one saide to the byshope that they had good trust that they shold serve fforthe there lyffe tymes, and he saide they shulde serve it out at cart then, for any other service they shold have bye that.

On Saterdaye in the Ymbre weke the kinges grace came in amonge the burgesis of the parliament, and delyvered theym a bille, and bade theym loke upon it and waye it in conscience, for he wold nott, he saide, have theym passe on it nor on any other thyng because his grace gevith in the bill, but they to see yf it be for a comyn wele to his subjectis, and have an eye thetherwarde. And on Wedynsdaye next he will be there agayne to here their myndes. Ther shalbe a proviso made for poore people. The gaylis shalbe ryde, the faultye shall dye, and the odre shalbe acquyte bye proclamacion or bye jure, and shalbe sett at libertie, and paye no fees; and sturdye beggaris and suche prisonars as can nott be sett a worke, shalbe sett a worke at the kynges charge, somme at Dover, and somme at the place where the water hathe broken in on the londe, and other mo placis. Then yf they fall to idelnes, tho idelers shalbe had before a justice of peace and his fawte writen; then yf he be takyn idle agayne in another place, he shalbe knowne where his dwellyng is, and so at the second menycion he shalbe burnyd in the hande; and yf he fayle the iij^{de} tyme, he shall dye for it. This saide burgis of the parliament. Men sayd that the sayntuary shall, aftre this settyng of the parliament, hold no man for dett, morder, nor felenye, nor for none other cause, nor West-mester, nor S. Martyns, nor seint Kateryns, nor none other sain-tuary. Other newis knowe I none, as knowith our Lord, who ever kepe us all. Writen in haste, the xiijth day of Marche, by your owne to his litle power.

It has been already stated that the Charter-house in London and the religious houses at Richmond, Syon, and Greenwich had been involved in the affair of the Maid of Kent, and had distinguished themselves by their opposition to the measures of the King. They thus became the first of the religious houses that were subjected to a reforming visitation, and some of the monks and nuns were treated with great harshness and severity. The following five letters, all written apparently in the year 1535, relate to these visitations. Thomas Bedyll and Richard Layton were both of them afterwards very active visitors of the monasteries, as we shall see a little further on.

The Charter-house (a name known at present by the celebrated school established on its site) was founded in the reign of Edward III. by the famous soldier Sir Walter Manny; its site was selected by him originally to serve for a burial place in the fearful plague of 1349-50, and about 50,000 bodies are said to have been interred there during its continuance. It afterwards became a monastery of Carthusians. A considerable number of the Charter-house monks refused obstinately to acknowledge the king's supremacy: John Houghton, the prior, was executed on the 27th April, 1535; two others, William Exmewe and Sebastian Newdigate, suffered on the 18th of June following; and Richard Bere, John Davy, Thomas Johnson, Thomas Green, Thomas Shryne, Walter Pierson, Robert Salt, Thomas Redyng, and William Horn, were executed on the 4th of August.

XIV.

BEDYLL TO CROMWELL.

[From MS. Cotton. Cleop. E. vi. fol. 252.]

Pleace it you to understand, that on Tuesday furthwith upon my departure from you I repaired to the Charter-house, and had with me diverse bokes and annotations bothe of myne owne and others against the primacy of the bisshope of Rome, and also of sainct Peter, declaring evidently the equalite of the apostelles by the law of God. And after long communication more than on howre and a half with the vicar and procurater of the house, I left thoes bokes and annotations with thaim, that they shuld se the holy scriptures and doctors thereupon concernyng the said maters, and thereupon reforme theim selves acordingly. And yesterday they sent me the said bokes and annotations againe home to my house by a servant of thairs, without any word or writing. Wherfor I sent to the procurater to com and speke with me, seing I kept my bed bi reason of siknes, and could not com to him. And at his commyng, I demaunded of him whether he and the vicar and other of the sennors had seen or herd the said annotations, or perused the titles of the bokes making moost for the said maters. And he aunswerd that the vicar and he and Nudigat had spent the tyme upon thaim tyl ix. or x. of the clok at nyght, and that they saw nothing in thaim wherby they wer moved to alter thair opinion. I than declared to him the daingor of his opinion, whiche was like to be the destruction of thaim and thair house for ever; and as far as I could perceyve by my communication with the vicar and procurator on Tuesday, and with the procurater yesterday, they be obstinatly determined to suffer al extremites rather than to alter thair opinion, regarding no more the dethe of thair father in word or countenaunce than he wer leving and conversant among thaim. I also demaunded of the procurater whether the residue of his bretheren wer of like opinion, and he aunswerd he was not suer, but he thought the wer al of one mynd. I shewed him that I thought that the spirit whiche appered affor God, and seyed he wold be a fals spirite in the mouthes of al the prophetes of Acab, had inspired thaim and sowed thys obstinacy in thaim. Finally I suppose it to be the wyl of God, that as thair religion had a simple begynnyng, so in this realme it shal have a strainge ende, procured by thaim selfes and by none others. And albeit they pretend holines in this behalf, suerly the ground of thair said opinion is hypocrisy, vayne glory, confederacy, obstinacy, to thentent they may be seen to the worle, or specially to suche as have confidence in thaim, more feythful and more constant than any other. From Aldergate strete, this mornyng of Ascention day. I am so trobyld with the fever, that I am fayne to kepe my house.

By your owne,

THOMAS BEDYLL.

XV.

ROLAND LEE * AND BEDYLL TO CROMWELL.

[From MS. Cotton. Cleopat. E. IV. fol. 10.]

Please it yow to understande, that on Saterday laste aboute vj. of the clock we receyved your lettres by the provynciall of the

---

* Roland Lee had been one of the King's chaplains, and performed the marriage ceremony between the King and Anne Boleyn: in 1534 he had been made Bishop of Coventry and Lichfield, and the King also conferred upon him the presidency of the council of Wales.

Augustyn ffriers, according to the which lettres we tooke our journey ffurthwithe towardes Richemount, and came thither betwixte x. and xj. at night, and in the mornyng ffolowing we had ffirst comunication with the warden and oon of the seniors named Sebastian, and after with the hole convent, and moved them by all the meanes and policies that we coulde devise to consent to the articles delyvered unto us by the saide provynciall, and requyred the confirmation of them by their convent seale; which warden and convent shewed them selfes very untowarde in that behalfe, and theruppon we were fforced to move the convent to putt the matter holly in the arbitrement of theire senyours, otherwise named distrettes, which were but iiij. in nomber, and that they iiij. havyng ffull auctoritie to consent or dissent ffor them all, and in the name of them all, shulde meate us at Grenewiche this day in the mornyng, and bring their convent seale with them; and so they did. And when we came to Grenewich we exhorted the convent likewise to putt the hole mattier in the handes of their seniors, or distrettes, to thentent to avoide superfluouse woordes and idle reasonyng, and specially to thentent that if the distrettes shulde refuse to consent, it were better after our myndes to strayne a ffewe then a multytude. But at Grenewiche we coulde in no wise obteyne to have the mattier put in the distrettes handes and arbitrement, but the convent stiffely affyrmed that wher the mattier concerned perticulerly every oone of their soules, they wolde aunswere perticulerly every man ffor hym self. And when, after muche reasonyng and debating, we requyred to have their ffinall and determynatt aunswer, which we demaunded of every oone of them perticulerly, we ffounde them in oone mynde of contradiction and dissent ffrom the saide articles, but specially agaynst this artycle, *Quod episcopus Romanus nihilo majoris neque auctoritatis aut jurisdictionis habendus sit quam ceteri quivis episcopi in Anglia vel alibi gentium in sua quisque diocesi.* And the cause of their dissent, as they saide, was by reason that that article was clerely agaynst their professyon and the rules of sayncte Frauncis, in which rules it is thus wrytten (as they shewed unto us): *Ad hec per obedientiam injungo ministris ut petant a domino papa unum de sancte Romane ecclesie cardinalibus, qui sit gubernator, protector, et corrector istius fraternitatis, ut semper subditi et subjecti pedibus sancte ecclesie ejusdem stabiles in fide catholica paupertatem et humilitatem, et secundum Evangelium Domini nostri Jesu Christi, quod firmiter promisimus observemus.* Wherunto thre aunswers: First, that saincte Frauncis and his brethern at the beginnyng were dwellyng in Italie undre the obedience of the bisshoppe of Rome, as all monkes not exempte be undre the obedience of the bisshoppe off Canterbury, and therfore it were no marvaile that saincte Frauncis wolde his brethern to be obedient to the bisshoppe of Rome, being their prelate; at which tyme of sayncte Frauncis, and long after, ther were none of his ordre in Englonde, and therfore thies woordes wer not ment by ffriers of Englonde. The seconde aunswere that we made was this, that the chapiter of saincte Frauncis rule which they alleyge makith mention of mynystres, and that they shulde desyer of the pope to have oone of the cardynalles which shulde be governer, protectour, and correctour of their brotherhode; and we shewed them that in our opynyon that chapiter was, no parte of saincte Frauncis rule, but was fforged sythens and planted into the same by some ambicious ff[ri]ar of that ordre, ffor, as we supposed, the name of mynystres was not founde out or spoken of when their rule was confyrmed; and it is to be thought that saincte Frauncis, being a holy man, was desyrous to have a cardynall to governe and correcte his brethern. Thirdely, we affyrmed unto them that they were the kinges subjectes, and that by the lawe of God they owed him their entier obedience; and that the pope and saincte Frauncis and they them selves, with their vowes, othes, or professions, coulde take away not oone jote of the obedience which they owe to the kinge by Goddis lawe. And we shewed them that none of the kinges subjectes coulde submytte himself or beare obedience to any other prynce or prelate, without the kinges consent. And if he did, he did the kinges grace greate injurye, and offendid God, breakyng his lawes commaunding obedience towardes prynces. And in this behalf we shewed that the king, being a christen prynce, was a spirituall man, and that obedience which they owed to the kinge by Goddes lawe was a spirituall obedience and in spirituall causes; ffor they wolde be obedient but only in temporall causes. But all this reason coulde not synke into their obstinatt heddes and worne in custome of obedience of the pope. Albeit we ffurther declared unto them that bothe archebissoppes of this realme, the bisshoppes of London, Wynchester, Duresme, Bathe, and all other prelattes and heddes, and all the ffamouse clerkes of this realme, have subscrybed to this conclusyon, *Quod Romanus pontifex non habet majorem jurisdictionem ex sacris literis in hoc regno Anglie quam quivis alius externus episcopus.* All this notwithstanding, their conclusion was, they had professed saincte Frauncis religion, and in the observance therof they wolde lyve and dye. Sory we be we can not bring them to no better fframe and ordre in this behalf, as our ffaithfull myndes was to doo, ffor the accomplishment of the kinges pleasure. From the Myles ende, the xvth day of June.

> By yower assurydly, ROLAND CO. ET LICH.
> Your owne, THOMAS BEDYLL.

To master Secretary.

XVI.

BEDYLL TO CROMWELL.

[From MS. Cleop. E. vi. fol. 168.]

After my moost due thankes and hertie commendations unto you, I do you to understand that, as it was agreed bytwixt you and me at your departing, I have deliverd al maister Dr. Fysshers bookes late bisshope of Rochester, devised by him in the defense of the kinges grace first unlawful marriage and against his secund lawful marriage, to my lord of Cauntrebury, to be seen and weyed by him and suche as gyve attendance on him at this tyme for thaunswer to be made to Cocleus* boke and others, trusting that my said lord and the said other lerned men wol make so substancial aunswer to the said M. Fisshers books and the seid others, that not only the peple of this tyme, but also suche as shal rede the said aunswers at al tymes hereafter, shall wel perceyve thereby that al the kinges procedinges in thoes maters have been grownded upon good reasons and auctorites founded in the law of God, which his grace was bounden in conscience to folow, notwithstanding any other assertion or intelligence.

I have also been at Syon sith your departing with my lord of London, where we have found the lady abbas and susters as conformable in every thing as myght be devised. And as towching the father confessor and ffather Cursone (whiche be the saddest men ther and best learned) they shewed thaimselfes like honest men; and I think the confessor wol now on Sonday next in his sermon make due mension of the kinges title of supreme hed, acording as he is commaunded. What towardnes or intowardnes we have seen in som other of the brethern there, I wol informe you at your retorne to Londone, and omitte it now bicause I have som hope that by the wisedome of the father confessor and father Cursone the residue shal shortly be brought to good conformite. And if not, there be two of the brethern must be weded out, whiche be sumwhat sediciose, and have labored busily to infect thair felowes with obstinacy against the kinges said title.

I had the father confessor alone in the very secrete comunication concernyng certen letters of the said M. Fisshers, of whiche father Rainold made mention in his examination, whiche the said Fissher promised the kinges grace that he never shewed to any

---

* Cocleus, a German theologian, was one of the foreign writers against the King's divorce from Catharine of Arragon.

other man, nouther wold. The said confessor hath confessed to
me that the said Fissher sent to him, to the said Rainold, and to
one other brother of thers decessed, whoes name I remember not,
the copy of his said letters directed to the kinges grace, and the
copie of the kinges aunswer also, but he hath sworen to me upon
his fidelite that the said copies tarried not with thaim but one
nyght, and that none of his brethern saw thees same but thees
thre affor named. He hath knowleged to me also that the said
Fissher sent unto thaim with the said copies a boke of his made in
the defense of the kinges grace first marriage, whiche he confessed himself to have in his keping, and which he hath willingly
deliverd unto me, and also Abels booke, and one other booke made
by the emperour his ambassitor (as I suppose).

My lord of Londone declared reasons for the confirmation of the
kinges title of supreme hed, and for the infirmation and extinc-
tion of the bisshope of Rome jurisdiction and power within this
realme, in such maner and fassion as was excellent and singuler.
And maister More hath used him self like a feithful true man to
his prince, and I wol ye wold write him som commendations or
thankes to recomfort him. Finally maister almaner and I wold
know your mynd and pleasure concernyng the boke whiche we
drewe out of my lord of Yorke his bothe devises, whereof we with-
drewe many thinges and likewise added. And where ye willed us
to adde thereto suche substancial mater for the purpose as we
shuld thinke convenient, that it myght be set furthe to printe,
albeit we have gathered suche mater as shal please you when ye
se it, yet we wol not be so bolde as put it to printe tyl ye se it
and allowe it.

I have kept Londone al this yere, and have had litel passetyme
abrode. If it myght please you to help me to a warrant or two in
Kent, at Ledys or elwher, or nyghe London, it wolde be muche to
my comfort, whiche am alwayes at your commaundement. From
London, the xxviij[th] day of July. By your owne,

THOMAS BEDYLL.

XVII.

DR. LAYTON TO CROMWELL.

[From MS. Cott. Cleop. E. IV. fol. 125.]

Hit may please your goodnes to understonde that Bisshope this day prechede and declarede the kinges title varawell, and hade a gret audience, the churche full of people. One of the focares in his saide declaration openly callede hym fals knave, with other folisshe wordes. Hit was that folisshe felowe with the curlede hede, that knelyde in your way whan ye came forthe of the confessors chambre. I cannolesse do but set hym in prison, *ut pena ejus sit metus aliorum.* Yesterday I lernede many enormouse thynges againste Bisshope in the examination of the lay brederen; firste that Bisshope persuadyt two of the brederyn to have gone ther ways by nyght, and he hymself with them, and to thaccomplicement of that they lakede but money to by the seculer apparell; further, that Bisshope wolde have persuadyt one of his lay brederen, a smyth, to have made a key for the dore, to have in the nyght tyme receyvide in wenches for hym and his felowe, and specially a wiffe of Uxbrige nowe dwellyng not far from the olde lady Darbie, nygh Uxbrige, wiche wiffe his olde customer hath bene many tymes at the graittes commonyng with the saide Bisshope, and muche he was desierouse to have hade hir conveyde in to hym. The saide Bisshope also persuadyt a nune, to whome he was confessor, *ad libidinem corporum perimplendam,* and thus he persuadyt hir in confession, makyng hir to beleve that whansoever and as offt as they shulde medle together, if she were immediatly affter confessede by hym, and towke of hym absolution, she shulde be clere forgyvyn of Gode, and hit shulde be none offence unto hir before Gode; and she write dyvers and sondrie letters unto hym of suche ther folisshenes and unthrifftynes, and wolde have hade his

brother the smythe to have pullede owte a bare of yron of that
windowe wheras ye examinede the lady abbas, that he myght have
gone in to hir by nyght, and that same windowe was ther commonyng place by nyght. He persuadyt the sexten that he wolde be
in his contemplacion in the churche by nyght, and by that meanes
was many nyghtes in the churche talkyng with hir at the saide
graite of the nunnes qwere, and ther was ther metyng place by
nyght, besyddes ther day communication, as in confession. Hit
were to long to declare all thynges of hym that I have herde,
wiche I suppos is trewe. This affter none I intende to make further serche, bothe of sum of the brederen and sum also of the
sisters, for suche lyke matters; if I fynde any thynges apparant to
be trewe, I shall, Gode willyng, therof certifye your mastershipe to
morowe by vij. in the mornyng, and affter this day I suppos ther
wilbe no other thynges to be knowyn as yett here, for I have
alredy examynede all the brederen, and many of them wolde gladly
depart hens, and be ryght wery of ther habite: suche religion and
faynede sanctitie Gode save me fro! If Mr. Bedyll hade bene here
a frear and of Bisshops cownsell, he wolde ryght well have helpede
hym to have browght his matter to passe withoute brekyng up of
any graite or yett cownterfetyng of keys, suche capacitie Gode
hathe sende hym. From Sion, this Sonday xij. Decembris. By
the spedy hande of your assurede poire preste,

RICHARD LAYTON.

XVIII.

BEDYLL TO CROMWELL.

[From MS. Cott. Cleop. E. iv. fol. 109.]

Right worshipful, after my moost hertie commendations, pleace
it you to understand that maister Leighton and I have had muche

busines with this house sythens your departing hens; and as for
the brethern, they stand stif in thair obstinacy as you left thaim.
Copynger and Lache were sent to my lord of London on Moneday. Here wer on Tuesday doctor Buttes and the quenys
amner to convert Wytford and Litell; and on Wensday here wer
doctor Aldrigge, doctour Curven, doctor Bawghe, and doctor Morgan, sent by the kinges grace for that purpose, but they nothing
proficted. I handled Whitford after that in the garden, bothe with
faire wordes and with foule, and shewed him that throughe his
obstinacy he shuld be brought to the greate shame of the world
for his irreligious life, and for his using of bawdy wordes to diverse
ladys at the tymes of thair confession, whereby (I seyed) he
myght be the occasion that shrift shalbe layed downe throughe
England: but he hath a brasyn forehed, whiche shameth at nothing. One Mathew, a lay brother, upon hope of liberte, is reformed. We wolde fayne know your advise what we shal do with
Whitford and Litell, and a lay brother, one Turnyngton, whiche
is very sturdy against the kinges title. We have sequesterd
Whitford and Litell from hering of the ladys confessions; and
we think it best that the place wher thes frires have been wont to
hire uttward confessions of al commers at certen tymes of the yere
be walled up, and that use to be fordoen for ever; ffor that hering
of utward confessions hath been the cause of muche evyl, and of
muche treson whiche hath been sowed abrode in this mater of the
kinges title, and also in the kinges graces mater of his succession
and mariage. On Wensday my lord Wyndesore came hither, sent for
by maister Leighton and me, and labored muche that day for the
converting of his suster and som other of his kynneswomen here;
and yesterday we had my lord of London here in the chapiter
house of women, and the confessor also, whiche bothe toke it upon
thair consciences and upon the perill of thair soulys that the ladys
owght by Godes law to consent to the kinges title, wherewith they
wer muche comforted; and wher we wylled al suche as consented
to the kinges title to syt styll, and al suche as wold not consent

therunto to depart out of the chapter-house, there was found none emong thaim whiche departed. Albeit I was informed this nyght that one Agnes Smyth, a sturdy dame and a wylful, hath labored diverse of her susters to stop that we shuld not have thair convent seal; but we trust we shal have it this mornyng, with the subscription of thabbes for her self and al her susters, whiche is the best fassion that we can bring it to. The persone whiche ye spak with at the grate, covyteth very muche to speke with you, seyng she hath suche thinges whiche she wold utter to no man but to you, and what they be I can not conject. We purpose this after none, or els tomorow mornyng, to awaite on the king grace, to know his pleasir in every thing, and specially towching the muring up of the howses of utterward confessions. Maister Leyghton hath wreten certen compertes unto you, and therefor I forber to spek any thing therof. The ladys of Sion besecheth you to be good maister unto thaim, and to thair house, as thair special trust is in you, and that they all run not into obloquy and slaunder for the mysbehavor of one person. A greate number of the ladys desired me to speke unto you that Bisshope and Parkere myght be discharged from the house of Sion, and Bisshope and Parker desire the same; I mervaile that they desire not likewise to be discharged of the person with whom ye talked at the grate, seing Bisshopes caus and that is one. From Sion, the xvij^th. day of December,

By yours, as your servant,

THOMAS BEDYLL.

The next letter forms a link in the long chain of evidence of the state in which the English monastic houses had fallen, when the visitation took place. The early history of the monastery of Stavordale in Somersetshire is very obscure. It is said to have been founded by Sir William Zouche. In the reign of Henry VIII. it was annexed to the Abbey of Taunton. There appears no reason for believing that Richard Zouche obtained the appointment which he here solicits.

XIX.

RYCHARD ZOUCHE TO CROMWELL.

[From MS. Cott. Cleop. E. iv. fol. 260.]

Sure, pleshyt your goode mastershype to underston that wer I dewlle ys a pore pryery, a fundacion off my nawynsetres, wyche ys my lorde my fatheres ynerytans and myne, and be the resone off a lewyde pryore that was ther, wyche was a schanon off Tawntoun afor, browytte hytt to be a sell unto Tawntoun, and now hys hytt dystryde, and ther ys but to chanons, wyche be off no goode levyng, and that ys gret petty, the pore howseholde be so yett yntretyd; werfor yff ytt may plese your good masterchyppe to be so good master to me to gett me the pore howse wyche ys callyd Staverdell, I wer bownde to pray for your masterchyp, and also I schal bere you my herty servys nextt the kynge ys gras, and be at your commayndment, be the gras off God, ho ever preserve your goode masterchype.

Your howyne pore servantt and bedman,

RYCHARDE ZOUCHE.

The following letter belongs, perhaps, to the next year, although it is strange that Sir Peter Dutton should address Cromwell by the simple title of *mastership* at so late a date. From documents given in Ormerod's History of Cheshire, it appears that the abbot of Norton refused to surrender his house, and that the attempt to enforce the orders of the court excited a serious insurrection, and the commissioners were obliged to take shelter in the tower of the priory church. The abbot and other persons concerned in this affair were arrested by Sir Peter Dutton, then Sheriff of Cheshire, and the former is supposed to have been executed. It may be observed, however, that this insurrection appears to have taken place at the beginning of October, 1536, whereas the present letter is dated at the beginning of August.

This little house was founded as a priory, about 1133 or 1135 at Runcorne in Cheshire, by William Fitz Nigel, and was moved by his son in the time of Stephen to Norton. Early in the fifteenth century it was changed from a priory to an abbey.

XX.

SIR PETER DUTTON TO CROMWELL.

[From MS. Harl. 604, fol. 54.]

Please it your gud mastership, my duetie remembert, thes to advertise you that I have taken the bodies of thabbot of Norton, Robert Jannyns, and the straunger, a connyng smythe, two of the seid abbottes servantes, also Rondull Breretone, baron of the kynges excheker of Chestre, and John Hale of Chestre, merchaunt, and have theym in my custody and kepyng. And the rest I entende to have as spedely as I can, and to be with you with theym, God willyng, in all convenyent spede as I possible may. Moreover, I haue causet dan Rondull Wylmyslow, the moncke of the Walle Royall, to cum up to you, for whom I spake unto your gud mastership, whiche is a gud religious man, discrete and wel groundet in lernyng, and hathe many gud qualites most apte to be a master of a religious howse then any other moncke of that howse. Wherfour it may please your gud mastership to be his gud master toward his preferrement that he may be admitted master of the same, and that I did promyse your mastership this seid moncke will accomplisshe accordyngly, wherefour I beseche your mastership that this berer and the seid moncke may resorte unto yow from tyme to tyme, to knowe youre pleasure therin, ensuryng you what ye do for me or my frynde, all is your owne, as knowithe our lord God, who mercifully preserve you. At Dutton, the iij^{de}. day of Auguste,

By youres assured,

PERUS DUTTON, K.

To the right honorable
  and his especiall gud master, maister Cromwell,
  secretary unto our sovereign lord the kynge.

The general visitation of the monasteries, which led to the suppression of the smaller houses, began in the autumn of 1535, under the immediate direction of Cromwell. One of his most active agents was Dr. Legh, mentioned in the following paper. Stowe, speaking of this event, says that the visitors " put forth all religious persons that would goe, and all that were under the age of foure and twentie yeeres : and after closed up the residue that would remeine, so that they shuld not come out of their places, and took order that no man should come to the houses of women, nor women to the houses of men, but onely to heare their service in the churches : all religious men that departed, the abbot or prior to give them for their habite a priestes gowne, and forty shillings of money; the nuns to have such apparell as secular women weare, and to go wher thei wold." The " closing up" of the monks in their houses is a circumstance frequently alluded to in the letters which follow.

The abbey of Wardon, or De Sartis, in Bedfordshire, was founded by Walter de Espec in 1135, and was furnished with monks from the abbey of Rievaulx. Henry Emery, the writer of the following paper, was the last abbot : he does not appear to have resigned his office till the surrender of his house on the 4th of December, 1538. Abbot Henry's " cawses" for resigning present a curious picture of the ignorance and turbulence of the monks.

XXI.

THE ABBOT OF WARDON'S REASONS FOR RESIGNING.
[From MS. Cotton. Cleopat. E. iv. fol. 163.]

Theis be the cawses folowing whi that I, Henri abbot off Wardon, have made labor to diverse of my frendis to resigne my office.

Firste, immediatele affter the kinges graces visitacion was executidd bi his commissioners master doctor Leighe and master Jo. ap Rece, and certaigne injunctions bi them to me and mi bretherne deliveridd to be observidd, mi saide bretherne toke occasion agenste me therat, and said amongest them that I was the cawser whi that thei wer enclosidd within ther monasteri, to this entent (as thei didd imagine) that I might do owtwardeli what I wollde, and they sholld not knowe it. From that tyme to this presente daie thei have vexidd me with many uncharitable surmises and obprobrius wordes, to muche and longe to be wreten.

Item, that whereas wee bi the said injunctions be commandid to have earlie lecture of divinite, whe have none ; and whan it is redd, few or non of the monkes cum to it.

Item, I ded assigne dampne Thomas Londone to rede the divinite lecture, and he undiscretele (unknowinge to me) did rede the bokes off Eccius Omelies, whiche bokes be all carnall and off a brutall understanding, and entret of many thinges clene anenst the determinacion of the churche of Endglonde. And so sone as I hadd knowledg off theis premisses, I toke from him his said bokes and sent to Londone to be deliverid to master doctor Leghe, and dischargid the said dan Thomas off his reding, and cawsid mi brother to rede the lecture; and then fewe or none of them wollde come at him.

Item, for as muche as I did perceave ignorance was a greate cawse whi that theis my bretherne wer thus farre owt of goode order and in continuall unquettnesse, to thentent that I wollde somwhat an inducedd them to understanding, I cawsid bokes of gramer to be bowghte for eche off them, and assignidd mi brother to enstructe theim, but ther wollde come non to him but one Richard Balldok and Thomas Clement.

Item, they be in nombre xv. brethern, and excepte iij. off them, non understand ne knowe ther rule nor the statutes off ther religione.

Item, in Lente I did sende forthe dampne Thomas Wardon in this housse besinesse, and he did sit at Shesforde all night at the ale howsse, and cam whom in the morning at matens tyme, for the wiche cawse I wollde a ministerid correccion to him, but he declaridd openle before the covent that I hadd no auctorite to correcte him, and steryd them sediciousli agenste me, in so muche that on dampne Cristofer thretenidd me and my servandes. Thus I was in suche fere that I did command my servandes to watche mi chambur iiij. nightis after, till ther furi was somwhat aswagidd.

Item, where above all other thinges I have often commandidd bothe the supprior and (as we call him) the *custos ordinis* that ther shulld no seculer bois be conversant with ony of the monkes, ne to lye in ther dortor; this notwithstanding ther is on Hewgh, that was a yonge monke here, and he lïethe in the dortor every night, but with whome I can not knowe; and the same Hewghe was here yester daie.

Item, the vth. daie of August Jhon Paxton and Henre Gibbeson did take the subprior in a hedge yn the vineyarde with a brethell woman, and he did promise viij^s. to the saide Gibbeson to kepe his cowncell.

Item, William Caringtone, Thomas Bikkliswade, Thomas London, Jhon Clifftone, Cristofer Wardon, be common dronkerdes.

I have not ascertained of what nunnery Margaret Vernon, the writer of the next letter, was abbess. The visitors, by putting in force the injunctions already alluded to, seem to have nearly emptied the house, all the sisters but one having quitted it voluntarily or by force: and the abbess herself appears to have been not unwilling to follow their example.

XXII.

MARGARET VERNON TO CROMWELL.

[From MS. Cotton. Cleop. E. iv. fol. 55.]

After all dew commendacyons had unto yowre good maystershyp, with my most umble thankes for the greate coste mayd on me and my pore maydyn at my last beynge with yowre maystershyp, furthermore plesyth yt yow to understonde that yowre vysytors hath bene here of late, who hath dyscharged iij. of my systers, the one ys dame Catheryn, the other ij. ys the yonge women that were last professyd, whyche ys not a lyttyll to my dyscomforte; neverthelesse I must be content with the kynges plesure. But now as towchynge my nowne parte, I most humbly beseche yow to be so specyall good mayster unto me yowre poore bedewoman, as to geve me yowre best advertysment and counseyle what waye shalbe best for me to take, seynge there shalbe none left here but my selfe and thys pore madyn; and yf yt wyl please yowre goodnes to take thys pore howse into yowre owne hondes, ether for yowre selfe, or for my nowne [maister] yowre sonne, I woyld be glad with all my hart to geve yt into yowre mastershypes hondes, with that ye wyll commaunde me to do therin. Trustynge and nothynge dowptynge in yowre goodnes, that ye wyll so provyd for us, that we shall have syche onest lyvynge that we shall not be drevyn be necessyte nether to begge, nor to fall to no other unconvenyence. And thus I offer my sylfe and all myne unto yowre most hygh and prudent wysdome, as unto hym that ys my only refuge and comfort in thys world,·besechynge God of hys goodnes to put in yow hys holy sprete, that ye maye do all thynge to hys lawde and glory.

By yowre owne assured bedewoman,

MARGARET VERNON.

The writer of the next letter was at the time visiting the abbey of Lacock, in Wiltshire.

XXIII.

DR. LEGH TO CROMWELL.

[From MS. Harl. No. 604, fol. 59.]

After my due and moste hartie commendacions, please it your mastership to be advertised, that whereas I have in all the places that I have ben at, according to myne instructions and to the kinges graces pleasure and yours, restrayned as well the heddes and masters of the same places as the brethern from going foorth of the precincte of the said places, which I adsure you greveth the said heddes not a litle, as ye shall well perceve by thinstant sutes that they shall make to the kinges grace and to you. It hathe ben reaported unto me sens my comyng to theis parties, that Mr. doctour Laitone hathe not doon the same in the places where he hathe ben, but licenced the heddes and masters to goo abrode, which I suppose maketh the brethern to grudge the more, whan they see that they be worse entreated than their master, which hath professed the same rule that they have. Wherfor, to thintent that an uniformitie maye be observed amongest us in all our procedinges, it maye please your mastershipp other to commaunde Mr. doctour Laytone to geve the same injuncions where he goeth and hath ben that I have geven in the places aforesaid, in which case yf ye see reasonable causes wherfor ye shulde release the same injunctions in some places ye maye at all tymes ; or els to advertise me of your pleasure therein, that I maye confourme myself to the same, and direct my proceding after one weye with you. Sir, yf ye go to Oxforde shortely, as ye ones intended, this bringer is a man of good experience and intelligence there and can declare you the state of the Universitie very well. Thus knoweth Allmightie God, who have your mastership in his blessed tuicion. From Laycok, the xxth of Auguste.

Yours ever assureyt,

THOMAS LEGH.

To the right honourable
M^{r}. Thomas Crumwell, principall
secretarie to the kinges highnes.

The account of the relics at Maiden Bradley, in Wiltshire, and of the frailties of the prior, given in the following letter, is amusing. This small priory was founded in the latter part of the twelfth century. It was originally a house for leprous women, established by one of the Bisets. The last prior was Richard Jenyn, who, after the dissolution of his house, obtained the rectory of Shipton Moyne, in Gloucestershire.

The visitatorial injunctions were very severe against relics, and the worship of images : one of them, as given in the Cottonian MS. (Cleop. E. iv. fol. 21), runs as follows :—
" Item, that they shall not shewe no relyques or fayned myracles for encrease of lucre, but that they exhorte pylgrymes and strayngers to geve that to the poore that they thought to offere to ther images or reliquies." In the lists of relics in other monasteries, we find many which were pretended to be preservative of women in labour ; they had previously been made an object of satire in Piers Ploughman's Creed.

XXIV.

DR. LAYTON TO CROMWELL.

[From MS. Cott. Cleop. E. iv. fol. 249.]

Pleasit your mastershipe to understonde, that yesternyght late we came from Glassynburie to Bristowe to Saint Austins, wheras we begyn this mornyng, intendyng this day to dispache bothe this howse here, beyng but xiiij. chanons, and also the Gawntes,* wheras be iiij. or v. By this bringar, my servant, I sende yowe relyqwis, fyrste, two flowres wrappede in white and blake sarcenet that one Christynmas evyn *hora ipsa qua Christus natus fuerat* will spring and burgen † and bere blossoms, *quod expertum esse,* saith the prior off Maden Bradeley; ye shall also receve a bage of reliquis, wherin ye shall se straingeis thynges, as shall appere by the scripture, as, Godes cote, Oure lades smoke, Parte of Godes supper *in cena domini, Pars petre super qua natus erat Jesus in Bethelem,* belyke ther is in Bethelem plentie of stones and sum qwarrie, and makith ther maingierres off stone. The scripture of evere thyng shall declare yowe all; and all thes of Maden Bradeley, wheras is an holy father prior, and hath but vj. children, and but one dowghter mariede yet of the goodes of the monasterie, trystyng shortly to mary the reste. His sones be tale men waittyng upon hym, and he thankes Gode a never medelet with marytt women, but all with madens the faireste cowlde be gottyn, and always marede them ryght well. The pope, consideryng his fragilitie, gave hym licens to kepe an hore, and hath goode writyng *sub plumbo* to discharge his conscience, and toc hoys M[r]. Underhyll to be his gostely father, and he to gyve hym *plenam remissionem,* &c.

I sende yowe also oure lades gyrdell of Bruton,‡ rede silke,

* Billeswyke Hospital, in the suburbs of Bristol, was also called Gaunt's from Maurice de Gaunt, by whom it was founded, before 1229.

† Burgen, *to bud.*

‡ The priory of Bruton or Brewetone, in Somersetshire, was founded about the year 1005, by Athelmer, earl of Cornwall. It was converted into an abbey in the beginning of the reign of Henry VIII.

wiche is a solemne reliquie sent to women travelyng, wiche shall not miscarie *in partu.* I sende yowe also Mare magdalens girdell, and that is wrappyde and coveride with white, sent also with gret reverence to women traveling, wiche girdell Matilda thempresse, fownder of Ferley,* gave unto them, as saith the holy father of Ferley. I have crosses of silver and golde, sum wiche I sende yow not now bycause I have mo that shalbe delivered me this nyght by the prior of Maden Bradeley hym self. To morowe erly in the mornyng I shall bring yow the reste, whan I have recevide all, and perchaunce I shall fynde sum thyng here. In casse ye depart this day, hit may please yowe to sende me worde by this bringer, my servant, wiche way I shall repaire affter yowe. Within the Chartar Howse hath professide and done althynges accordyng as I shall declare yow at large to morowe erly. At Bruton and Glasenburie ther is nothyng notable ; the brethren be so straite keppide that they cannot offende, but faine they wolde if they myght, as they confesse, and so the faute is not in them. From Sainte Austines withoute Bristowe, this saint Bartilmews day, at iiij. of the cloke in the mornyng, by the spedy hande of your moste assurede poir preste,

RYCHARDE LAYTON.

John Bartelot, the subject of the following letter, is probably the same person who will be found a little later concerned in a somewhat similar discovery to that here mentioned. His transaction with the prior of the Crutched friars is not greatly to his credit : and the chancellor appears to have formed no very unjust opinion of him.

XXV.

JOHN BARTELOT TO CROMWELL.

[From MS. Cotton. Cleopat. E. iv. fol. 134.]

Pleas it your honourable mastership to be advertisid, that in the tyme of Lent last past your contynuell oratour John Bartelot,

---

* Farley, in Wiltshire, was a small house dependent on the priory of Lewes, founded by the second Humphrey de Bohun. The empress Matilda was a benefactress, as appears from the confirmation charter of Henry III.

with other to the noumber of v. personez of good conversacion, ffound the prior of the Crossid Fryers in London at that tyme beyng in bedde with his hoore, both nakyd, abought xj. of the clok in the for none, upon a Fryday, at which tyme the said priour, to thentent his mysdemeaner and shamfull facte shuld not be knowen wherby he shuld susteyn opyn shame, knelid upon his kneez, and not only desyrid your said oratour and his cumpany to kepe secret his said acte and not to disclose in any wise the same, but also for the same entent frely of his owen mocion yaf amonges theym about xxx^{li}. which he then was possessid of, of the which summe your oratour hadde by the said yef* abought vij^{li}. And also the said priour promysid to yef amonges the said company xxx^{li}. more by a certen day. And after by mediacion of ffrendes of the said priour, the said xxx^{li}. was releasid to the summe of vj^{li}, which vj^{li}. the said priour bound hym self to pay to your oratour by his bill obligatorie at a certen day in the same lymittid. Yet this notwithstonding, for because your said oratour for nonpayment of the said vj^{li}. did arrest the said ffryer, he hath so heynously enformed the lord chauncellour ayenst your oratour, that he not oonly will put hym to suertie, making the premisses a heynous robery, sayeng opynly that your oratour is worthy to be hangid, but also will by his high auctorite compell your oratour to repay ayen to the said ffryer the summe of xxx^{li}., oonles your moost charitable goodnes be therin otherwise shewid. Yt may therfor pleas your good mastership, of your aboundaunt goodnes, to provyd that the premissez may be duly examyned according to equite, for this is the very and hole truth in the same. And your said oratour shall pray to God for your honour and preservacion long to endewer.

      By your humble to his pour duryng his lif,

JOHN BARTELOT.

To the right honourable master secretory.

* Gift.

The abbeys of Rievaulx and Fountains, mentioned in the following letter, are well known at the present day by their extensive and picturesque ruins. The former, a house of the Cistercian order, was founded in 1131 by Walter Espec; the latter was founded in the year following (1132) by a colony of monks of the abbey of St. Mary at York. This letter can hardly be by the same Thomas Legh who was so active a visitor, and whose signature occurs so frequently to other letters.

XXVI.

THOMAS I. LEGH TO CROMWELL.

[From MS. Cotton. Cleopat. E. iv. fol. 137.]

Pleasithe it your mastershyp to be advartesyd that, according unto your commandement, with most diligence I hawe deliverd your letter, also attymes most convenient referryd unto the kynges commyssionars at Riwax siche credance as yower pleisar and equite wolde, whyche uppon the abbott of Funtans partt was butt lyghtly regardyd, and playnly expressyd of the same, that suche letter as I deliveryd and credance relatyde was ffrom M. Crumwell onley, and nott ffrom the kinges hyghnesse, wheropon, by the councelles of docter Spensar and Boyear, a procter, after evidence prove be wyttnessys, and the abbott of Rywax confession publishyde, the said abbott amonge other exceptions dyd laye thys excepcion, *Quod vigore literarum nulla commissionariis nec illorum alicui competit aut competere potest jurisdictio contra prefatum abbatem de Rievalle, pro eo videlicet et ex quo dicte littere regie fuerunt et sunt dolose, surreptitie, quod sunt tacita veritate et expressa falsitate per dolum et fraudem ac hujusmodi (?) serenissimi principis nostri circumventione impetrate,* who in hys obstinacie and parrvarse mynde adhering to the rulles of hys religion, as he said, departyd from Riwax, and wolde nott accordingli unto your letters thare remayne for the accomplyshment of the kinges commaundement, notwithstondyng that I often tymes desiryd hym and commaundyd hym in the kinges name to tarry and make prosses according to justice withowt forder delay; whyche rebelliouse mynde at this tyme is soo radicate, not only in hym, butt also in money of that religion,

as in the abbott of Rywax wryting thys letter here inclosyde to
the slaundare of the kinges heygnes, and after the kinges lettars
receivyd dyd imprison and otharways punyche divers of hys
brethern whyche ware ayenst hym and hys dissolute lywing; also
dyd take ffrom one of the same, being a wery agyd man, all hys
money whyche he shulde hawe made hys jubili withalle, that as
persons almost nothing regarding God and veri lytyll owr grett
maister the king, under the pretence of the rwlles of there religion, lyvythe as persones, *solute ab omni lege seu obedientia et Deo
et regi debita,* being abowghtwardes, as yt semythe to me, to rwlle
the king by ther rulles, whyche ys a perverse ordre that so noble
a hedde shulde be rulyd by so putride and most corrupte membres. *Sed Cato inquit, obsta principiis.* All the cuntre maykythe
exclamacions of thys abbot of Riwax, uppon hys abhomynable
lywing and extorcions by hym commyttyd, also many wronges to
divers myserable persons don, whyche evidently duthe apere by
bylles corroboratt to be trwe, wythe ther othese corporale in the
presens of the commissionars and the said abbott takyn, and
opon the same xvj. witnessys examynyd, affermyng ther exclamacions to be trwe. Therfore, *tempore jam instante,* the kinges
magiste consideryd, whome they hawe knowligyd to be *supremum
caput totius ecclesie Anglicane,* the honor of my lorde of Rutland *
in thys besynes remembryd, your worshyp and also my pore
honeste not forgotton, they wolde ether quykli be lokyd opon and
shortly, or elles ther dessolute lywing with rebelliose demeanour
shall every day increase more and more, to the dysplesour of God,
disquietnes of the kinges prerogative, and reproche slanderouse
unto ther religion, with troble of suche cuntres as they ar inhabytyd
in. The abbot of Funtance had knowlige at hys being at Riwax,
the erle of Cumberlond † to have a commission for to inqwyer upon
hys demenars, whyche causyde hym in ther businesses to playe

---

* Thomas Earl of Rutland, as a descendent of Walter Espec, was the patron of
Rievaulx. After its dissolution he obtained a grant of the site.

† Henry Clifford, created Earl of Cumberland in 1525. He shared largely in the
spoils of the monasteries.

twe partes, *nam tunc sua res agitur paries cum proximus ardet.*
Thes premysses consyderyd, I trust ye wyll thinke hym not worthe
to be visitour of hys religion ony longer by the kinges auctorite.
And in thys cause of the abbot of Riwaxe, the other commyssionars
hathe precedide according to the lawe, and yowr credence by me
to theyme relatyde, and condignlie hathe remowyd hym from the
rewlle of hys abbacie and admynistracion of the same. With my
slawe wryting I besiche yow to tak no displesur, and of the cause
therof I shall at my cummyng to London make trwe relacion
unto yow. Wrytten in hast, the fyrst day off Septembar, ffrom
Belver.

By your servand,

Thomas I(?) Legh.

I pray yow noote there presumptuose myndes, most alienat
ffrom religion, hawing nothing of ther own, ne may have ther
accomptes made, whiche oonly to be calyd an abbatte will con-
tende contrare to ther obediencie with the kinges highnes, the
fownders, and all other, to the great slandar of the religion, dis-
qwiettnes and extreme costes and charges of ther howse.

To the ryght worshypfull master
Thomas Crumwell, oon of the kinges
most honorable councell, thys
be delyverde wythe spede.

In the following letter we find the Abbot of Glastonbury, one of the greatest abbeys
in England, petitioning against some of the visitatorial injunctions. We shall find him
afterwards acting more decidedly in opposition to the wishes of the court, for which he
was at last brought to the scaffold.

XXVII.

JOHN FITZ-JAMES TO CROMWELL.

[From MS. Cotton. Cleop. E. iv. fol. 39.]

My singuler gode master, after moste humble recommendacion,

with like thanckes for your great payne of late taken with me to my great comforte, this shal be to advertyse your saide gode mastershipp that I have spoken with my lorde abbot of Glaston concernynge suche injunccions as weer yeven hym and his covent by your deputie at the last visitacion there.   Wherof there be foure articles * in this papar here ynclosede, and as to too the first articles extendyth generally to every moncke yn the howse, but to suche as be exceptede in the seccound article, to infourm your mastershipp of the trothe, ther be certen officers brodirs of the howse whiche have allway be attendaunt apon the abbot, as his chapleyn, steward, celerer, and on or too officers moo; if they schuld be bounde to the firste too articles, it schuld muche disapoynt the order of the howse, whiche hathe longe ben full honorable. Wherfore if it may pleas your saide gode masterschipp to licence the abbot to dispence with thoo too firste articles, yn my mynde ye schall doo a verie gode dede, and I dare be suertie he will dispence with none but with suche as schalbe necessarie.   And to the thirde article they have used allwayes to make ther leesses by on of the religion and ceculer men appoynted to hym, whiche leesses have comenly be made at a courte and letten by copie of the courte roll, and the covent never made previe to the leese, and if they schuld make no leese but by assent of the more parte of the covent, it schuld be verie tedyous bothe to them and to ther tenauntes.   Wherfore, if it may pleas your gode masterschipp to discharge that thirde article, the abbot weer muche bounde to your gode masterschipp.   And to the iiijth article, peraventure there

* The paper containing these four articles appears to be lost, and a slip with four articles in no point answering to the description given in the letter is attached to it in the letter.   One of the injunctions of the visitors was, " that no monke or brother of this monastery by any meanes goo forthe of the precynct of the same."   Another injunction, which appears to be that alluded to by the abbot of Glastonbury in his third article, was, " Also that the abbot and president of this house shall make no waste of the woodes pertayning to this house, nor shall set out unadvisydly any ffermes or reversions without the consent of the more parte of the convent."   See the draught of the visitatorial injunctions in the Cottonian MS. Cleop. E. iv. fol. 21.

be sume of his brodirs would be gladd to be abrode, and to make untrew surmyse, so the abbot may paye for ther costes. Wherfore, it may pleas yow to ordre that clawse to be spared to tyme the abbot may wayte on your gode masterschipp the next terme, or elles to make it if the complaynaunt prove his complaynt to be trew than to have his costes, or elles not, the abbot weer muche bounde to yowe. Other articles ther be whiche they thincke verie strayt; howbeit they will sue to your gode masterschipp ffor that at more leyser, and yn the meane tyme I dowte not they will kepe as gode religion as any howse of that order withyn this realme, as knowith God, who longe preserve your saide gode masterschipp. At Redliche, the ij^{nd}. day of Septembre.

Your humble daylye oratour, as he is moste bownd,

JOHN FFIT JAMES.

This is the second letter from Dr. Legh on the subject of that part of the injunctions which confined the monks and their superiors to their houses. His coadjutor Dr. Leighton appears to have been inclined to more indulgence on this head, to which Cromwell seems to have been not unfavourable.

XXVIII.

DR. LEGH TO CROMWELL.

[From MS. Cotton. Cleop. E. IV. fol. 54.]

After my dewe commendations to your good maistershipp, please it you to be advertised that I have receyved youre gentill and loving lettres, yn which ye wolde that at my discretion I may licence the heddis for their necessary busynes and affaires to go furth of theire monasteries in suyche discrete maner and fourme as no brute* may be made thereof. Sir, it was not myne entent in my

* i. e. *noise, report.*

CAMD. SOC. K

lettres to have any autoritie to dispense with the saide heddes in this case, but as in tymes past so I doo yet think it very necessary that they have not libertie so sone after their injuctions, partely because it will be some occasion to think the other may as well be broke, and partely because their inferiors shall think that they have no litell injury so to be bounden, and their hed, which hath professid the same religion and shulde be in all hardenes as a lanterne and example to theym, thus to be losid. Besides this, if ye had withdrawen your hand a while herein, they shuld have had gret occasion to seke uppon the kinges favour and yours, and so it might have lyen in your handes to gratifie theym daily to their great hartys ease and your no litell commoditie. And also dyvers other causes there be, as ye shall knowe by the compertes in this visitation, why it is not expedient as yet that some of theym shuld have suych libertie. Wherfore, notwithstonding your gentill licence geven to me in this behalf, I entende to release none before that I speke with your maistership, or els that ye send me strayte commaundement so to doo. Praying you hartely that ye well consider whome ye send to the universities of Oxford and Cambrige, where other will be founde all vertue and goodnes or els the fontayne of all vice and myschief, and if all be well orderid there, no dowte both God and the king shall be well servid in these affaires, and your maistershippes office well discharged. Thus I commit you to Allmightie God. From Willton, the third daie of Septembre.

Yours ever assureytt,
THOMAS LEGH.

Our next letter introduces us again to the monks of the Charter House at London, who continued obstinate in their non-conformity with the desires of the court. It is an interesting picture of the state of the house at this period.

XXIX.

JASPAR FYLOLLE TO CROMWELL.

[From MS. Cotton. Cleop. E. iv. fol. 35.]

My dewtye to your good maistershipe humbly premyside, pleasithe hit the same to understande that with this my rude letter I have sent to you a paper of suche proportyon of vyttell and other as the lay brothers hyre tellyth me of necessite muste be provydyde for them, whiche will not be borne with the revenuce of the howse, ffor the yerly revenuce of the howse is vj^c. xlij^{li}. iiij^d. ob., and the provysion in that proportyon amountythe to vj^c. lviij^{li}. vij^s. iiij^d. And yet sythyns the makyng of that proportyon, whete is risen iiij^s. in every quarter, and malte xx^d. in every quarter, and comunely all other vittell rysithe therwith. I lerne her among this laye broders, that hertofore when all vittell was at a convenyent price, and allso when they were fewer persons in number than thei now be, the proctowr hath accomptyde for M^{li}. a yere, theyr rent of asyse beyng but as above vj^c.xlij^{li}. iiij^d. ob., whiche costlow fare, buyldynges, and other, was than borne of the benevolence and charyte off the citie of London. Nowe they not regarding this derthe, nether the encrease of ther superfluus nomber, nether yet the decay of the said benevolence and charyte, wold have and hathe that same fare contynuall that then was usid, and wold have like plentye of brede and ale and fyshe gevyn to strangers in the butterye and at the butterye dore, and as large lyvere of bredde and ale to all ther servantes, and to vagabundes at the gate, as was than uside, wich can not be. Wherfore, under the favor of your mastershipe, hit semythe to be moche necessary to mynyshe eyther ther number or deyntye fare, and allso the superfluus lyvere of brede and ale.

These Charterhowse monkes wold be callyde solytary; but to the cloyster dore therbe above xxiiij. keys, in the handes of xxiiij. persons, and hit is lyke in letters, unprofytable tales and tydinges, and sumtyme perverse concell commythe and goethe by reason therof. Allso to the buttrey dore ther be xij. sundrye keys, in xij. mens handes, wherin symythe to be small husbandrye.

Nowe is the tyme of the yere when provysion was wont to be made of lyng, haberdens, and of other salt store, and allso of ther wynter vesturys [to] theyr bodyes and to ther beddis, and for fuell to ther cellys, wherin I tarye tyll I may knowe your mastershippis pleasure therein.

I thinke, under correctyon of your mastershipe, that hit were very necessary to remove the ij. lay broders from the buttery, and sett ij. temporall persons ther in that rome, and lykewyse yn the kychine, ffor in those ij. officys lye the waste of the howse.

In the beginnynge of Auguste laste paste, my lorde of Caunter-burye sent for ij. monkes her, Rochester and Rawlyns. His lord-shipe sent Rochester home again, but he kepithe Rawlyns styll with hym, and I understand he hathe chaungid his habytt to seculer prestes clothing, and eatyth fleshe. I know that summe of them, and I thinke that dyverse moo of them, wold be glad to be lycencyde to the same.

Oon lay brother *apostata*, late of the ile of Axalme,* as he said, being sycke yn the greate syckenes, was secretlye withowt my know-lege receyvyde her into the cloyster, wher he dyed within iiij. days. Oon of the lay brothers kepte him in his siknes, and is now sike in the same great sycknes. Goddis wyll be performyde.

Wher the lorde Rede, late chife justyce of the comon place, hath her foundid a chantrye of viij^{li} yerly for terme of xxx. yeris, his chaplen dyed the first day of September, and ther is yet xiiij. yers to cum. Maister John Maydwell, comenly callyd the Scot-tysshe frere, hath bin hir with danne John Rochester, William Marshall and other than being present, and hath exhortyd him to the best, but they cowd fynde no good towardnes in him, but after an howres communicacyon they lefte him as they fownde him.

* The Charterhouse of Axholme will be mentioned further on.

Than I entretyd Rochester and iiij. or v. of the monkes to be contentyde to hyr him preche oon sermon amo[n]g them, oon day that weke, wherwith they were than contentyd; but on the next day, when they had spokyn with ther other broders, they sent me worde that I shuld not bryng him among them, for if I so dyd, they wold not hire him, by cause they harde tell of him that he prechide agaynst the honoryng of images and of sayntes, and that he was a blasphemor of saynctis. And I said that I mervayled moche of them, for ther can be no gretter heresie in any man, specyally in a relygius man, than to say that he can not preche the worde of God, nether will not hire hit prechid. And they say that they wyll reade ther doctors, and go no farder; and I tellyd them that suche doctours hathe made sum of ther compaynye to be strong traytours and traytorusly to suffer dethe. Now, sir, standing the case in the premisses as I have now wryttyne, I dare do nothing tyll I know sumwhat of your mastershipis pleasure. For I have lernyde of my felowe John Whalley, that your pleasure is that I shuld breke noone old ordir of the howse; but your commandement onys knowyne, I trust to endevor my self to folowe and accomplisshe hit, with suche diligence and discrecion as I am able, and as God will geve me grace, and as I thinke to aunswer to your mastership yn dred of your displeasure, as knoweth God, who ever ledde you ffrom henceforth forwarde, as he hathe done hiderto, yn his holye spiryte, the comforte of our mooste christen and mooste catholike prince, the kynges highnes, and of all his noblemen, and all other his true subjectes. At the Charterhowse nexte to London, the v. day of September.

Your humble servant, JASP. FYLOLLE.

Sur, I have sowyde to the byll of proporcion a parchement contaynyng the names of the whole howshold of the Charterhouse, and by cause ye shall not mervell upon the ordyr of that byll, in the first lyne is set byfore every mans name that hath confessyd hym selfe to be the kyngs trew man, ther is set a g. for good, and before the other a b. for badde.

In the secunde lyne ys sett the letter that standyth upon his cell dore. The thyrde lyne is the number of the persons.

We have already seen several allusions to the intended visitations of the Universities, as connected with the visitation of the monasteries, for it is clear that the Universities were at this time looked upon and treated as at least in great part monastic establishments. The following letter from Dr. Layton affords us a kind of sample of what was done at Oxford. It is a curious picture of the state of learning at the moment when our island was about to participate with the continent in its restoration.

XXX.

DR. LAYTON TO CROMWELL.

[From MS. Cotton. Faustina C. vii. fol. 205.]

Pleasit your goodnes to be advertisyde that in Magdelen Colege we fownde stablisshede one lecture of divinitie, two of philosophie, one morale another naturale, and one of Laten tonge, well kept and diligently frequentede. To thes we have adjonede a lecture in the Greke, that is, the grammer in Greke perpetually to be rede there, and all the yewthe therunto to have confluence for ther principulles. In New Colege we have stablisshede two lecturres publique, one of Greke, another in Laten, and have made therfore for evermore an honeste salarie and stipende. In Allsowllen Colege we have in lyke maner stablesshede two lecturres, one of Greke, another in Laten, with a goode stipende and salarie therunto assignede for ever. In Corpus Christi Colege we fownde two lecturres stablesshede by the founder, one in Greke, another in Latten, publique for all men therunto to have concourse. We have further stablessede a lecture in Laten tonge, publique, in Marten Colege; and another in Qwenes Colege; and have assignede and made a sufficient stipende for either of thes for evermore. Bicause we fownde all other the colegeis not able in londes and revenewis to have within them lectures publique, as the other afore rehersede hathe, we have injoned the saide poire colegeis that they and evere of them shall frequent and have dayly concourse unto the saide lectures. *Penam imposuimus* to evere scoler within the universitie not heryng at the leste one of thes lectures, for that day that he shalbe absent from one of the saide lectures to be punissede in the losse of his commons for that day, the saide paine evere day *tociensquociens absens fuerit, nisi concurrenti causa aliqua legitima, approbanda tamen per prepositum collegii sive aule.*

We have sett Dunce * in Bocardo, and have utterly banisshede hym Oxforde for ever, with all his blinde glosses, and is nowe made a comon servant to evere man, faste nailede up upon postes in all comon howses of easment: *id quod oculis meis vidi.* And the seconde tyme we came to New Colege, affter we hade declarede your injunctions, we fownde all the gret quadrant court full of the leiffes of Dunce, the wynde blowyng them into evere corner. And ther we fownde one Mr. Grenefelde, a gentilman of Bukynghamshire, getheryng up part of the saide bowke leiffes (as he saide) therwith to make hym sewelles or blawnsherres to kepe the dere within the woode, therby to have the better cry with his howndes.

We have also, in the place of the canon lecture, jonede a civel lecture, to be rede in evere colege, hale, and in.

We have further, in visitynge the religiouse studenttes,† emongyste all other injunctions adjoyned that none of them for no maner cause shall cum within any taverne, in, alhowse, or any other howse whatsoever hit be, within the towne and the suburbs of the same, upon payne onse so taken by day or by nyght to be sent imediatly home to his cloister whereas he was professede. With-

---

* Duns Scotus.

† The *religiouse studenttes* were the students sent to the university with exhibitions from the monasteries. One of the visitorial injunctions, in allusion to this class of students, directs :—" Also that the abbot or president kyep and fynd in some universite one or two of his brethren, accordyng to the habilite and possessions of this house, which brethern, after they be lernyd in good and holly letters, when they retorne home, maye instruct and teache ther brethern and diligently preache the worde of God."

oute doubte we here say this acte to be gretly lamentede of all the duble honeste women of the towne, and specially of ther laundres that now may not onse entre within the gaittes, and muche lesse within ther chambers, wherunto they wer ryght well accustomede. I doubt not but for this thyng onely the honeste matrones will sew unto yowe for a redresse.

Other thynges moo wiche ys to tediouse and long to conceve by writyng we have done, wiche all I shall declare unto yowe at my cummyng. This Sonday by nyght we shall make an ende ; for all this day we repaire to colageis for the redresse of division and complaintt put unto us. To morowe by vij. of the cloke in the mornyng I wilbe in the chapitre howse at Abyngton, and I truste to bring yow the trewthe of evere thyng for that howse ; and therof doubte ye not. On Wedinsday by nyght, at utermoste, I truste to be with yowe at Winchestre, Gode willyng, who sende yowe as goode helthe as your hert desierith. We fynde here all men applyng and glade to accomplisshe all thynges. From Oxforde, thys Sonday the xij[th] day of Septembre,

by your moste assurede poire preste and servant,

RYCHARDE LAYTON.

To the ryght honorable Mr. Thomas Cromwell,
   cheffe secretarie to the kynges hyghnes.

The letter which follows appears to have been written about the same time as the preceding. The abbey of Rewley, or *De regali loco*, in the suburbs of Oxford, was founded by the will of Richard king of the Romans, brother of Henry III. The last abbot (the writer of this letter) was Nicholas Austen.

XXXI.

THE ABBOT OF REWLEY TO CROMWELL.

[From MS. Cotton. Cleop. E. iv. fol. 269.]

Ryght honorable and my syngular good master, my dutye remembred, I humblye commend to yow, glad to here of youre helth,

welth, and prosperyte, the which I pray Jhesu long to contynewe
to your hertes desyre, and thanckyng your mastershipp for your
greatt kyndnes shewid to me att all tymes, whereas itt pleasyd
yow that so sone I shold come to your speache, with so lytell ex-
pense in lyeng att Londone, and also for your good and gentle
wordes, kynde and lovyng offre and profre, nott havyng for the
same pleasure or commodytie of me as yett, trustyng by some
specyall gyfft of grace to acqwyte itt x. fold. And whereas I had a
letter sende me, that our monasterye shold be gyven to Mr. Archard,
your servant, and that itt was also in the commyssyon, I submytt myselfe fulle and holle to your mastershipp, as all my refuge,
helpe, and socor is yn yow, glad of my voluntarye mynde to be
bounde in obligacion of one hunderd powndes to be payed to your
mastershipp, so that our house may be savyd, although itt be converted intoo thuse of a college, to have both lernynge and lernyd
men go forwardes theryn. I was loth to attempt your master-
shypp any ferther, seyng I had such gentle answeres, onlesse the
greatt rumour of the towne and universite compulsed me, bycause
of the fforsaid gyfft to the said Mr. Archard, besechyng your
mastershipps kynde letter agaynst the surveyoures comyng to dyscharge them, that itt may be as a sheld or buckler to defende me,
that yow may gett yow a memoryall to be prayed for for ever. And
thus almyghty Jhesus send your mastershipp longe lyfe and moche
honour.

NICOLAS by the grace of God abbott of Royallyen.

Sir Thomas Audley, afterwards baron Audley of Walden, in Essex, lord chancellor
of England, the writer of the following letter, was a zealous promoter of the dissolu-
ion of the monasteries, and obtained large grants of the estates which came to the
rown by that great measure.

Barking, or Berking, in Essex, was one of the oldest nunneries in England, having been founded by Erkenwald bishop of London in 677.   It was remarkable also for its riches. Dorothy Barley was the last abbess, and surrendered the house to the King on the 14th of November, 1539.

XXXII.

SIR THOMAS AUDLEY TO CROMWELL.

[State Papers, Vol. I. p. 450.]

After my right herty commendations, these shalbe to advertyse you, that I have sent forth wryttes for prorogacion of the parlament, commyssions and proclamations for corne, and also proclamations for clothiers, accordyngly as ye heretofore advertysed me that it was the kynges plesure that I shuld so do. I have also made redy wryttes for adjournement of the terme til Halowmas, and also sent letters in your name and myne for certificate of the residewe of the bokes of the spiritual possessions yet beyng onretourned; wherin the comyssioners, I promyse you, have been very necligent. I send to you a boke of the instructions for courne. I have usid my poor wytt in yt, trustyng it shalbe taken in good part. I am enformed that doctour Lee is substitute by you to visite al the religeous houses in the diocese of London. My sute at this tyme ys to you, that it may plese you to spare the visitation of the house of Barkyng, til your retourne into these partiez, that I and you may speke together, and ye shal comand me as moche to my power. If it like you that this abstynens may bee at my request, I then hertely desire you to direct your letters to doctour Lee for the same. In good fayth, my request ys, not for any defaut or suspect that I have in doctour Lee, for I here not but that he suith hymself right indifferently in the execution of his charge; but it is for other considerations that I wold be a sutour to you for the said house. And when ye and I have spoken togethir at your retourne, do as ye shal seeme best; trustyng for my sake, and at my contemplation, ye will use the more favour to the house. Praying you to remembir al my requestes in my last letters to you directyd, and eftsones desire you to make myn most humble recommendations to the kinges highnes and to the quenes grace. And thus fare ye as hertely well as I wold my self. Wryten the morow after Michaelmas day. Your assured to al his power,

THOMAS AUDELY, k. chauncelour.

To his hertie loving frend,
  Mr. Secretary, be this
  yoven.

The following account of the capture of the abbot of Langdon's concubine is singularly ludicrous. Langdon, or West Langdon, in Kent, was a small abbey of Premonstratensians, founded and endowed by William de Auberville, in 1192. The name of the last abbot was William Sayer. The private posterns or " startyng hoilles " of the monasteries are frequently mentioned by the old satirists. One of the injunctions (MS. Cotton. Cleop. E. iv. fol. 21) seems to have been particularly aimed against such houses as that of Lanngdon. " Also, that ther be *no enteryng into this monastery but one*, and that by the great for-gate of the same, which diligently shalbe watchyd and kept by some porter specially appoynctyd for that purpose, and shalbe shute and openyd by the same bothe daye and nyght at convenyent and accustomyd howres, which porter shall *repell all manner women* from enteraunce into the said monastery."

XXXIII.

DR. LAYTON TO CROMWELL.

[From MS. Cotton. Cleop. E. iv. fol. 127.]

Pleasit your goodnes to understonde, that one Friday xxij°. Octobris, I rode bake with spede to take an inventarie of Fowlstone,* and from thens I went to Langden. Wheras immediatly discendyng from my horse, I sent Bartlett, your servant, with alle my servantes, to circumcept the abbay, and surely to kepe alle

* At Folkestone in Kent, Eadbald king of Kent founded a nunnery, on the site of which Nigellus de Mandeville founded a priory in 1095. This house was surrendered on the 15th of November, 1535, as will be seen by a subsequent letter in the present volume.

bake dorres and startyng hoilles, etc. I my self went alone to the abbottes logeyng jonyng upon the feldes and wode, evyn lyke a cony clapper fulle of startyng hoilles, a goode space knokkyng at thabbottes dore, *nec vox nec sensus apparuit*, saveyng thabbottes litle doge that, within his dore faste lokked, bayede and barkede. I fownde a short polax standyng behynde the dore, and with yt I dasshede thabbottes dore in peisses, *ictu oculi*, and set one of my men to kepe that dore, and aboute howse I go with that polax in my hande, *ne forte*, for thabbot is a daingerouse desperate knave and a hardy. But for a conclusion, his hore, *alias* his gentle womman, bestyrrede hir stumpis towardes hir startyng hoilles, and ther Bartlett wachyng the pursuet towke the tendre damoisel, and affter I hade examynede hir, to Dover ther to the maire to sett hir in sum cage or prison for viij. dais, and I browgt holy father abbot to Canterbury, and here in Christeschurche I will leve hym in prison. In this soden doyng *ex tempore* to circumcept the howse and to serche, your servant John Antonie his men mervelede what felow I was, and so dyde the reste of thabbay, for I was unknowyn ther of al men. At last, I fownde hir apparel in thabbottes cofer. To tell yowe all this commodie, but for thabbot a tragedie, hit were to long. Now hit shalle appere to gentilmen of this contrey, and other the comons, that ye shall not deprive or visite but upon substanciall growndes. Surely I suppos Gode hym self put hit in my mynde thus sodenly to make a serche at the begynnyng, bycause no chanon apperede in my syghte; I supposede rather to have fownde a hore emongiste them then in thabbottes chambre. The reste off alle this knaverie I shall differ tyll my cumyng unto yow, wiche shalbe with as muche spede as I can possible, doyng my assurede deligence in the reste. This mornyng I ryde towardes the archebisshop to visite hym; now whan I have visite hys see, this nyght I wilbe at Feversham abbay.* This ys to advertise yowr maistershipe.

* The abbey of Faversham in Kent was founded about 1147, and filled with Cluniac monks from Bermondsey.

Scribullede this Satterday, an writen with the hasty hand of your assurede servant,

RYCHARD LAYTON, Preste.

The following letter was written by the same William Barlow, who wrote the letter printed before at page 6. He appears to have been moved, at his desire, from the priory of Haverfordwest to that of Bisham, which he quitted on the 22nd of February 1535-6, for the Bishopric of Asaph, which in the following April (1536) he exchanged for that of St. David's. His predecessor in the latter see, against whom he here complains, was Richard Rawlins, appointed in 1523.

The priory of Haverfordwest was founded before the year 1200 by Robert de Haverford, the first Norman lord of this district. The ruins are still visible by the river side, near the town.

XXXIV.

WILLIAM BARLOW TO CROMWELL.

[From MS. Cotton. Cleop. E. IV. fol. 107.]

Pleasith your good maistershipe with compassion to advertise the complaynt and unfayned peticion of your humble oratour, disquietly vexede without cause or any pretenced occasion motioned of your saide oratours partie. Whereas the quene of here graciouse bounte advouched me unworthy the priorshipe of Haverfordwest under here graces foundacion, syns the tyme of my ther contynual residence, consideryng the hungry famyne of heryng the worde of God and desolate scarcete of true prechers, I have endeveryd my self with no smalle bodely daunger agenst Antichrist, and all his confederat adherentes, sincerely to preche the gospell of Christ, whose verite as hit is invincible so is hit incessantly assautyd of faythles false perverters; by reson wherof they whiche of dutie ought to fortifie me in mayntenyng the truthe maliciously have concevid a malivolent mynde causles to maligne agenst me, in suche wise that I was forced ffrom theire tyranny to appele unto the kyng his honorable councelle, as playnly apperithe by the un-

true surmised articles falsely contrived by the blacke ffreere of
Haverfordwest, whiche though I presented to your maistershipe
as thacte of his onely doing, yet was hit the mayntenans of the
busshope and his ungostly spirituall officers, whiche is evident by
the rewarde of the busshope to the ffreere at his departyng, also by
his letters directed to Mr. dean of tharches and to doctoure Huys,
diligently to sollicite that I myght be suppressed in my just matter.
And where they sithe perceive that (praise be to God !) under the
favour of your righteouse equite they cannot prevaile agenst me as
they wilfully wulde, yet cesse they not wrongfully to vex suche as
pertayne to me, troblyng them with tyranny for my sake, no
suche cruelte deservyng ; as where of late I sent a servaunt home
about certen busynes, immediatly aftre his commyng the busshops
officers ascited hym to apperans, and ransacking his house forced
hym to delyver suche bokes as he had, that is to saye, an Ynglysshe
Testament, thexposicion of the iiijth, vth, and vjth chapters of
Mathewe, the Ten Commaundementes, and the Epistelle of Saynt
Johan, violently withholding them with vehement reproches and
clamarouse exclamacions agenst heretikes, as if to have the Testament in Ynglysshe were horrible heresie, to no litle dismaying
and ferefull discomfort of the sincere favorers of Godes word.
Moreover, they charged in the kynges name the maire of Tynby,
in payne of fyve hundreth merckes, to putt in warde the said poore
man, his wiff, and a certen honest widowe of inculpable fame, with
whom they were at host, laying certen articles to theyre charge whiche
they never thought nor spake ; and aftre most shamefull rumors
raysed uppe to theyre dyffamacion, with slaunderouse wonderment
of the towne, alle crafty meanes assayde to bryng in false witnes,
when no accuser wuld appere openely, as a true certificat undre
the townes seale largely dothe testifie, the above mencyoned officers, without any charitable satisfaction to the said parties wrongfully imprisonede, badd the maire do with them as he lusted, and
so thens departyng made ther advaunt * in places where they came

* Their boast.

of theire valyaunt actes agenst heretikes, meanyng therby the favorers of Christes gospell. In consideracion wherof hit may please your singuler goodnes to provyde a redresse, that ffrom the terroure of suche tyrannes the kynges faythfulle subjectes youre poure oratours maye peaceably lyve according to Goddes lawes, without any suche unchristen empeschement and combrouse vexacyons. Furthermore, unfaynedly to assertayne your maistershipe, in what petious case gretely lamentable the kynges faithfull subjectes the poore resians * in the dioces of saynt David your suppliaunt oratours ar miserably ordred undre the clergye, requyreth a farre larger processe then here maye conveniently be comprised ; for though we have semblably to other dioceses in outwarde auctorite and exterior ceremonies a busshop, a suffrigan, archdeacons, deans, commissaries, and other busshoplyke officers intitled with spirituall names, also a multitude of mounckes, chanons, ffreers, and secular pristes, yet among them all, so many in nombre and in so large a dioces, is ther not one that sincerely prechithe Goddes word, nor scarce any that hertely favorithe hit, but all utter enemyes theragenst, whose stubburne resistence cannot be without froward rebellion agenst the kynges graciouse actes establisshed uppon the verite of Goddes word. And concernyng the enormyouse vices, the frawdulent exactions, the mysordred lyvyng, and hethyn idolatry, shamefully supported undre the clergies jurisdiction, whiche by sequele of theyre blynd wilfull ignorans do consequently folowe, no dioces I suppose more corrupted nor none so farre out of frame, without hope of reformacion, except your maistershipe shall see a redresse, in whom under the kynges grace the trust of all those that meane well onely consistyth. Fynally theyr abused fasshions at lengithe to discover, at your commaundement, I shalbe redy with suche certente of truthe, that no adversary shalbe able to make contrary denyall ; whiche so performed, hit may then please youre good maistershipe to licence me for to departe, under the laufull favour of youre protection, without the

* Inhabitants, residents.

whiche nether can I without parell repaire home, nor ther in saffte contynue among so odiouse adversaries of Christes doctrine, by whose tyranny that I may not be unjustly oppressed, I most humbly beseche your assistent ayde, howbeit no farder then the verity of Scripture will justifie my cause, nether for no carnall commodite of any worldly preferment, but alle onely for tha-vauncement of Christes gospell, to the honor of God, who ever-more graciously preserve your maistershipe in honorable felicite.

Your humble oratour,

WILLIAM BARLO, prior of Haverfordwest.

To the right honorable maister Thomas
Crumwell, chief secretary to the
kynges highnes.

The priory of Bridlington, situated on the coast of Yorkshire, was founded early in the reign of Henry I. by Walter de Gaunt, whose father (Gilbert de Gaunt) had re-ceived a grant of the manor from William the Conqueror. The second Gilbert de Gaunt, eldest son and heir of the founder, confirmed his father's charters, and added liberal donations of his own. The following letter has been printed by Mr. Prickett, in his History of Bridlington, but with a wrong date. The writer was William Wode, the last prior, who in the year following (1536) took an active part in the insurrection commonly called the "Pilgrimage of Grace," and was executed along with the abbots of Fountains, Rievaulx, and Jervaulx, also implicated in that rebellion.

XXXV.

THE PRIOR OF BRIDLINGTON TO CROMWELL.

[From MS. Cott. Cleop. E. IV. fol. 53.]

Right wourshipfull, my dewtie in my moste humble maner re-membred, I recommende me to your gude maistershipe, and for somuche as your sayd maistershipe by your last lettres to me directed advised me, and in like maner counselled me, to recognishe the kynges highnes to be our patrone and ffounder, forasmuche as noe article, worde, sentence, or clause in our originall graunte to

hus mayde by sir Gilbert de Gaunte, cosyne to our originall ffounder, appered to the contrarie whie of equitie his highnes owght
not so to be, or elles to appere before your maistershipe and other
of his graces counsell the laste day of Octobre, as I wolde awoide
his graces highe displeasour. In this matter, even so humblie as
I canne, I shall besuche your gude maistershipe to be gude maister to me and your poour and cotidiall oratours my bretheren; for
notwithstondinge the kinges grace his noble progenitours titles
and clames hertofore mayde to our said patronage and founder-
shipe (thoghe all we ar and ever will be at his moste graciouse
commaundement and pleasour), yet we have ever benne dimissed
clere withowt any interruption in this behalfe nighe this two hundreth yeres, as shall appere before your gudnes under substanciall
evidence of recorde. And so I besuche your maistershipe we may
be at this tyme, for in your maistershipe our holle truste in all our
gude causes remaneth. And where as I ame detenede withe
diverse infirmities in my body, and in lyke maner ame feble of
nature, so that withowt great yeopardie of my liffe I cannot nor
ame not hable to labour in doinge of my dewtie to appere before
your [gude] maistershipe, I shall right humblie besuche your gudnes
to have [me] excused, and in lyke maner to accept this berar my
brother as my lauful deputie in this behalfe, who shall mayke
your maistershipe aunswer as concernynge thes premisses, to
whome I besuche your maistershipe yeve firm credence, of whome
also ye shal resave a poour token frome me whiche I eftsones
besuche your gude maistershipe to accept, thankfullie with my
poour hert and cotidiall prayers, of whiche ye shall be assured
enduringe my liffe, as is my dewtie, Gode willinge, who ever
preserve your gude maistershipe, in muche wourshipe longe to
endure. Frome our monasterie of Bridlingtone, the xxiijrd day
of Octobre, by your humble and cotidiall oratour,

WILLIAM, prior of the same.

The next letter relates to the priory of Fordham, in Cambridgeshire. This house, which Tanner calls " Fordham *alias* Bigynge," is said to have been founded by Robert de Fordham, for canons of the order of Sempringham.

XXXVI.

DR. LEGH TO CROMWELL.

[From MS. Cotton. Cleop. E. iv. fol. 229.]

My hartye recommendatyons presupposid, pleasith yt your mastership to undrestand, that ther ys a pryory namyd Byggyn in the towne of Fordham, in the dyocesse of Norwyche, wher as ys but the prior and his moncke, and the moncke is in extreme age and at dethes doore, and my lorde of Northehumberland ys fownder ther, of whom I suppose ye maye very easely opteyne his title and interest. Yt is a propre howse, and yt stand commodyously and pleasauntly, and yt maye spend xxx^{li}. by the yere in temporall landes, besyde spyrytualtyes, whyche ys a benefyce of xvj^{li}. by the yere. Also I desyre you to send me worde, what shall be doon with thes relygyous persons whiche knelyng on ther knees, howldyng up ther handes, instantly with humble petycyon desyre of God, the kyng, and you, to be dymyssyd from ther relygyon, sayyng they lyve in yt contrary to Goddys lawe and ther conscyens, trustyng that the kyng of hys gracyous goodnes and you wyll set them at lybertye owte of this bondage, which they ar not able lenger to endure (as they saye), but shuld fall into dysperatyon or elles ronne awaye, with many other lamentable petycyons whiche war now to long to wryte, but yt war a dede of charyte that they myght lyve in that kynd of lyvyng whiche myght be moste to the glorye of God, the quyetnes of ther conscyens, and most to the commonwelthe, who so ever hathe informyd you to the contrary, for your harte wold lamente to here them as I doo, as thys berer your servauntec an shewe you. As consernyng thes thynges, I shall desyre your mastershyp of farder knowlege what I shall doo, and I shalle be redy to accomplyshe your mynde in thes and

in all other thynges with dylygens to thuttermost of my poore,
desyryng that you wyll remembre God herein (as I dowte not
but ye wyll), who ever accomplyshe your good mynd in all
thynges.   From Ely, the fyrst daye of Novembre.

Yours ever assuryd,

THOMAS LEGH.

In the last edition of the Monasticon there appears to be some error or confusion
relating to the date of the following letter, and to the last abbot of the Premonstratensian abbey of West Dereham, who is said to have been Roger Forman, and to have
held the same office from 1522 to the time of the dissolution of his house.   It is stated
in the same work that " John Maxey, bishop of Elphin, was commendator of Welbeck, A.D. 1520."

The abbey of Premonstratensian canons of Welbeck, in Nottinghamshire, was begun
in the reign of Stephen, and the foundation completed under Henry II.   The bishops
of Ely, having bought the manor, were afterwards considered the founders or patrons.
The abbey of West Dereham, in Norfolk, formed by a colony of canons brought from
Welbeck, was built in 1188 by Hubert, then dean of York, afterwards bishop of Salisbury.

XXXVII.

THE COMMENDATOR OF WELBECK TO CROMWELL.

[From MS. Cotton. Cleop. E. iv. fol. 43.]

Jhesu.

Please hit you, maister secretarie, to understonde, I receyved
the xxvj[th] day of Octobre a certificate from the convent of West-
dorham under there convent sele of the dethe of my brother abbot
ther (whose soule God pardon !), and the sele of his office also,
accordinge to the old custome and usage that hath ben all wayes
usid in timys past, to be sent unto the father abbot from all his
filiall chirches, and also accordinge to ye private statutis of our
religion.   Sir, I perceyve that the kynges grace visitors (doctor

Lee) be forthe in those parties, and whether hit be your maister-shipis plesure that he shall medle in that eleccion or noo I dissire humbly to know your plesur, ffor I insure you I wolde do no-thinge but that which my3t stonde with your lawful favore, seinge that ye are and hath ben alwaye so gud maister to me and unto my pour religion. Notwithstondinge, as your maister-shipe knowes well that the kynges grace hathe gyven to me and unto the pour monastery of Welbeck (*imperpetuum*) under his brod sele for all eleccions of al the ordre of Premonstraten. within this realme and Walis. Howbehit I intend to do nothinge but that shall stond withe the kynges grace plesur and yours bothe, humbly dissiringe to know your maistershipis plesur in writing what I shall do herein. Your maistership said unto me, at my last be-inge withe you, that when any eleccion fell in my religion I shuld do my duety lyke as I have done before tyme, and accordingly unto the kynges grace graunt. Also ther hathe ben a prest (the person of Brandon Ferre), and maid a sequestracion of all the gudis ther, both within and witheout, moveable and unmovable, but whether your maistership knowes of hit or not I can not say. Sir, as towching all suche communicacions as I hade at my last being withe yow, (God willing) I shall performe at my commyng upe at Candlemas next commyng. And thus Jhesu preserve yow in helthe with myche honore. From Welbeck, the ij^{de} day of Novembre.

        Yours to hys little poure,

          JOHN ELPHIN and commendatar off Welbek.

ʊ The commissioners appear to have found little in the large Benedictine monastery of Bury in Suffolk to report, except a list of superstitious relics.

XXXVIII.

JOHN AP RICE TO CROMWELL.

[From MS. Cotton. Cleop. E. IV. fol. 120.]

Please it your mastership, fforasmoche as I suppose ye shall
have sute made unto yow touching Burie er we retourne, I thought
convenient to advertise yow of our procedinges there, and also of
the compertes of the same. As for thabbot, we found nothing
suspect as touching his lyving, but it was detected that he laye
moche forth in his granges, that he delited moche in playng
at dice and cardes, and therin spent moche money, and in
buylding for his pleasure. He did not preche openly. Also that
he converted divers fermes into copie holdes, wherof poore men
doth complayne. Also he semeth to be addict to the mayntenyng
of suche supersticious ceremones as hathe ben used hertofor.

As touching the convent, we coulde geate litle or no reportes
amonge theym, although we did use moche diligence in our examinacion, and therby, with some other argumentes gethered of
their examinacions, I fermely beleve and suppose that they had
confedered and compacted bifore our commyng that they shulde
disclose nothing. And yet it is confessed and proved, that there
was here suche frequence of women commyng and reassorting to
this monastery as to no place more. Amongest the reliques we
founde moche vanitie and superstition, as the coles that Saint
Laurence was tosted withall, the paring of S. Edmundes naylles,
S. Thomas of Canterbury penneknyff and his bootes, and divers
skulles for the hedache; peces of the holie crosse able to make a
hole crosse of;* other reliques for rayne and certain other super-
stitiouse usages, for avoyding of wedes growing in corne, with
suche other. Here departe of theym that be under age upon an
eight, and of theym that be above age upon a five, wolde departe

---

* The immense number of pieces of the *true* cross possessed by different religious
houses, both on the continent and in England, was a frequent subject of ridicule among
the earlier reformers.

yf they might, and they be of the best sorte in the house and of best lernyng and jugement. The hole nomber of the covent before we cam was lx., saving one, beside iij. that were at Oxforde. Of Elie I have written to your mastership by my felowe Richard a Lee. And thus Almightie God have you in his tuicion. From Burie, vth. Novembre.

Your servant moste bounden,

JOHN AP RICE.

The following letter is an additional evidence of the eagerness with which the country gentlemen and the courtiers were looking out for shares in the abbey lands. The small priory of Ingham in Norfolk was founded in the fourteenth century, by Sir Miles Stapleton, of Bedale in Yorkshire.

XXXIX.

RICHARD WHARTON TO CROMWELL.

[From MS. Cleop. E. iv. fol. 122.]

Ryght woorshypfull syr, as I am most bownde of dewtye, with my humble recommendacions to your mastershyppe, syr, yt shall please yow to be athvertysyd that here ys an abbey callyd Ingham in Norfolke, not fare frome Seynt Benettes abbeye, the fownder therof ys on sir Frawnses Calthrope, and after hys dethe one Edwarde Calthrope, nevewe and heyer unto the sayd syr Fraunses, whoo hathe maryid a nere kynswoman off myne. The prior and covent of the same abbye, by the covent seale, hathe solde the hole abbye with all the londdes therto belongyng, to one Wylliam Wodhowse a nere dweller to the same, wythowght the knowlege of the fownder, and allso contrary to the promysse of the sayd prior and covent, who promyssyd the sayd Edward Calthrope that in case they dyde eyther selle or aleyne the same or ony parte therof, that the same Edwarde shulde have yt before any other man, forasmyche as yt was ffowndyd by hys awnsetours, and the sayd Edward allso nexte heyer to the fowndacion. Yett notwithstondyng hys promysse, he hathte solde yt to the sayde Woodhowse by the covent seale, as afore mensionyd, and the same Woodhowse now beyng at London to serve owght the recoverye of the same. Soo as the same Edwarde Calthrope for ever shall loose hys fowndacion, and allso hys bargeyne of the prior and covent, onlesse yt wyll please your mastershype, at thys my power sewte, to be soo goode master to the sayde Edwarde Callthrope to stoppe the recovere incontinent with spede, tyll your mastershype shalbe further instructyd and sewyd unto by the sayd Edwarde Calthrope and other of hys fryndys. And forasmyche as the sayde Edward ys the fownder and allso hade a speciall promyse of the prior and covent to bye the same in casse they dyd sell yt, after my power mynde yt ware moste reason that he shulde have the barganye and profarment before ony other. Yf yt please yower mastershyppe to helpe hym and stonde hys good master, I dowght with yower helpe he maye recover hys sayd bargayne in the same, and for the paynys that yower mastershyppe shall take therin, the same Edward shall gyffe yow an hondryde powndes, and yow shall bynde hym and alle hys frynddys to be yower sarvaunttys and bedemen whyll they doo lyve. I beseche yow, syr, that I maye be athevertysyd of yower pleasure herein by my servaunt thys brynger. Syr, I am allwayse bolde to crave to yower mastershyppe for eyde and helpe for me and my frynddys, not able to requite yower goodnesse but with my power harte and sarvyse, wyche ys and shalbe at yower commaundment; and thus I beseche God to preserve yower mastershyppe to long lyffe and good prosperytye. Frome Bungeye, the vij. daye of Novembyr.

Att yower mastershyppes commawndment,

RYCHARD WHARTON.

The subject of the following letter is a continuation of the report previously given at p. 75, of the present volume.

XL.

THE COMMISSIONERS IN KENT TO CROMWELL.

[From MS. Cott. Cleop. E. iv. fol. 219.]

Right worshipfull sir, itt maye youe to understond, that we receyved your lettre this present Tewesdaye att nyght, about vij. of the clok, by the handes of John Antony your servaunt, advertesyng youe that before the receyt therof we have been att the monasteries of Langdon, Dovour, and Folkston, and have taken a clere surrender of every of the same monasteries under ther covent seales, beyng also recognized in ther chapter houses, accordyng to your wille and commaundement, wheruppon dyverse tenauntes belongyng to the seid monasteries have openly attorned unto the kynges grace.

We have also receyved into your custodye the covent seales of the seid monasteries, and have in lyke maner receyvd all the evidence belongyng to the monasteries of Langdon and Folkston, and have likewyse receyved parte of the evidence belongyng to Dovour, such as we thought most expedyent, and the residue we have putt into a suer chiste under lock, wherof we have the key in our custodye.

We have also lefte the chanons and monkes still in ther houses, withoute any clere dyscharge of them, butt have putt them att ther liberte and choise whether they wille abide ther untill the kynges graceis plesure be ferther knowen therin, or eles to goo from thens to ther fryndes, wherof the most parte desire to have capacitees, and somme to be assigned over to other places of religeon. Which monkys and chanons att the tyme of the receypt of your seid lettre (as we trust and thynk) ar remaynyng still in ther houses.

Advertesyng your mastership fferther of the estate of the seid monasteries, wherin (as yett) we toke none inventories, by cause the inventories were taken allredy, as your mastership knowes.

Fyrst, the house of Langdon is sore in decaye, and no maner of grayne or other vittalles for the realeff of the house. Thabbott therof (as he is reported) a veray unthrifte yvell housbond, and of yll rule, and his covent veraye ignorant and poore.

The house of Dovour is a goodly house and well repayred in all places, as fer as we cowd perceyve; and that the prior (as itt was reported unto us) ffound the house att his ffyrst comyng thither indented in ix^{xx}li., and hath reduced and brought that to c^{li}. as itt is said, of whose nowe case dyverse of the honest inhabitantes of Dovour shewe them selves veray sory.

The house of Folkston is a littill house, well repayred, and the prior a veray honest parson, and a veray good husbond,* and no les belovyd emonges his neypours.

We have consulted uppon your letter that Herry Polsted, John Antony, and Antony Ager shall accomplish the same in all thyng with all convenyent spede. And thus the Holy Goost contynewe yowe in good helth [and] welffare. Writton at Canterbury, the xvj. daye of November.

Your owne, THOMAS BEDYLL.
Your servaunt, HERRY POLSTED.
Your servant, JOHN ANTHONY.

The next letter is altogether undated, but it appears to have been written about this time, and is placed here from its connection with the proceedings in Kent, a portion of which form the subject of the preceding letter. We have already seen the prior of Christ's Church, Canterbury, excusing himself from having any connection with Elizabeth Barton.

-----

* *i. e.* a careful housekeeper.

XLI.

CHRISTOPHER LEVYNS TO CROMWELL.

[From MS. Cott. Cleop. E. iv. fol. 124.]

Pleasithe hit your mastershype to understonde, that one Sondaye was senyghte I delyveryde unto your servaunt mayster Filoll
a certayne bill of complaynte ayenste the priour of Christe Churche
in Cantreburye, wheryne I openyde unto your mastershipe that
dyverse brethren of the same howse hadde shewyde unto me that
the sayde pryour hadde takyne a collette ffor the bysshoppe of
Rome by name of Pope, contrarye to his othe and a lawe made in
that behalffe,* and allso delyveryde unto hyme the copye of an
inventorye latelye exhibityde by hym unto your maistershipe of
the juelles and plate belongynge unto the same monasterye, with
a remembraunce of certayne parcells of sylver, golde, and stone to
the value of thowsandys of poundys, as the brethren of the same
house reporte, willffullye lefte owte of the sayde inventorye, contrarye unto an injunction to hyme gevynne by doctor Leyghtone,
vysitour there under your mastershipe. Whether your maistershipe have knowelege of the same byll or no, I knowe not; but
the sayde priour ys departyde to his howse, and I verylye thynke,
that those his brethren or monkes whiche have openyde thys
matter, whome he knowith ryght well, that after his comynge home
they shall never come forthe to depose in thys matter that he
hathe done ayenste our soverayng lorde the kynge, but other shalbe
poysenyde or murtheryde in prysone, as the commen reporte of the
monkes of the same house ys that he hathe murthredde dyverse
other. And bysydys thys, hit ys not to be dowbtyde that he,
knowynge hyme selfe to be gyltye in the mater before rehersyde,
wyll eloyne owt of the same howse into the handys of hys secrett

* The act of parliament abrogating the " usurped power of the bishop of Rome,"
in this island, who was no longer to receive the name of *pope*, was passed in the
session of the 25 Hen. VIII.

fryndys thowsandys of poundes, wiche is well knowen he hathe, to hys conforte herafter, to the greate hynderance of our soveraing lorde the kynge, whiche ys justelye intytyllydde by his lawes ther-unto, upon thys offence done, to have the hole moveable goodes of the howse. Whiche hynderaunce to our sayde soveraing lord, and dangers unto these poore men hys brethren, in thys behalfe consyderyde, hit may please your mastershipe to take summe order by your highe discressyon. Wryten by your bedman and the kynges trewe subjecte,

CRISTOFER LEVYNS,

To the right honorable
maister Thomas Crumwell
hyghe secretarye to the
kynges hyghnes.

Towards the end of the year Layton and Legh set out on a visitation journey towards Yorkshire. The following letter caries them as far as Lichfield.

XLII.

DR. LAYTON TO CROMWELL.

[From MS. Cotton. Cleop. E. iv. fol. 131.]

Hit may please your mastershipe to understande, that in goyng northwardes from London I towke in my way towardes Lichefelde, wheras I appointede to mete with doctor Leig, firste a prorie of Gylbertyns and nunnes inclosede and closse;* wheras they wolde not in any wisse have admittede me as vysiter, I wolde not be so answerede, but visitede them, and ther fownde two of the saide nunnes not baron; one of them *impregnavit supprior domus,* an other a servyng man. The two prioresses wolde not confesse this, nother the parties, nor none of the nunnes, but one old beldame;

---

* This was probably the priory of Chicksand in Bedfordshire, founded about 1150 for canons and nuns of the order of St. Gilbert of Sempringham.

and whan I objectede agayns the saide prioresses, that if they
cowlde not shewe me a cause resonable of that ther conseilement,
I muste nedes and wolde punnisshe them for ther manifeste perjurie, ther answer was that they were bownde by ther religion never
to confesses the secrette fawttes done emongiste them, but onely
to ther owne visiture of ther religion, and to that they were
sworne evere one of them at ther firste admission.   Another
priorie callede Harwolde,* wherin was iiij. or v. nunnes with the
priores; one of them hade two faire chyldren, another one and no
mo.   My lorde Mordant,† dwellyng nygh the saide howse, in-
tyssede the yong nunnes to breke up the cofer wheras the covent
sealle was; sir John Mordant his eldyste son then present, ther
perswadyng them to the same, causede ther the prioresse and hir
folysshe yong floke to seale a writyng made in Latten; what therin
is conteynede nother the priores nor hir sisters can telle, sayyng
that my Lord Mordant tellith them that hit ys but a leasse of a
benifice improperite, with other small tenanderyse.   They say all
they durste not say hym nay; and the priores saith planely that
she never wolde consent therto.   This was done sens Michaelmas.
To cale my lorde Mordant to make answere thus by power and
myght in his contrey to use howses of religion of the kinges
foundation (me semith) ye can no lesse do by your offes, unleste
ye will suffer the kinges foundations in continewaunce by every
man to be abusede.   At Saint Androse in Northampton‡ the
howse is in dett gretly, the landes solde and morgagede, the fermes

* At Harewold, or Harwood, in Bedfordshire, there was a priory of nuns of the
order of St. Augustine, founded in the middle of the twelfth century. Very little is
known of its history.

† Sir John Mordaunt, who had been sheriff of Bedford and Bucks in the first year
of Henry's reign, and had been employed by that monarch in several important occasions.   He was summoned to parliament as a baron in 1532.

‡ The date of the original foundation of the priory of St. Andrew in Northampton
is somewhat uncertain.   In 1084, Simon de St. Liz, the first Norman Earl of Northampton and Huntingdon, repaired and newly endowed this house, and placed in it a
company of Cluniac monks.   The last prior is said to have been Francis Abtree, *alias*
Leicester: it is stated in the last edition of Dugdale that he is called by Layton in this
letter John Petie, the words "I have petie" having been mistaken for a proper name.

let owte, and the rent recevide before hande, for x., xv., xx. chaun-
teres fowndett to be paide oute of the londes, and gret bondes off
forfaitures therupon for non payment; the howse is iiij. hundreth
powndes in revenewys. The kinges fowndation thus to be man-
gellede by the quondam, I have petie ; the prior now is a bacheler of
divinitie, a gret husbond, and a goode clerke, and petie hit is that
ever he cam ther : if he were promotede to a better thyng, and the
kinges grace wolde take hit into his handes, so myght he recover
all the londes agayne, wiche the prior shall never. In my retorne
owte of the northe I will attempte hym so to do, if hit be your
pleasure. The colege of Newarke * here in Lecestre of the kinges
fowndation, with an hospitale, is welle keppede, and honeste men
therin, iij. hundreth powndes in ther trezarewre howse before
hande. The abbay here is confederyde, we suppos, and nothyng
will confesse. The abbot is an honeste man, and doth varawell,
but he hath here the moste obstinate and factiouse chanons that
ever I knewe. This mornyng I will objecte aganste divers of them
bugrie and adulterie, *et sic specialiter discendere,* wiche I have
lernede of other (but not of any of them) ; what I shall fynde I
cannot tell. This mornyng we depart towardes Lichefelde churche,
and from thens to certayne abbays upon Trent syde, and so to
pase on to Sothewelle,† and to be at Yorke within a day affter the
xijth day, we intende, and thus to make spede with diligence and
trew knowlege of everethyng is our intent. My lorde of Lincolne‡
commaundyt the prechers here of Newarke colege that they
shulde no more preche, but onely in ther owne benifices. Why
shulde he inhibite any man to preche the worde of Gode ? He

---

* The College of Newark, or St. Mary's the greater, in the city of Leicester, was
founded by Henry duke of Lancaster, and the buildings completed by John of Gaunt.
The church was destroyed after the dissolution.

† The collegiate church of Southwell in Nottinghamshire is said to have been
founded by Paulinus archbishop of York about A.D. 630. Subsequently in the twelfth
century it consisted of sixteen canons. After its dissolution, it was restored by
Henry VIII. and still exists.

‡ John Longland, consecrated in 1521, and no very zealous reformer.

visitede here at Lecestre, and thorow his dioces in thes parttes, at
Lent laste, onely to prevent the kinges visitacion; he cannot
visite but *de triennio in triennium,* and he preventede his tyme
more then half a yere, so to prevent the kinges: *et sic visitavit
pendente visitatione metropolitica,* to the derogation off my lorde
of Canterburies power and prerogative metropolitan, gyvyn hym
by the kinges hyghnes. If he will so suffer his power to be con-
temnede, hit is petie he shulde have his mitre. From Lichefelde,
crastino divi Thome. By the spedy hande of youre assurede
preste and servande,

RYCHARDE LAYTON.

The small priory of Newstead, called in Latin *De Novo Loco juxta Stanford,* for
which the bishop of Lincoln writes in the following letter, was founded in the beginning of the reign of Henry III. by William de Albini. The last prior was Richard
Lynne, so that it is probable that the bishop's recommendation was not listened to.

XLIII.

THE BISHOP OF LINCOLN TO CROMWELL.

[From MS. Cotton. Cleop. E. iv. fol. 48*.]

Myn humble duety remembred unto your good mastershippe,
with my bounden thankes for your grette goodnes always and att
all tymes shewed unto me, ytt may please you to understand that
the pore house of Newsted besydes Stamford hathe bene voyde
sence the xxix^th day of October, by the resignation of the late
prior ther. And forasmoche as ther ar nowe butt twoo chanons
in the sayd house, my lord of Rutland, ther ffounder, hathe nominate ther unto sir John Blakytt, chanon, whiche semyth to be a
right honest sobre man, and hathe compounded for the firste
fructes. And for that your mastershippe commaunded me nott to
medle with eny religious houses, I wilnott intermedle in these
premisses, nor eny other lyke, withoute knowledge of your pleasour.

In consideration whereof, I beseche you I may knowe the same by this berer, wheddre itt may stand with your said pleasour to lycence me to admytte the said nomination, and to gyve *mandatum* to tharchedekon for his installation, for the ease of the said poore house. And thus the blessyd Trynyte have you in his tuicion. Wryten att Wooborne, the xth day of January. Your bownden bedisman,

JOHN LINCOLN.

To the right honourable master
secretary, this may be delyveryd.

One of the objects of the mission of Legh and Layton to the North, appears to have been to intimate the wishes of the court to the archbishop of York (Edward Lee), who was looked upon with some suspicion as a favourer of the monks and of the old religion. In the year following he was drawn into the " pilgrimage of grace" rebellion, but excused himself on the ground of having acted under compulsion.

XLIV.

DR. LEGH TO CROMWELL.

[From MS. Cotton. Cleopat. E. IV. fol. 104.]

Ryght worshipfull syr, my dewty presupposid, this is to advertise you that master doctor Layton and I the xj. daye of January war with the archebushope of Yorke, whom we accordyng to your pleasure and preceptes have vysyte, injoynyng him to preache and teache the word of God according to his bownd dewty to his cure committid unto hym, and also in the knowlege concernyng the prerogatyve poore that the kynges grace have, and to see other here in his jurisdiction being enduyd with good qualites, havyng any respecte either to God, goodnes, vertue, or godlynes, to performe the same; injoyning moreover to hym to bring up unto you hys fyrst, second, and thyrd fundations, wherupon he enjoiythe hys office and prerogatyve poore, with the grawntes, privelegis, and concessions geven to hym and to his see apperteynyng. The

whiche whan that you have red them, and knowen in all poyntes
the hole effect of them, I doo not dowte but that you shall see and
rede many thynges wordy reformation, by the knowlege wherof I
suppose the kynges hyghnes and you wyll be glad, and to thyncke
it mete that every bushope war in leke wyse orderyd, then shuld
they them under ther governauns edyfye moche in Christ, in his
doctrine and teachynges, and then the poore ignoraunte persons,
now by blyndenes and ignoraunce sedusid, myght therby be
browght to lighte and knowlege, wherby they shuld profitt môche
the welthe of ther owne sowlys and the commynaltye.　And it
shuld be gretly expedient to the concervacion of ther fidelite
toward ther prince, and to hys graces succession now begotten, or
hereafter to be begotton.　Now that I have enformyd your mastership of our actes and dedes, doon to a good ende, as our opinion
serve us, yt shall lye in your circumspecte prudencye and wysdom
to order all thynges as ye shall thincke to your approvyd dyscre-
tion most mete, and to the farderans of the glory of God and preservation of the common welthe most expedient and necessary.
For in the same injunctions geven heretofore, eyther augmentid or
diminyshyd, to be mynystred to other bushopys, as shall be
thowght to your wysdom most convenyent, I doo not dowght
but it shall be moche profitable and commodius bothe to the kynges
highnes and to your mastership, as knoweth God, who ever preserve your mastership.　From Yorke, the xiijth daye of January.

Yours ever assureyd,
Thomas Legh.

To the ryght honerable
master Thomas Cromwell,
chyeff secretary unto the
kynges highnes, and master
of his rollys, this be delyveryd.

The mitred abbey of St. Mary at York, mentioned in the following letter, dated from the eleventh century. According to some it was founded by earl Siward; according to others, it sprang from a colony of monks who came thither from Whitby. It was enlarged by William Rufus, and became in course of time a very rich house. The last abbot was William Thornton or Dent.

XLV.

DR. LAYTON TO CROMWELL.

[From MS. Cotton. Cleop. E. iv. fol. 115*.]

Hit may please your mastershipe to be advertissede, that here in Yorkeshire we fynde gret corruption emongiste persons religiouse, evyn lyke as we dyde in the sowthe, *tam in capite quam in membris*, and wurse if wurse may be in kyndes of knaverie, as, *retrahere membrum virile in ipso punctu seminis emittendi, ne inde fieret prolis generatio*, and nunnes to take potations *ad prolem conceptum opprimendum*, with suche other kindes of offences lamentable to here. This day, we begyn with Saint Mare abbay, whereas we suppos to fynde muche evile disposition bothe in thabbot and the convent, wheroff, Gode willyng, I shall certify yowe in my next letters. The dean of Yorke was never fully concludede with the tresareure here for the deanrie. The dean wolde not resign unto hym, unleste he wolde leffe hym other possessions; for pension he wolde none have, fearyng suche lyke debaytment therof as was of pensions in the laste Parliament. To have takyn the tresareureshipe for the lieu of a pension he was onse content, wherunto the tresareure wolde not agre, unleste he myght have hade his prebende also with his deanrie, wiche the dean wolde not, and so they broke; the tresareure wolde have hade the dean to have wryten unto yowe of sum towardnes in the premisses at suche tyme as the tresareure came up laste to London, wyche the dean then refusede to do, bycause therof he persavede no gret towardnes of any conclusion. This is the deans taile to me, and this I fynde trewe; wherfore I shall desier your mastershipe to continewe your goode mynde towardes me, and in the mean tyme ye shalbe faste assurede of my faithfull servyce in all suche your affaires as ye commite unto me, and for no corruption or lucre frome my loyaltie to swerve in doyng my princès commaundement for your discharge, whyche hath put your truste and affiance unto me. Frome Yorke, xiij° Januarii, by your assurede poire preste,

RICHARDE LAYTON.

While Legh and Layton were in the North, Bedyll was occupied in Cambridgeshire, and the fen district. The celebrated abbey of Ramsey was founded soon after the middle of the tenth century. The charter of King Edgar is printed in the Monasticon. The last abbot was John Wardeboys, *alias* Lawrence: he was appointed to that place as early as 1507, and must have been an old man at the time he surrendered his house to the King, which he did very willingly.

XLVI.

BEDYLL TO CROMWELL.

[From. MS. Cotton. Cleop. E. iv. fol. 204.]

In my moost hertie wise I commende me to you, doing you to understand that I am now at Ramesey, wher in myne opinion the abbatt and convent be as true and as feythful obedienciaries to the kinges grace as any religious folkes in this realme, and live as uprightly as any other, after the best sort of lyving that hath been emong religious folkes this many yeres, that is to sey mor gyven to ceremonies than is necessary. I pray God I may fynd other houses in no worse condicion, and than I wolbe right glad that I tok this jorney. Your cosyn Mr. Richard * was her on Thursday, by whom I sent letters unto you, whiche I thinke ye have

---

* The term *cousin* was applied in a very general manner to all kinds of distant affinity. Richard Cromwell was the secretary's nephew.

not yet receyved.* Muche of the mater of my letters concerneth a charter of king Edgar, whiche I found in this house, wreten in a very antique Romane hand, whereof the subscription is this, *Signum Edgari illustris Anglorum imperatoris;* And it is subscribed with vj. dukes whiche were in Edgars tymes. The said Edgar exempteth the abbat and his convent and al his men from the power of al bisshops, and maketh thaim immediatly subject to him self; and albeit they were then excepted, the bisshop of Rome had never to do with thaim. Ther may be good notes gatherd out herof, as I have wreten mor playne in my said letters delivered to Mr. Richard. Here in this monastery of Ramsey be two brethern whiche have gyven thes billys enclosed unto me, very affectuosly desiryng to have liberte to go from thaire cloyster by the kinges grace auctorite, or els to have licence to repair to my lord of Cauntrebury to sue thaire capacites. I have steyed thaim as wel as I can, with suche counsels and exhortations as I could gyve thaim; but I fere, if they can have no liberte graunted thaim, they wol take it of thaire owne auctorite. I beseche you to write a word or two how I shal use me self towardes thaim and al other whiche wol make like suyt, in no smal number as I think, whereof som occasion hath growen by that that docter Lee now at Christmas gave liberte to half the house of Sawtre † to depart (as I am informed), whiche Sautre is within v. myles of Ramsey. The religious men thinketh that I have like auctorite as docter Lee, and that moveth thaim to make this suyt. Nevertheless I wol no thing do therein, or presume suche hyghe maters, without your advise and counsel, beseching you to write your mynd in this behalf, and in suche other thinges whiche ye wold me to do in this

---

* This letter is preserved in the same volume, but is not of importance, as it chiefly contains a copy of part of the charter.

† The abbey of Saltrey, or Sawtrey, in Huntingdonshire, was founded in 1146, when Simon earl of Northampton established there a convent of Cistercian monks from the abbey of Wardon in Bedfordshire. The last abbot was William Angell.

jorney. If it pleased you to grant me a commission to visit the religious houses unvisitted in Lyncoln diocese, whiche shal be nyghe my jorney, it shuld be muche to my commodite. From Ramsey the xv. day of January.

By your owne,

THOMAS BEDYLL.

To the right honorable and my singuler
frende, M. Thomas Cromwel,
the kinges grace secretarie moost worthy.

The next letter relates to the mal-practices of the abbot of Fountains, who has been already mentioned in a previous letter. He was a few months afterwards condemned and executed for his activity in the rebellion of 1536.

XLVII.

LAYTON AND LEGH TO CROMWELL.

[From MS. Cotton. Cleop. E. iv. fol. 114.]

Pleasit your mastershipe to understonde, that thabbot of Fontance hath so gretly dilapidate his howse, wastede ther wooddes, notoriously kepyng vj. hoorres, diffamede here *a toto populo*, one day denyyng thes articles with many mo, the next day folowyng the same confessyng, thus manifestely incurryng perjurie. vj. days before our accesse to his monasterie he committede thefft and sacrilege, confessyng the same. At mydnyght causede his chapelaine to stele the sextens keis, and towke owte a jewel, a crosse of golde with stones. One Warren, a goldsmith of the Chepe, was with hym in his chambre at that owre, and ther they stole oute a gret emerode with a rubie; the saide Warren made thabbot beleve the rubie to be but a garnet, and so for that he payede nothyng, for the emerode but xx^{li}. He solde hym also then plate withoute weyght or ownces: howe moche thabbot therfore therin was decevide he cannot tell, for the trewith ys he ys a vara fole, and a miserable ideote. We pronuncede hym perjurede, and willede hym to shew us a cause why he owght not of ryght and justes to be deprivede, and reheresyde and rede unto hym his owne rule, wiche deprivede hym for the premisses, with other many his transgressions mo, wiche were to long to write. He cowlde not denye but that by those his owne rulles he owght to be deprivede, if ther hade bene no nother lawe made or written for deprivation; and for a conclusion he hath resignede privelie into our handes, noman therof yet knowyng. We have acceptede and admittede his resignation, *et declaravimus monasterium jam esse vacans,* and sufferith hym to ministre in all thynges (for the avoidance off suspicion) evyn as he dyde before, tyll we knowe your further pleasure. Ther is never a monke in that howse mete for that rowme. Yf the erle of Comerlande knewe that hit were voide, he wolde make all labor he cowlde possible for the scelerer ther, wiche I inseure yowe is not mete therfore, for suche causes as I knowe ye will alowe, whan I shall declare them unto yow. There is a monke of the howse callede Marmaduke, to whom Mr. Timmes lefft a prebende in Repon churche, nowe abydyng upon the same prebende, the wysyste monke within Inglonde of that cote and well lernede, xx^{ti} yerres officer and rewler of all that howse, a welthie felowe, wiche will gyve yowe syx hundreth markes to make hym abbot ther, and pay yowe immediatly affter the election, withoute delay or respite, at one payment, and as I suppos withoute muche borowyng. The first fruttes to the kyng is a thowsande powndes, wiche he with his pollicie will pay within iij. yerres, and owe noman therfore one grote, as he saith, and his reason therin is vara apparant. Yf ye have not therfore providede or promisede suche a rowme for any other your frendes, this man we thynke were mete both for the kinges honour and for the discharge of your conscience, and the profett of the howse; for I am sure all thabbottes of his religion will thynke hym a ryght apte man hereunto, and the moste mete of any other. What shalbe your pleasure forther in this behalffe, other in preferryng this man, or other ways as ye thynke beste, we advertissede of your pleasure shalbe glade, with all diligence and dexteritie that shall ly in us, to accomplisshe that your mynde, disieryng yowe that by this bringer my servant with spede hit may please yowe to certifie us of the premisses. And we suppos that many other of the beste abbottes mo, affter they have commonede with your mastershipe and us, will cum to lyke preferment. And wheras we have herde that thabbot of Whitbie * hath by his letters certifyede yowe heretofore that he wolde resigne, if he be so myndett at our cumyng thether (wiche shalbe shortly) or if we fynde any cause of deprivation, whom hit shall please yowe then therunto to prefere, if ye be prefixede of any, hit may also please yowe to certifie us, or if ye be not determinede of any, then if hit be your pleasure to commite that to our discretion we shall fynde yowe a man habile both for the kinges honoure and discharge of his conscience and for your wurshipe and also profite. This monke of Repon hath a prebende of xl. powndes, wiche ye may bestowe also upon your frende, if ye make hym abbot.

Ye shall do well to sende for Warren the goldesmith, and lay unto hym thefft and sacrilege, and the recept therof, and to know what other thynges he hath hade of thabbot this viij. or ix. yerres paste. And thus I pray Gode sende yow as goode helth as yowre hert desierith. From Richemont, xx° Januarii, by your assurede poire prestes and faithful servandes,

RYCHARDE LAYTON AND THOMAS LEGH.

To the ryght honorable
master Thomas Cromwell,
cheffe secretarie to the
kinges hyghnes.

* Whitby was one of the most ancient monastic houses in the north of England, founded by the abbess Hilda about A.D. 657 (the land having been granted by Oswy king of Northumberland as a nunnery by the name of Streoneshalch. After the conquest it was refounded as a monastery of Benedictine monks. The abbot reigned in 1537, and Henry Davell, who was appointed by the king to succeed him, surrendered the monastery in 1540.

The following able letter was written by John Shepey, *alias* Castelocke, the last abbot of Faversham in Kent. The commissioners appear to have wished to wrest his house from him on the ground of his advanced age; and he must have been old, for he was abbot as early as the 14th Hen. VII. (A.D. 1498). He voted for the King in the question of the divorce : and, with the prior and others of the house, he subscribed to the King's supremacy on the 10th Dec. 1534. He finally surrendered the abbey on the 8th of July, 1538.

This abbey, which stands at a little distance to the north-east of the town of Faversham, was founded about 1147, for a convent of Cluniac monks brought from the priory of Bermondsey in Southwark.

XLVIII.

THE ABBOT OF FAVERSHAM TO CROMWELL.

[From MS. Cotton. Cleop. E. iv. fol. 34.]

Right worshipfull syr, after humble recommendations according to my most bounden dutye, with lyke thankes for your benevolent mynde alwayes shewid toward me and my poore house to your goodnes had and used; it may please you to be advertised, that I latelye receyvid your lovyng lettres dated the viij[th]. day of this present moneth, concernyng a resignation to be had of the poore house which I under God and the kyngis highnes my sovereigne lorde of longe tyme (though unworthye suche a cure) have hadde mynistration and rule of, and that by cause of thage and debilyte which ar reported to be in me. So it is, right worshipfull syr, I trust I am not yet nowe so ferr infeobled or decayed, nether in body nor in remembraunce, either by ony extremytie of aege whome debilitye lightlye for the most part alway accompanyeth, either by ony immoderate passion of ony greate contynuall infirmytie, but that I may aswell (high thankes be unto God therof!) accommodat my self to the good ordre, rule, and governaunce of my pore house and monastery as ever I myght sith my first promotion to the same, though I may not so well percase ryde and journey abrode as I might have done in tyme passed. But admytte the peculier office of an abbat to consiste (as I must nedes refell, for we professe a rule myche dyverse therunto) in journeying forth and surveying of the possessions of his house, in which case agilytie and pacyence of labour in journeying weer myche requyred indeede : though I my self be not so well able to take paynes therin as I have been in my yongre yeeres, at which tyme I trust I toke suche paynes that I nede lesse surveying of the same at this present tyme, yet have I suche feithfull approved servauntes whome I have brought upp in mye poure house from their tendre yeres, and those of suche witt and good discretion joyned with the long experyence of the trade of suche wordely thinges, that they ar able to furnysshe and supplye those partes, I knowe right well, in all poyntes myche better then ever I my self coulde, or then it had been expedyent or decent for me to have doone. Ayen, on that other side, if the cheif office and profession of an abbat be (as I have ever taken it) to lyve chaste and solitarylye, to be separate from the intromeadlyng of worldelye thinges, to serve God quyetlye, to distribute his facultyes in refresshing of poore indigent persons, to have a vigilant eigh to the good ordre and rule of his house and the flock to hym commytted in God, I trust your favour and benevolence obteyned (wherof I right humbly requyre you) I my self may and am aswell able yet nowe to supplye and contynue those partes as ever I was in all my lief, as concernynge the sufficyencye of myne owne persone. Yet doubtlesse myche more ease and quyet might it be unto me, as ye in your seid lettres right freendly and vehementlye have persuaded, for to make resignation of my seid office uppon the provision of suche a reasonable pension as your good maistreshippe shulde thinke meete and convenyent, wherin surely I wolde nothing doubte your worshipe and conscience, but in the same have myche affiaunce, not onely for the greate goodnes and good indifferencye which I here every where commenly reported by you, but also for the greate favour and benevolence which I have alwayes founde in you. And percase in myne owne mynde I coulde right well be contented and fully persuaded for as myche as concerneth myne owne part so to doo for the satisfaction and contentacion of your lovyng motyon, for I am nothing lesse then ambicyous; but I do more esteeme in this thing the myserable state and condition that our poore house shuld stond in, if suche thing shoulde com to passe, then I doo myne owne pryvat office and dignitie, thadmynystratyon wherof though it be somwhat more paynefull unto me then it hath been accustomed heretofore, yet God forbydde that it shulde seme unto me hirkefull or tedyouse. Moreover I [pray] your good maistership, to whome I wolde all these thinges weere as opynlye and manyfestlye knowen as to my seilf, our seid poore house and monasterye by meane and occasion of dyverse and many importable costes and charges which we have susteyned aswell toward the kinges highnes as otherwise: partelye by reason of dyvers greate sommes of money which it was left indebted in, in the tyme of my last predecessour there (which as it is well knowen in the countrey was but a right slendre husbande to the house): partelye by meane of dyvers and many greate reparations, aswell of the edifyces of our churche as of other houssing, which weere suffred to fall in greate ruyne and decaye, insomoche that som of theym weer in maner lykelye to fall clene downe to the grounde, as in the innyng of dyvers marsshes belongyng to our seid monasterye which the violent rages and sourges of the implacable see hadde wonne and occupyed, beyng nowe sith my tyme well and sufficyently repayred and fully amended, as the thing it seilf may sufficyently declare, to thinestymable costes and charges of our poore house: partely ayen by the meane of the greate costes, charges, and expenses which we have hadde and susteyned by and thorough thoccasion of dyvers and many sondrye suetes and actions which we have been compelled to use and pursue ayenst dyvers of our tenauntes for the recoverye of dyversse rightes of our seid monasterye of long tyme injustelye deteigned and by the same tenauntes obstynatlye denyed; and partlye also by meane of dyvers and many greate sommes of money which we have payed and lent unto the kinges highnes, aswell in dysmes and subsidies as otherwise, amountyng in all to the som of ij^{M.li}. and above, to our greate empoverysshing, and is yet nowe at this present tyme indebted to dyvers of our frendes and creditours above the som of cccc.li. as ye shalbe ferther instructed of the particulers therof whensoever it shall please you to demaunde a ferther and more exact declaration therin. Which sommes, if it might please Almighty God that I might lyve and with your good favour contynue in my seid office by the space of six or sevyn yeres at the ferthest, I doubte not but I shulde see theym well repayed and contented ayen. But if I shoulde nowe at this present tyme resigne my seid office (the case stonding as it doth) undoubtedlye our poore house, beyng nowe so ferre endebted alredy by meane of thoccasyons before remembred (thimportune charges of the first frutes and tenth which wolde be due unto the kinges highnes nowe immediatlye uppon the same resignation hadde therunto added and accumulat), shoulde be cleerelye impoverysshed and utterly decayed and undone for ever in my mynde, which I am right well assured your goodnesse wolde ne coveiteth not to bring to passe. And therfore Christe forbidde that ever I shulde so heynouslye offende and commytt ayenst Almightye God and the kinges highnes and sovereigne lorde, that by my meane or consent, so godlye and auncyent a foundation, buylded and dedicat in the honour of Saynct Savyour of so noble and victoryouse a prynce and one of the kynges most noble progenytours, whose very bodye, togither with the bodyes of his deere and welbeloved quene and also the prynce his sonne, there lyeth buryed in honourable sepulture, and ar had all thre in perpetuall memorye with contynuall suffrages and commendations of prayers,* shuld be utterlye and irrecuperablye decayed and undone, as it must nedes of verey necessitie followe if ony suche resignation shuld nowe be had. Wherfore, the whole premysses tendrelye considered and deliberatly perpended, right worshipfull syr, I doubt not but ye will contynue your accustomed favour and benevolence

---

* King Stephen, his queen Matilda, and their son Eustace Earl of Boulogne, were buried in the church of Faversham Abbey.

which ye have alwayes borne toward our poore monasterye, and so doyng ye shall not only please and content Almightye God our Savyour, but also byende us to be your contynuall bedemen and pray to God duryng our lyves for the prosperous astate of your good maistreship longe to endure with myche increase of honour. Dated at oure poore monasterye aforeseid, the xvjth day of this present monethe of Marche, anno Domini 1535.

By youre bedeman and dayelly oratour
JOHN abbott of Faversham.

To the right honorable his especiall
good maistere secretarye, be this
letter delyveryd.

At the time when the foregoing letter was written the first grand step in the destruction of the monasteries had been made.   Towards the end of February, 1535-6, the bill for the dissolution of the lesser monasteries passed the English parliament.   Grafton, p. 454, says, " in this time was geven unto the King, by the consent of the great and fatte abbottes, all religious houses that were of the value of three hundred marks and under, in hope that their great monasterys should have continued still.   But even at that tyme one sayde in the parliament house, that these were as thornes, but the great abbottes were putrifyed olde okes, and they must needs folowe : and so will other do in Christendome, quod Doctor Stokesley bishop of London, or manye yeres be passed." In fact there were few people of any penetration who did not forsee that it was but the beginning of a more general confiscation of the monastic property.

The act now passed was entitled, " An Acte wherby Relygeous Houses of Monkes, Chanons, and Nonnes, whiche may dyspend Manors, Landes, Tenementes, and Heredytamentes, above the clere yerly value of ij. c. li. are geven to the Kinges Highnes, his heires and successours, for ever.   (27° Hen. VIII. cap. 28).—The preamble runs as follows,—" Forasmoche as manifest synne, vicious, carnall, and abhomynable lyvyng, is dayly used and commytted amonges the lytell and smale abbeys, pryoryes, and other relygyous houses of monkes, chanons, and nonnes, where the congregacion of suche relygyous persones is under the nomber of xij. persons, wherby the gouvernours of suche relygyous houses and thir covent spoyle, dystroye, consume, and utterly wast, aswell ther churches, monasteryes, pryoryes, principall houses, fermes, granges, landes, tenementes, and heredytamentes, as the ornamentes of ther churches and ther goodes and cattalle, to the high dyspleasour of Almyghty God, slaunder of good relygyon, and to the greate infamy of the kynges highnes and the realme, if redres shuld not be hadde therof ; and albeit that many contynuall vysytacions hathe bene

hertofore had by the space of two hundreth yeres and more, for an honest and charyta-
ble reformacion of suche unthrifty, carnall, and abhomynable lyvyng, yett neverthelesse
lytell or none amendement ys hytherto hadde, but ther vycyous lyvyng shamelesly
encreasseth and augmentith, and by a cursed custome soo rooted and enfested that a
greate multytude of the relygyous persones in suche smale houses doo rather chose to
rove abrode in apostasy than to conforme them to the observacion of good relygyon;
soe that without suche small houses be utterly suppressed, and the relygyous persons
therin commytted to greate and honorable monasteries of relygyon in this realme,
where thei maye be compelled to lyve relygyously for the reformacion of ther lyves,
ther canne elles be noo reformacion in this behalf. In consideracion wherof the kynges
most royall majestye beynge supreme hede in erthe under God of the churche of
Englonde, dayly findyeng and devysyng the increase advauncement and exaltation of
true doctryne and vertue in the seid churche, to the onelye glorye and honor of God and
the totall extirpyng and dystruccion of vyce and synne, havyng knowledge that the
premysses be true, as well by the comptes of his late vysytacions as by sondry credyble
informacions, consyderyng also that dyverce and greate solempne monasteryes of this
realme, wherin, thankes be to God, relygyon is right well kept and observed, be destytute
of suche full nombers of relygyous persons as they ought and maye kepe, hath
thought good that a pleyne declaracion shuld be made of the premysses aswell to the
lordes spirituall and temporall as to other his lovyng subjectes the commons in this
present parliament assembled; wherupon the seid lordes and commons by a greate de-
liberacion fynally be resolved, that yt ys and shalbe moche more to the pleasour of
Almyghty God and for the honor of this his realme that the possessions of suche spirituall
relygyous howses, nowe beyng spent, spoyled, and wasted for increase and mayntenance
of synne, shuld be used and converted to better uses, and the unthryfty relygyous
persons soo spendyng the same to be compellyd to reforme ther lyves. And therupon
most humbly desire the kynges highnes that yt may be enacted by auctoryte of this
present parlyament, that his majestie shall have and enjoye to hym and his heires for
ever all and synguler suche monasteryes pryoryes and other relygyous houses of monkes,
chanons, and nonnes, of what kyndes or dyversyties of habyttes, rules, or orders soo
ever thei be called or named, which have not in landes and tenementes, rentes, tythes,
porcions and other heredytamentes, above the clere yerely value of two hundreth
poundes; and in lyke maner shall have and enjoye all the scytes and circuytes of every
suche relygyous houses, and all and synguler the manors, granges, meases, londes,
tenementes, revercions, rentes, servyces, tythes, pencions, portions, churches, chapelles,
advowsons, patronages, annuyties, rightes, entres, condycions, and other heredytamentes
apperteynyng or belongyng to every suche monasterye, pryory, or other relygyous house,
not havyng as ys aforeseid above the seid clere yerely value of two hundreth poundes,
in as large and ample maner as the abbottes, pryours, abbesses, pryoresses, or other
governors of suche monasteryes, pryoryes, and other relygyous houses now have or
ought to have the same in the right of ther houses. And that also his highnes shall
have to hym and to hys heires all and synguler suche monasteryes, abbeis, and pryoryes
whiche at eny tyme, within one yere next aftre the makyng of this acte, hath be gevyn

and graunted to his majesty by any abbot, pryour, abbes, or pryores, under the covent
seales, or that otherwyse hath be suppressed or dyssolved.   And all and synguler the
manors, londes, tenementes, rentes, servyces, revercions, tythes, pencions, portions,
churches, chapelles, advowsons, patronages, rightes, entrees, condicions, and all other
interestes and hereditaments to the same monasteryes, abbeys, and pryoryes, or to any
of them, apperteynyng or belongyng.   To have and to holde all and synguler the premysses with all ther rightes, profyttes, jurysdyccions, and commodytyes, unto the
kynges majestye and to his heires and assignes for ever, to doo and use therwyth his
and ther owen wylles to the pleasor of Almyghty God and to the honor and profytte of
thys realme.''

After some provisions in favour of persons holding rents, &c. out of the possessions
of the abbeys to be dissolved, the bill goes on to say,—'' Provyded alweis and be yt
enacted, that, forasmoche as dyverce of the chief governours of suche relygyous houses,
determynyng the utter spoyle and destruccion of ther houses, and dreadnyng the sup-
pressyng therof, for the mayntenance of ther detestable lyves, have lately fraudelently
and craftely made feoffamentes, estates, gyftes, grauntes, and leasses under ther covent
seales, or suffred recoveres of ther manors, londes, tenementes, and heredytamentes in
fee symple, fee tayle for terme of lyf or lyves or for yeres, or charged the same with
rentes or corrodyes, to the greate decaye and dymynycion of ther houses, that all suche
craftye and fraudelent recoveres, feoffamentes, estates, gyftes, grauntes, and leasses,
and every of them, made by eny of the seid chief governors of suche relygyous houses
under the covent seales within one yere next afore the makyng of this acte, shall be
utterly voyde and of none effecte.

'' Provyded alweys that suche person and persons as have leasses for terme of lyf or
yeres wherupon is reserved the olde rentes and services accustomed, and such as have
eny offyce, fees, and corrodyes that hathe bee accustomed or used in such relygyous
houses, or hath bought any liverye or lyvyng in any suche houses, shall have and
enjoye ther seid leasses, offyces, fees, corrodyes, lyveres, or lyvynges, as if this acte
hadde never be made.

'' And yt ys also enactyd by auctoryte aforseide that the kynges highnes shall have
and enjoye to his owen propere use all the ornamentes, jewelles, goodes, catalles, and
dettes which apperteyned to eny of the chief governours of the seid monasteryes or
relygyous houses in the right of ther seid monasteryes or houses at the furst day of
Marche in the yere of oure Lorde God M^l.D.xxxv. or eny tyme sythen, whersoever and
to whose possession soever they shall comme or be founde : except onely suche beastes,
grayne, and woodes, and suche other lyke catalles and revenues, as have ben sold in the
seid furste daye of Marche or sythen for the necessarye or resonable expences or
charges of eny of the seid monasteryes or houses.

'' Provyded alweis that suche of the seid chief governours which have be elect or
made abbotte, prior, abbesse, or priores, of eny of the seid relygyous houses sythen the
furst daye of Januarye which was in the yere of our Lorde God M^l.D.xxxiiij., and by
reason therof be bounden to paye the furst frutes to the kynges highnes at dayes to
comme lymyted by ther bondes made for the same, that in every suche house such chief

governour and the suertyes of every of them shalbe clerly dyscharged by auctoryte of this acte ayenst the kynges highnes and all other persones for the payment of suche sommes of money as thei stonde bounden to paye for ther seid furst frutes or for eny parte therof.

"And forasmoche as the clere yerely value of all the seid monasterys, pryoryes, and other relygyous houses in this realme, is certefyed into the kynges excheker amongest the bokes of the yerely valuacions of all the spirituall possessions of this realme, amongest which shall and may appere the certentye and number of suche small and lytell relygyous houses as have not in londes, tenementes, rentes, tythes, porcions, and other heredytamentes, above the seid clere yerely value of two hundreth poundes ; be it therfore enacted by auctorytie aforseid, that the kynges highnes shall have and enjoye accordyng to this acte the actuall and reall possession of all and syngler suche monasteryes, pryoryes, and other relygyous houses, as shall appere by the seid certyfycate remaynyng in the kynges eschequer not to have in londes, tenementes, rentes, tythes, porcions, and other heredytamentes above the seid clere yerely value of two hundreth poundes : soo that his highnes maye lawfully gyve, graunte, and dyspose them or any of them at his wyll and pleasour, to the honor of God and the welth of this realme, without further inquysycion or offices to be had or founde for the same.

"In consyderacion of whiche premysses to be had to his highnes and to his heires as ys aforseid, his majestye ys pleasyd and contentyd, of his most excellent charyte, to provyde to every chief hed and governour of every suche relygyous house duryng ther lyves, suche yerely pencions or benefyces as for ther degrees and qualytyes shalbe resonable and convenyent ; wherein his highnes wyll have most tender respect to suche of the seid chief governours as well and truly conserve and kepe the goodes and ornamentes of ther houses to the use of his majestie without spoyle, waste, or embesylyng the same, and also his majestye wyll ordeyne and provyde that the coventes of every suche relygyous house shall have ther capacytes, if thei wyll, to lyve honestlye and vertuously abrode, and some convenyent charytie dysposed to them toward ther lyvyng, or elles shalbe commytted to suche honorable great monasteryes of this realme wherin good relygyon ys observed, as shalbe lymyted by his highnes, ther to lyve relygyously duryng ther lyves.

"And yt ys ordeyned by auctoryte aforseid, that the cheff governours and coventes of suche honorable great monasteryes shall take and accept into ther houses from tyme to tyme such nomber of the persons of the seid coventes as shalbe assigned and appoynted by the kynges highnes, and kepe them relygyously duryng their lyves within ther seid monasteryes in lyke maner and forme as the coventes of suche great monasteryes be orderyd and kept."

Some clauses follow relating to the payments of tithes and subsidies out of the monastic estates, and to the payment of debts due from the monasteries dissolved. The bill then proceeds,—" Provyded always that the kynges highnes, at eny tyme after the makyng of this acte, may at hys pleasure ordeyne and declare by hys lettres patentes under his greate seale, that suche of the seid relygyous houses which his highnes shall not be dysposed to have suppressyed nor dyssolved by auctoryte of this acte, shall

stylle contynue, remayne, and be in the same bodye corporatt and in the seid essencyall
estate, qualite, and condycion, aswell in possessions as otherwyse, as thei were afore the
makyng of this acte, without any suppression or dyssolucion therof or of any parte of
the same by auctoryte of this acte ; and that every suche ordinaunce and declaracion
soo to be made by the kynges highnes shalbe good and effectuall to the chieff governours of suche relygyous houses which his majestye will not have suppressyd and to
ther successours, accordyng to the tenours and purportes of the lettres patentes therof
to be made ; any thyng or thynges conteyned in this acte to the contrary hereof
notwythstondyng."

After some other provisoes not necessary to be repeated here, the act goes on,—
" Savyng alweys and reserved unto every person and persons beyng founders, patrons,
or donours of eny abbeys, pryoryes, or other relygyous houses that shalbe suppressyd by
thys acte, ther heires and successours, all suche right, tytle, interest, possession, rentes,
annuityes, fees, offyces, leses, commons, and all other profyttes whatsooever, which any
of them have or shuld have had wythout fraude or covyn, by any maner meanes, otherwyse then by reason or occasyon of the dyssolucion of the seid abbeys, pryoryes, or other
relygyous houses, in, to, or upon any the seid abbeis, pryoryes, or other relygyous houses
wherof thei be founders, patrons, or donours, or in, to, or upon eny the londes, tenementes, or other heredytamentes apperteynyng or belongyng to the same ; in lyke maner
forme and condycion as other persones and bodyes polytyke be saved by this acte as ys
afore rehersed, and as if the seid abbeis, pryories, or other relygyous houses had not be
suppressyd and dyssolved by this acte, but had contynued styll in ther essencyall
bodyes and estates as thei be now in, eny thyng in this acte to the contrary hereof
notwithstondyng.

" And ferther be yt inacted, ordeyned, and establysshed by auctoryte aforeseid, that all
and syngler personnes, bodyes polytyke and corporat, to whom the kynges majestye, his
heires or successours, hereafter shall gyve, grante, lett, or demyse any scytt or precynct
with the houses therupon buylded, together with the demeanes of any monasteries,
pryoryes, or other relygyous houses that shalbe dyssolved or gevyn to the kynges
highnes by this acte, and the heires, successours, executours, and assignes of every suche
person, bodye polytyke and corporate, shalbe bounden by auctoryte of this acte, under
the penalytyes hereafter ensueng, to kepe or cause to be kept an honest contynewell
hous and houshold in the same scyte or precynct, and to occupye yerely asmoche of
the same demeanes in plowyng and tyllage of husbondry, that ys to saye asmoche of the
seid demeanes which hath ben commonly used to be kept in tyllage by the governours,
abbottes, or pryours of the same howses, monasteryes, or pryoryes, or by ther fermer
or fermers occupyeng the same, wythin the tyme of xx^{li} yeres next before this acte : and
if any person or persons, bodyes polytyke or corporat, that shalbe bounden by this acte,
doo not keep an honest house, houshold, housbondry, and tyllage in maner and forme as
ys aforeseid, that then he or thei soo offendyng shall forfett to the kynges highness for
every moneth soo offendyng vj^{li}. $xiij^s$. $iiij^d$. to be recovered to his use in any of his
courtes of record.

" And over that yt ys enactyd by auctoryte aforeseid, that all justyces of peas in

every shire where any suche offence shalbe commytted or done contrary to the true
meanyng and intent of this present acte, shall in every quarter and generall sessyons
within the lymyttes of ther commyssyon inquyre of the premysses, and shall have full
poar and auctoryte to hier and determyn the same, and to taxe and assesse noo lesse
fyne for every the seid offences then ys afore lymytted for the same offences, and the
extretes therof to be made and certefyed in the kynges excheker accordyng and at such
tyme and forme as other extretes of fynes, yssues, and amercyamentes ben made by the
same justyces."

The following paper appears to have been written in the time of Queen Elizabeth,
by some one who had witnessed the dissolution of the religious houses, and who here
sets down his recollections of the causes and manner of that great revolution in the
social condition of our island.

XLIX.

THE MANNER OF DISSOLVING THE ABBEYS BY K. H. 8.

[From MS. Cotton. Titus F. iii. fol. 266.]

The furst entraunce was a president gewen by cardinall Wolsey,
who under pretense of and four better abilitie to bilde his sumptuous colledge, dessolved certaine small housses, and by that doinge
of himselfe, I doubt not with good warrant from Rome, he did
make loose in others the conscience towardes those houses.
After him there came to the kinges service Mr. Cormwell, whoe
had served the cardinall in these former doinges.

That Cormwell was the man that by his zeall, his wisdome,
and his couradge, was Goods instrument to carrie all to good
effect. These meanes he used. He firste found meanes to perswade the king that it might lawfully be done; that for his
crowne and state in saftie it was necessarie to be done, four that he
made appeare to the kinge howe by their meanes the pope and
clergie had so greate aucthoritie, revenue, alliaunce, and princi-
pallye captivitie of the sowles and obedience of subjectes, that
they were able to put kinge in hazarde at their will; that for his

revenue and maintenaunce of his estate, warres, and affaires both in peace and in warre, at home and abroade, with others, it was moste profitable to dissolve them for augmentacion of his treasure.

He allyed the king so stronglie with mightie forces in Germanie and that league of religion, so as with there forces and his treasure and the consideracion of common perill by there common enemie the pope, he was able to withstande and encounter any foren princes that at the popes irritacion and prostitutinge of his kingdome to the occupante woulde make any attempt against him : this allyaunce was bothe by league with Saxonie and other, and the marriadge with the sister of Cleve.

The emperor and French king were so in hostilite, that either of them was glade to wine king Henrie to his part, wherby either of them feared to irritate him, least he joyninge with the other mighte make to harde a match againste the other; wherby I thincke that the same hostilitie was the raither cherrished by Cromwells policie : whereuppon grew the play in Fraunce, wherein were shewed the emperor and the Frenche king plaing at tenise, and the king of England paieng four the balles;* besides that thoughe they had not ben in hostillitie, yet neither of them durst suffer the other to overgrowe by impropriatinge to him selfe any thing in England, and so the emperor him selfe was glad to set still, althoughe the principall ground in shewe of the quarell touched him in heiour repudiatem (?).

Cromwell caused preachers to goe abroade, and maintayned them to instructe the people, and so to perswade the subjectes consciences to stand fast to the king without feare of the popes curse, or his desolving of his allegience.

He caused to be placed in the archebushopes place Cranmer, and in divers other bushoprickes and hier places in the clearge

* This is a curious and early example of political caricature. Another similar notice, relating to the same period, will be found in Ellis's Letters, second series, vol. ii. p. 44.

divers protestantes, by meanes wherof he was able to execute greate thinges amonge them selves, and they were not able so muche as to enter into any full and perfect counsell against them, muche lesse to put any thing in publicke execution, as against the former kinges of theis realme.

He knewe that the clargie had in king Richardes the secondes time suborned an other with pretense of a next title to depose the kinge; he knewe that his clargie were attemptinge the like with the marquies of Exetar.

He perswaded the king by maintteininge of *equum jus*, and by holdinge-downe the over-emminent power of soche greate ones as in time paste, like bell-wethers, had led the sheppeshe flockes of England against their prince, to knett fast to him the love of his commons and specially of his cittie of London.

He placed abbottes and ffriers in divers great housses divers lerned men, and perswaded against these supersti[ti]ens, which men were readie to make surrender of their houses at the kinges commaundement.

He caused the king to restrayne all payment at Rome, and all resorte of his subjectes thither, either for suites, appells, faculties, or other causes, wherby both he kept treasure and held it from his ennemies, and restrained his ennemies from fliinge to foren partes or conference with them.

He caused visitacions to be made of all the reeligious houses touching their conversations, whereuppon was retourned the booke called the Blacke Booke, expressing of everie suche house the vile lives and abhominable factes, in murders of their bretherne, in sodomyes, in whordomes, in destroying of children, in forging of deedes, and other infinite horrors of life, in so muche as devidinge of all the religious persons in England into three partes two of theise partes at the least were sodomites: and this appeared in writting, with the names of the parties and their factes. This was shewed in parliament, and the villanies made knowen and abhorred.

He caused the king of the abbes possessions to make suche

dispersion, as it behoved infinite multitudes for their owne intrest to joyne with the king in hollding them downe, whiche he did by divers meanes, and these amoung other: by ffownding divers bushoprickes and colleges with these possessions, selling many of them to many men four reasonable prises, exchainging many of them with the nobilitie and other for their auncient possession to their greate gaine with whome he exchainged, preferring many sufficient persons to the kinges servis who were sone raised to nobilitie and to worshipe and good calling, and all indewed with maintenaunce out of the revenewes of abbyes.

Here is all I can remember.

There was also used for the manner of dessolution—

First, divers abbotes and other that could be thereunto perswaded, or were some of them four the purpose placed by the king, made surrender of their houses and conveied them to the kinge by order of lawe, and had competent pencions both them selves and their companie during their lives. Somme beinge detected by the said visitacion, to have the kinges favour not to punishe them with rigour, not to publishe their infamie for their vile factes, were likewise content to surrender.

For all the rest, which were not then many, the parliament being made acquainted with their vile lives, were redely contented both to confirme the surrender, and geive their consyntes to the geving of all the reaste to the kinge.

CHAPTER II.

FROM THE DISSOLUTION OF THE SMALLER HOUSES TO THE PASSING OF THE ACT FOR THE DISSOLUTION OF THE LARGER MONASTERIES.

No sooner was the act for the dissolution of the smaller monasteries passed, than we find Cromwell beset by two classes of suitors ; on one side the heads of houses where the fewest irregularities had been discovered hoped to have advantage of the clause which left it in the power of the king to preserve at his discretion such houses as might appear deserving of exception, while on the other many of the gentlemen and noblemen of the court eagerly sought to obtain a share of the spoils. Among the letters which follow will be found examples of both these classes of applications. The fate of the nuns appears to have excited on the whole more compassion than that of the monks and friars. The following petition is from the prioress and sisters of Legborne, or Lekeburn, in Lincolnshire, a nunnery founded by Robert Fitz-Gilbert towards the end of the twelfth century. Little is known of the history of this house, and it is not clear how Cromwell came to be considered the representative of its founder.

L.

THE PRIORESS AND NUNS OF LEGBORNE TO CROMWELL.

[From MS. Cotton. Cleop. E. iv. fol. 270*.]

Right honourable oure most synguler maister and ffounder, oure duetie in the humblest wise presupposed, with dayly prayer as youre perpetuall and religious beedwomen, please yt youre goodnes to understonde, that whereas almyghty God hath indued you with just title ffounder of the pryory of Legborne, to the great comfort of me and all my systers, we doo and shall alweyes submyt oure selfes to youre most rightuouse commaundement and ordre, oonly puttyng oure comfort in youre goodnesse for all causes concernyng youre poure pryory of Legbourne. And whereas we doo here that a grete nombre of abbyes shalbe punysshid, subprest, and put downe, bicause of theire myslyvyng, and that all abbyes and pryoryes under the value of cc^{li} be at oure moste noble prynces pleasure to subpresse and put downe, yet if it may pleas youre goodnes we trust in God ye shall here no compleyntes agaynst us nother in oure lyvyng nor hospitalitie kepyng. In consideracion wherof, if it may please youre goodnes in oure great necessitie to be a meane and sewter for youre owne powre pryory, that it may be preserved and stond, you shalbe a more higher ffounder to us then he that first foundid oure howse. We have noon othir comfort nor refuge but oonly unto youre goodnes, and we hooly submyt our selfes to the pleasure of God, to the pleasure of oure prynce, and to the pleasure of you oure ffounder, and howsoever it shall please God that we shalbe orderid, we shall contynue youre faithfull and dayly bedewomen, as knoweth owre Lorde, who ever preserve you to youre most comfort.

> Your owne dayly beadwomen, Jane
> Messyndyne, pryores, and systers of
> the pryory of Legborne.

The next letter relates to two of the smaller religious houses in Devonshire. The priory of Totnes was founded by Judhel or Johel in the reign of William the Conqueror, as a cell to the great benedictine abbey of Angers. The patronage descended from the original founder to the Zouches, in which family it remained till their attainder after the accession of Henry VII., when it was conferred by the crown on Sir Peter Edgcumbe. Thomas Rychard appears as the last prior of this house.

The priory of Cornworthy was a poor house of Austin nuns, also in the patronage of the Edgcumbes, although it appears doubtful whether the original founder was of that family, or whether, like the priory of Totnes, it was derived from the Zouches. The following letter supports the latter supposition. The last prioress appears to have been Avicia Dynham.

LI.

SIR PETER EDGECUMBE TO CROMWELL.

[From MS. Cotton. Cleop. E. IV. fol. 258.]

Affter my most harty recommendacyons, with lyke thanckes for your goodnes to me att tymes schewyd, and this ys to advertyse

yow that here ys moche communycacyon and brutes * that all abbays, pryorys, and nunrys under the cler yerly valew of cc[li]. schall
be suppressyd, nottwithstondynge hyt ys nott as yett in thes parties oponly knowen the occacyon off suppressyon, nor who schall
take most benyffyte therby, nor to whate usse hyt schall rest at
lengthe. But trew hyt ys, that I am by the kyngges ffather by hys
graunt to my poare ffather made to hym and hys isue male,
ffounder off the pryory off Tottenes and the nunry off Cornwor-
thye in Devonsschyre, and every off them be under the valew off
cc[li]. And as to Tottenes, the pryour ther ys a man off goode ver-
tuus converssacyon, and a good viander, and I can do no lesse
with my truthe and dewty but to advertyse yow off that I know
trew in this causse, hartely besechynge yow so to advertysse the
kyngges highnes, and that I in my most umbyll maner beseche hys
grace to order me in this causse as onne that wyll juberd † lyff and
goodes to do hys grace trew servyce, and hartely beseche allmyghty God longge to preserve hys most nobyll persson, and
yow so to serve hys highnes. From my poare howsse, the daye
off annuncyacyon off our lady, ywr aun,

P. EGGECOMBE.

    Mr. secretory, in casse hyt be sso that the kyngges pleasure maye
be by ywr meanys so good that the prior of Tottenes maye enjoye
the spirituall promocyons, and hyt wyll be no bettere ffor hym and
hys bredere to leve on, and I to have the temperall possessyons yn
parte theroff, the sunnere ffor concyderacyons that I am ffownder
off bothe howsys, I promyse yow by this my wrytynge to concyder
yowr ffavor and sute, as I trust to plese yow, and yff ye thinck my
sute not ressonabyll, I refferre me and my causse to yor order
under the kyngges highnes above all others lyvynge, and so I
trust yow, and herin I hartely praye yow to know ywr pleasure.

---

      * *Brutes*, i. e. reports, rumours.
      † Jeopard.

Boxgrave in Sussex was an alien priory, founded in the reign of Henry I. by Robert de Haye, as a cell to the benedictine abbey of Essay in Normandy. On its dissolution, the site and premises were granted to Sir Thomas West lord Lawarr, who was patron of the priory as representative of the Hayes, by possessing their estate and residence of Halnaker House, the 'pore howse' mentioned in the letter. The last prior was Thomas Myles.

LII.

LORD LAWARR TO CROMWELL.

[From MS. Cotton. Cleop. E. iv. fol. 234.]

Right worshipfull sir, in my most hartes wise I recommend me to you, verey desyrus to here of youre good helthe, thankyng you of your provyd goodnes shewed to me undeservid, for the whiche you bynd me to be youres dewryng my lyffe, and so shall ye ffynd me to the best of my letyll powre. Pleasythe you to be adver-tysed, that I have perffyt word that the acte is past that all howses off relygyon that is under three hundred markys ys gevyn to the kynges highnes, bothe the landes and gooddes, and that by the said acte his highnes may by his letters patentes under his grete seale gyve lysence to as many as shall stand with his gracys pleasure to contynewe unsubpressyd. And so it is, that I have a power howse called Boxgrave, very nere to my power howse, wherof I am ffounder, and there lyethe many of my aunsytorys, and also my wyffys mother; and for bycawse hyt is of my ffoundacyon, and that my paryshe churche is under the roofe of the churche of the said monastery, and have made a power chapell to be buryed yn, wherfor yf hit myght stand with the kynges gracys pleasure, for the power servyce that I have doyn his highnes, to fforebere the subpressyng of the same, or else to translate hyt ynto a college of suche nombre as the landes wyll bere; and yf hyt may not stand so with his gracys pleasure, then I wold lowly beseche hys grace to have the prefarment of the farme, with all such other thynges as the pryor yn his tyme had for the provysyon of his howse; wherffore I wyll beseche you that I may have youre lawfful ffaver, good wyll, and helpe hereyn. And suerly, syr, I shall recompence youre goodnes, kyndnes, and payne hereyn, so that I trust that

for soe powere a thyng that you shalbe contentyd and pleasyd, besechyng you to be as good to me hereyn as you may be, as my
most trust ys in you, as knowythe the blessyd Trinite, who long
preserve you. Wryttyn at my powere howse, upon owre Lady
day.

Your owen assuryd,
THOMAS LAWARR.

As was before stated, the latter part of lord Lawarr's request was granted, and he
obtained both the property and even the furniture of Boxgrave priory. The priory
church afterwards became the parish church of the town, and the tomb of his father
is still preserved. It is rather singular that in the following letter, which must have
been written at this time, Cromwell is addressed by the title of *lord*: this however
may have been a mere piece of flattery from an inferior, as a compliment to his political
station.

LIII.

JOHN MORISE TO CROMWELL.

[From MS. Cotton. Cleop. E. iv. fol. 234*.]

Right honorable and my synguler goode lorde, I humbly recommende me unto yowe; this shalbe to advertyse your lordshippe,
that syr John Dawtree, master Palmer, and I, according to the
kynges commyssion and instruccions, have dyssolved the pryorie
of Boxgrave in the countie of Sussex. The besenes of dissolucion
therof was fynysshed the xxvjth. day of this present moneth, at
which tyme I receved your lordshypps lettre in ffavor of my lord
Lawarre, which according to your lordshypps commaundment by
that sent of other joynt commyssioners wyth me I have folowed,
so that my seyd lord Lawarre, as I trust, is contented. The valure
of the goodes that he hath bowght cummys to cxxv^{li}. xiij^s. iiij^d.
wherof he hath payed xl^{li}. and for the rest I have taken his owne
bond to the kynges use to be payed at suche dayes as he hym selff
hath desyred, that is to sey, Myghelmas next and Ester ffolowing,

wherwyth I trust the kynges grace wilbe pleased by meanes of yowre good lordshyppe, and the rather for that his grace, by the vygylant circumspectyon and dylygent dewte of the seyd lord Lawarre, hath more proffett there then in any other howse dissolved in Sussex. And, as I verely thynke, the kyng is not better answered nor more trewly of the goodes apperteynyng to his highnes by reason of any howse dyssolved in Inglond, then he is also there, as almyghty God knowith, who long preserve your lordshippe with the increase of honor to his pleasure. From Boxgrave, the xxvijth day of Marche.

Att your comaundment glad to do serves,

JOHAN MORES.

To the right honorable
and my synguler good
lord, the lorde preve
Seale, yeve this.

The following letter is another suit for a grant of abbey lands. The priory of Fineshed, or (as it was more anciently called) Castel Hymel, in Northamptonshire, was founded by Richard Engayne the elder, who died in 1208. After the dissolution it appears to have been retained for some time in the king's hands, and it was finally granted to John lord Russell. The last prior was Christopher Harpeworth. This, as well as the priory of Worspring in Somerset, was one of the smaller houses. The latter was founded in 1210 by William de Courteney. The last abbot or prior of this house was Roger Thorynton.

LIV.

HUMPHREY STAFFORD TO CROMWELL.

[From MS. Cotton. Cleop. E. IV. fol. 209.*]

Right worshipfull, yn my most humblyst wise I can I comend me unto your good mastership, thanckyng your mastership ever for the great kyndenes and ffavour shewed unto me alweys, and where it may please your mastership to call to your good remembrauns that ye promysed me to be good master unto me when the tyme came : sir, your mastership shall understond that whereas yet I am not able to doo suche acceptable service unto the kynges highnes my master, as my poore and true hert wold, and if I hadd wherwith to maynteyn it, so it is, pleasith it your mastership to understond, that where I desyred Mr. Bryan to be so good master unto me as to moshion unto your mastership to helpe me to the gifte of the priorie of Fynshed, a house of chanons yn the countie of Northampton, of the yerly value of lvj^{li}. x^s. xj^d. ob. yn case it be subpressed, sir, your mastership shall understond that sens that tyme my naturall ffather willed me to write to your mastership, and to non other, for to be good master unto me for a house of chanons yn Somersett shiere called Worspryng, where my seyd ffather is ffounder therof, and as I doo subpose of like value or theraboutes.   And if it wold please your mastership to be so good master unto me as to helpe me to Worspryng priorie, I were and wylbe wylst I leve your bedman and alweys redy to your mastership suche poore service and pleasure as shal become me to doo, whillest I do leve, God wyllyng, who ever have your mastership yn his tuysshon.   From Bletherweke,* thus present Palme Sonday, by your own assured to his litle power,

HUMFFRAY STAFFORD, esquyer.

To the right honorable sir
Thomas Cromwell, knyght, secretorie
to the kinges hyghnes, d.d. thus.

The following letter from Edward Lee, archbishop of York, relates to some of the small houses dependent upon his see.   The abbots and monks, perceiving the dissolution of these houses to be inevitable, seem in many instances to have turned to their own advantage the movables and jewels which were in their hands.   The sale or embezzlement of these articles was afterwards placed among the heaviest charges against certain obstinate abbots.

* Blatherwick Hall, in Northamptonshire.   The old mansion is still standing.

LV.

THE ARCHBISHOP OF YORK TO CROMWELL.

[From MS. Cotton. Cleop. E. iv. fol. 239.]

Right honorable, aftre my hartiest commendation, accordeng to
your requeste made to me in your lettres, I have furthwith upon
the receipte of the same sent commawndement to certayne monasteries beeing nie to Yorcke, where I was than, and nowe I have
given commaundement to all archdeacons to warne all monasteries
of lesse yerelie valewe than ij^c li. being within their archdeaconries,
that they shall no thing imbecille ne alien; and if theye have,
that theye shall agayne call suche thinges aliened or imbecilled to
their handes. Some that were noted to have received some
goodes of suche monasteries I called and warned that they shold
in no wiese meddle with anye suche goodes, and that if they had
anye suche, that they shold restore them, and ferthermore, if anye
suche goodes shalbee offred to them, that they shold give me
warneng. And for bicause most resorte for suche propose is to
the citie of Yorke, I have warned the maiour of Yorke, and oother
of his brodren therof, and speciallie the maister of the mynte,
upon their peril and daunger that theye receive no goodes of anye
suche monasterie, and ferther herin I entend to doo, from tyme
to tyme, as I shall see neede, and dailie doo warne suche as doo
resorte to me, that they meddle not with anye suche goodes, that
by them this commawndiment maye bee the more published, as I
trust it shalbee nowe by tharchdeacons officialles, wiche be nowe all
abrode, and have speciall commawndiment to sett furthe this
propose.

Sir, I entierlie praye you to bee good to me for ij. places of the
patronaige of the archbushoppes of Yorke, that if you shall
thinke opon suche considerations as I shall alledge that I have
reason to sue for them, that you woll helpe me with your good
word, that theye bee not suppressed. The tone of them, named

Saincte Oswaldes, is not of foundation a monasterie of religiouse men, but is *libera capella archiepiscopi*. No man hathe title in it but the archbushoppe : the priour therof is removable at my pleasure and accomptable to me, and the archbushoppe maye put ther, if he woll, seculer prestes, and so wold I have doone at my entre, if I had not ther founde oone of myne acquayntaunce whome I judged meete to bee ther undre me. And morover tharchbushoppes of Yorke had it given to them by William Rufus in exchaunge for recompense as well of landes, as jurisdiction taken from them at the commeng in of William Conquerour, as apperethe in my registres and oodre old bookes. And in the same it apperethe that the saied chapell enjoyethe all privilaiges lieke as all oother the kinges free chapelles ; for it was some tyme *libera capella regia*, and for the defense of the saied privilaiges, and jurisdiction ther, my predecessours have alwaies had writtes from the king agaynst all disturbers, bicause it is no oodre but *libera capella*, and some tyme was the kinges.

The toodre is called Hexham,* upon the borders of Scotland, and was some tyme *sedes episcopalis*, and manye holie men some tyme busshoppes ther bee in that churche, sainctes of name ; and wiese men, that knowe the borders, thinke that the landes therof, althoughe theye were x. tymes as moche, can not contrevaile the damaige that is lieke to ensue if it bee suppressed, and some waie ther is never a house between Scottland and the lordshippe of Hexham ; and men feare if the monasterie goo downe, that in processe all shall bee wast moche within the land. And what comfort that monasterie is daylie to the contre ther, and speciallie in tyme of warr, not onlie the contre men doo knowe, but also manye of the noble men of this realme that hathe doone the kinges highnes service in Scotland. I doubt not but that the land of that

---

* Hexham was a bishop's see under the Anglo-Saxons. The monastery, called by the Anglo-Saxons Hagustald, dated from the seventh century. The last prior was Edward Jaye.

monasterie is better than twoo hundred pound by yere, as liek-wiese tharbushoppes landes war moche bettur if they laie in a quiet place. Some of my predicessours have had ther xiij^c. marces by the yere, and nowe it is *communibus annis* undre ij^c li. I entierlie praye you, if you thinke that I have reason to sue for these ij., that you woll helpe me to save them. And as for Hexham, I thinke it is necessarie to bee considred, as I thinke theye that knowe the borders woll saie.

Sir, according to the kinges commawndiment, I have generallie given commawndment that no prechers shalbee suffred that with-ow3te discretion preache novelties, and, as you right wieselie con-sidered, doo rather sowe seedes of dissention than doo anye good, and some suche as I have herd to use suche preacheng I have discharged, and yet they preach, but I make processe agaynst them, and some of them saie theye wooll get licence of the king to preache. If theye obteigne anye suche licence, I then ame dis-charged for them that have suche licence ; but I trust that you woll suffre no suche licence to passe, but that I shall knowe therof, and what your pleasure is, than if they preache suche novelties I praye you I maye knowe by this bearer. Some saie theye have licence of my lord of Cantorburie; but I trust theye have no suche, and if theye have, none shalbee obeyde here, but onlie the kinges and youres. And thus in my hertiest maner ffare you well. From Cawode, the xxiijth. of April, 1536.

Your owne ever assured,

EDOUARDE EBOR.

The next letter relates to the pensions which were granted to the heads and monks of the dissolved houses. It appears that these were often small, and the monks had probably sometimes difficulties in establishing their claims. Cokesford in Norfolk was a priory of Augustine canons, founded in the reign of Stephen by William Cheyney. The site was granted on the 9th of May, 29 Henry VIII. to Thomas Howard duke of Norfolk. John Matthews, the last prior, had subscribed with his canons to the king's supremacy.

LVI.

THE PRIOR OF COKESFORD TO CROMWELL.

[From MS. Cotton. Cleop. E. iv. fol. 269*.]

Ryght wyrthfull sir, with dwe reverens my duty remembred, desiryng and hartely prayng your masterthep to be good maister to me and help me to my pore levynge and pencion, for the wyche I thynke longe to know wherto I xall hold me, and, sir, for the love of God and of your charitabyle disposicion youe bere towards me, of your goodnes and nothynge of my deservynge, it may lyke youe to se the order of it and redy sped for my por comfort and levynge, and that it may so be ordered by your best advyse and cownsell that I may have it without further vexacion or trobyle in getyng on leveynge of my forsed por levynge, for I fer me without your good helpe and ayd and comfort it wylbe hard to combee. I have no frend to make my compleynt to but to yow alonly; wherfore I besche yow to take informacions of Mr. Balley of the Francys, my frynd this brynger. Mr. doctor Lee wylbe good to me with your good helpe, in home ys all my trost; he promysed me at Londone to have xx^{li}. for my pension, I trust to have that with better, and my chambre, with all that bylongynge to that same, with ij. beddys, one for my self and another for my servant. In thes thynges, with all other, I submit my self to God and to your good wyll, and I, your chaplene and dayly orator, with alle trew and diligent servys and promysys, by me befor promysyd, as ever xalle lye in my lytyll pore, as knowith our Lord, how ever have youe in his glorius tuiscion, after your wyrschipfull hartes desyre. Wretynge at Cokesford, this Sonday next before the Invencion of the holy crose.

Alle yours and at your comaunment, your dayly oratour and chaplen, Johan Mathewe, latt pryor of Cokesford.

Calwich, or Calewych, in Staffordshire, was originally a hermitage or small cell founded before 1148, and given by Nicholas de Greselei Fitz Nigel to the priory of Kenilworth. A small convent of black canons was also placed here. Very little appears to be known of the history of this house, and almost all the information contained in the following letter is supplementary to the account given in the last edition of the Monasticon.

Rowcester, or Rocester, in Staffordshire, was an abbey of black monks, founded by Richard Bacon about the year 1146. The last abbot was William Grafton.

LVII.

RICHARD STRETE TO CROMWELL.

[From MS. Cotton. Cleopat. E. iv. fol. 236.]

My duty done, according to your lettres datyd *penultimo die Aprilis* I have ben at Calwich, and takyn an inventary of the goodes of that house by indenture, and committyd the keping and garding of all thinges ther to thabbott of Rowceter ij. myles thens, and on of his brethren abidith at Calwich to overse them who hath kept the sequestre syns the departur of the late prior. The valour of the goodes and laundes foloith.

Inprimis, household very course, as doith appere by particlars in the inventary	xv^{li}.	xiij^s.	ij^d.
Item, in catall, as oxen, kye,* horses, mares, shepe old and yonge . .	lxxix^{li}.	xv^s.	iiij^d.
Item, in corne apon the grounde . .	xj^{li}.	vj^s.	viij^d.
Item, stuff for the church, as chales and vestmentes, etc.	x^{li}.	ix^s.	viij^d.
Summa,	cxvij^{li}.	iiij^s.	x^d.

* *Kye,* i. e. cows.

Item, the demeanes lyen roundabowt the house, and ben worth yerely . .	xxiij^{li}.	xij^s.
Item, other tenthes yerely . . .	xvij^{li}.	viij^s. j^d. ob.
Item, the paroch church of Glaston to that monastery appropriat, besyde the vicar indoment	xiij^{li}.	vj^s. viij^d.

In these is no harde peneworth: the house and other byldinges be in mean good state of reparacion. I have dischargyd and put forth such persons as were not mete to be ther, and laft such as be husbaundes, and I have made sure the convent saill, and the evidence.

The first founder ther was Nich. Gresley, in whose title nowe claymyth Mr. Longford (as men here report). Ther be diverse benefactours that hath gyffyn landes to that house, as it doith appere, viz. my lord Stuard, sir Henrie Saucheverell, Mr. Oker, and other thair ansetors. And thus ye may partly perceyve, and what I can do ferther shalbe redy by God his grace.

Item, to the last part of your lettre toching demeanour and the payment to the collectours, in the archdeaconry of Coventry, Derby, Staff., and Salop; the collectors have amoste made an ende in these iiij. archdeaconrys, as fer as I can perceyve is no denying, and as for the collectour of tharchdeaconry of Chester, I never herd from hym, so I supposyd he had good spede in his gedring. And how and in what maner all thynges is ther ye shalbe acertenyd shortly. I trust no man in that archdeaconry wolde be obstinate, if thay be well handlyd. Mr. parson Molenex told me this weke that the collectour as yet askyd hym no money, ner gaf hym warnyng, and whether faute be in the collectour or other, ye shalbe shortly acertenyd, and money sent with spede, by God his grace. The deithe of my lord and his wilfull and parciall cessing, defferrith all this, as knowith God, who kepe you. Lich., xij°. Maij.

Yours, RICHARD STRETE, preist.

The following letter relates to the proceedings of the commissioners in Northampton-shire. At Chaucomb, Chacomb, or Saucomb, there was a priory of Augustine canons, founded by Hugh de Chacombe in the reign of Henry II. The last prior was Thomas Stoner. Ashby Magna, in Leicestershire, was a manor belonging to the nunnery of Catesby, or Catteby, in Northamptonshire, which house was founded by Philip de Esseby or Ashby, or by his son Robert, about the reign of Richard I. The last prioress is said to have been named Jocosa, i.e. Joice. From a subsequent letter it appears that this letter was addressed to the Chancellor of the Augmentations.

LVIII.

THE COMMISSIONERS IN NORTHAMPTONSHIRE TO SIR R. RICH.(?)

[From MS. Cotton. Cleop. E. iv. fol. 209.]

Ryght honorable, after all humble recommendacions, theis shalbe to advertyse you that we have byn yn execucion off the kynges commission directed unto us, begyngnyng at Chacumbe, wher we accomplysshed alle thynges acordyng unto our commyssion, and frome thens we repayred to Assheby, where after on days tar-reyng we werr ffayne to departe thens unto Catesby nunrey, by oc-cacion of sykenesse, where we have also accomplisshed the kynges commyssion accordyng to his high commandement and our poore distreccions. Which howse of Catesby we ffounde in verry perfett order, the priores a sure, wyse, discrete, and very religyous woman, with ix. nunnys under her obedyencye as relygious and devoute and with as good obedyencye as we have in tyme past seen or belyke shall see. The seid howse standyth in sueche a quarter muche to the releff off the kynges people, and his graces pore sub-jectes their lykewyse mooche relewed, as by the reporte of dyvers worshyppfulles nere therunto adjoynyng as of alle other yt ys to us openly declared. Wherefore yf yt shulde please the kynges highnesse to have eny remorse that eny suche relygous house shall stande, we thynke his grace cannot appoynt eny house more mete to shewe his most gracious charitie and pitey one than one the said howse of Catesby. Ferther ye shall understande, that as to her bounden dewtye towardes the kynges highnes in theis his affayres, also for discrete enterteynment of ws his commys-sioners and our company, we have not fownde nor belyke shall

fynde eny suche of more dyscrecion. And lese peraventure theyr
may be labor made to her detryment and other undoyng, before
knowleg showlde cum to his hyghnesse and to yow frome us, yt
may therfore please yow to sygnefy unto his hyghnesse the effecte
of theis our lettres, to thentent his grace may stay the graunte
theyrof tyll suche tyme we may ascerteyn yow of our fulle certy-
fycat and compartes in that behalfe accordyng. Frome Catesby,
the xij. day off this present moneth off May; from the kynges
commyssioners at your commandement.

EDMOND KNYGHTLEY.
JOHN LANE.
GEORGE GYFFARD.
ROBT. BURGOYN.

The priory of St. Petroc at Bodmin in Cornwall was founded in Saxon times, and
was refounded for Augustine canons in 1120. The site with demesnes were granted,
after its dissolution, to Thomas Sternhold, the celebrated translator of the Psalms.
The last prior was Thomas Vivian, alias Wannyworth: he was suffragan bishop of
Megara in Greece, and his tomb is still preserved in the church.

LIX.

THE PRIOR OF BODMIN TO MR. LOK.

[From MS. Cotton. Cleop. E. IV. fol. 116.]

Master Lok, I harttili recommend me unto you, so thankyng
you for your gret kyndenesse and payne that ye have take for me,
which I trust wons God wyllyng to recompens. Syr, I am sore
disquietid with a sett of unthryfty chanons, my convent and there
berars, which of longe contynuans have lyvyd unthriftili and
agene the gode order of relygyon, to the grete sklaunder of the
same, as all the contrey can telle. For the reformacyon thereof,
the buschope yn hys late visitacyon gave certayne and dyvers injuncions, commaundyng me straytle to see observyd and kept,

which are noo hardar thane ower owne rule and profession byndis us, and as alle other relygyus men use and observe where god relygioun is observid and kept; wherewith they be sore grevid, and yntend the most parte of them to depart with capacitise withowt my concent and wylle, and won of them hathe purchesid a capacyte the last terme withowt my lycence, which is agene the wordes of his capacite, wherefor I have restraynyd his departyng, for no gret los that I showld have of hym, but for the yl exemple to othere; for yf I showld suffer this man to depart yn this maner, I shall have never a chanon to byde with me. I am sore threttynyd with won master Roger Arundell, a gret berar and mayntynar of my bretherne agenst me, and the procurar of there capacites, to be browght before the kynges grace honorable councell, for that I have not sufferd this lewde chanon to depart with his capacite acordyng to there yntent. I pray you harttili to shew this mater to my gode master secretary, desieryng hym, as my speciall trust ys yn hym, yf anney complayntes cum to hym, as I dowt not but that there wol, yt may plese hym to refer the examynatioun of the mater to sir Johan Arundell, sir Peter Eggecumbe, sir Johan Chamond, or any other discrete gentilmen yn the contrey whatsoever, so that I cum not to London, as there purpose ys, which showld be to gret a charge for me to bere, my hows beyng sore yndettid alleredy. This gentilman hathe procured a commyssion, as I am informyd, to pull downe a were longyng to my pore hows, whiche hathe stande us thes ccccc. yere and more. If nede be, I wol wryte more of this mater by mastre Hill. Thus fare ye as wel, as your gentil hart can thynke, and alle my gode frendes and lerners to honour (?) pray you have harttili commendid. From Badmyn, 25 May, by your owne for ever,

THOMAS, priour there.

To the ryght worshipfull
master W. Loke, mercer, dwellyng yn the
Chepscyde, at the syngne of the
Padlok, this be dd. with spede.

The following letter from Richard Beerely, a monk of Pershore, is a curious illus-
tration of the state of the religious houses. His request appears to have been granted,
as we do not find his name among the list of monks who received pensions at the dissolution of the house. The Benedictine abbey of Pershore in Worcestershire, was
founded towards the end of the seventh century. The last abbot appears to have been
John Stanewell or Stonywell.

LX.

RICHARD BEERLY TO CROMWELL.

[From MS. Cotton. Cleop. E. iv. fol. 161.]

Most reverent lord yn God, second person yn this rem of
Englond, ynduyd with all grace and goodnes, y submytt my selfe
unto your grace and goodnes, desyuryng you myckely to be
good and gracyus lord unto me synful and poor creatur, my lowly
and myck scrybullyng unto your nobull grace at thys tyme ys
gruggyng yn my conchons that the relygyon wyche we do obser
and keype ys no rull of sentt Benett, nor yt no commandyment of
God, nor of no sentt, but ly3th and foulysse serymonys, mayd sum
yn old tyme and sume yn our tyme, by ly3th and ondyscrytt
faders, wych have done ther dutys and fulfellyd ther owne serymonys, an lett the preceps an commandymentes of God go. And so
have y do thys syx yere, wych doth now greve my conchons sore,
that y have bye a dyssymblar so long tyme, the wych relygyon
say sent Jamys, ys yn vayne and bryngyng forth no good fruttes;
bettur owtt then yn the relygyon, except yt were the tru relygyon
of Chryst. Also we do nothyng seyrch for the doctryn of Chryst,
but all fowloys our owne sensyaly and pleser. And thys relygyon, as y supposse, ys all yn vayne glory, and nothyng worthy to
be except nather before God nor man. Also, most gracyus lord,
ther ys a secrett thyng yn my conchons wych dothe move me to
goo owt of the relygyon, an yf yt were never so perfett, wych no
man may know but my gostly fader, the wych I suppss yf a man
mothe guge yn other yong persons as yn me selfe, for Chryst say,

nolite judicare et non judicabimini; therfore y wyl guge my
nowne conchons fyrst, the wych fautt he shall know of me heyr-
after more largyorly, and many other fowll vycys don amonckst
relygyus me[n], not relygyus men, as y thynk the owtt not to be
cald, but dyssymblars with God. Now, most gracyus lord and
most worthyst vycytar that ever cam amonckes us, helpe me owt
of thys vayne relygyon, and macke me your servant, hande-mayd,
and beydman, and save my sowlle, wych sholdbe lost yf ye helpe
yt not, the wych you may save with on word speckyng, and mayck
me wych am now nawtt to cum unto grace and goodnes. Now y
wyll ynstrux your grace sumwatt of relygyus men, and how the
kynges grace commandyment ys keyp yn puttyng forth of bockes
the beyschatt of Roms userpt power. Monckes drynk an bowll
after collacyon tell ten or xii. of the clock, and cum to mattens as
dronck as myss, and sume at cardes, sume at dyyss, and at ta-
bulles, sume cum to mattens begenynge at the mydes, and sume
when yt ys allmost done, and wold not cum ther so only for boddly
punnysment, nothyng for Godes sayck, wyth many other vycys
the use, wyche y have no leser now to express. Also abbettes,
monckes, prest, don lyttyl or nothyng to put owtt of bockes the
beyshatt of Romes name, for y my seylfe do know yn dyvers
bockes wher ys name and hys userpt powor upon us ys. No
more unto your nobul grace at thys tyme, but Jesu preserve you
to pleser. Amen.

Your commyssary commandyd me to wrytt my mynd unto
your nobul grace, by my outhe I toyk of hym yn our chaptur
hows.

> Be me, your beydman, dan. Ryc. Beerley, now
> monck yn the monastery of Pershor.

To my nobull and gracyus lord
vycytar yn the kynges cortt be
thys byl delyveryd yn hast.

The writer of the following letter was William Walle, abbot of Kenilworth, from the 8th to the 29th Hen. VIII. He was not the last superior of this house, having been succeeded by Simon Jekys, or Jakys. The abbey of Kenilworth was founded about 1122 by Geoffrey de Clinton, chamberlain and treasurer to Henry I. Broke, in Rutland, was a very small priory, subordinate to the abbey of Kenilworth : its last prior was Roger Orwell.

LXI.

THE ABBOT OF KENILWORTH TO CROMWELL.

[From MS. Cotton. Cleop. E. iv. fol. 214.]

Ryght honorable and my synguler good master, my covenable duety with condygne recommendacyons humbly unto your master-shypp remembryd, maye it please you to be further advertisyd of such matter as at thys daye, I and my pore house ar muche per-plexid and unquietid in, concernyng our maner or cell of Broke, in the county of Rotteland, whych by the injust and wntrewe demean-our and behavour of such my chanon as I sent thider for to have the governaunce and rule thereof, and for that he had not suche profitable and commodyous pencyon assygned and made sure unto hym duryng hys lyfe as he and his consell wold and could devyse and aske, hath entytled the kynges hyghnes in his court of augmentacyons unto the hoole tytle and interest thereof; whyche woll and shalbe, onles your mercyfull favor be ministrid and shewid therein, a utter undoyng and distruccyon of my house and monastery for ever. For it is not unremembred, I dowte not, unto you, that when I fyrst receyved your lettres concernyng the said house, at my next sendyng after of the saide your lettres, I offrid the fferme and lesse of the same unto ony frend of yours, yf it please you to name thereunto, and so entred into bargeyn and lesse, and dimisid it after suche forme and facion as ye knowe, with bond of a M. marc unto the lesse for his surety and state therein accordyngly, wych yf it cannot be performed by us, we be dangred in the seid sum by the lawes of this realme. Wherefore it maye please you of your goodnes and perfitt charite to be a meane unto the kynges highnes, and to oder of his counsell that shalle have the heryng, ordryng, and determynacion of the said matter, that our juste, trewe, and perfitt interest of the said maner of Broke, with the appertenauntys, whyche war pperpetually and freghley gyven unto our monastry of Kenellworth in pure all-messe, as it is moost evydently apparaunt in evydence, maye stylle belonge to apperteyn unto our saide howse, accordyng as thys lawis and ryght doth requyre and aske. And for that it shalle not becum me to stond in contencyon and traverse with his highnes, or to defend or prosecute any thyng that his grace and counsell do suppose and deme to be his ryght and title by his lawis newly made and ordenyd, it may please your mastershyppe, for and in my name, to be solicytour and mediatour, that I and my house maye have and enyoye of the lesse of our saide sovereyghne lord the residwe of all the londis and tenementes at this daye belongyng unto the said cell of Broke, for suche resonable rent as they now be demysid by me, and for lyke yerys in ffee fferme, to thentent that suche my lesse as nowe hath them by me may enyoy and contynue suche dimyssion as is dymisid unto them in salvacion of the bond of the said Mᵈ. marcs, whereunto I and my house stand chargyd. And where it plesid the kinges hyghnes for my good and trewe servyce done to his grace at the insurrexion at Coventre to my grett charge, to promyse me his favour in ony my reasanable suyte concernyng ryght of my house, I shalle, for his goodnes to me in this case shewid, accept my selfe well recom-pensid, and what end so ever your mastershyppe shalle take I shalle at alle oures abyde, for in you nowe is all my trust, as God know-ith, who ever prosper you in honor. Att Kenellworth, the xvij^th daye of Junij.

Your humble orator,

WILLIAM, abbat ther.

George Giffard, the writer of the following letter, was one of the commissioners for the dissolution of the smaller religious houses, and was now on his progress through Staffordshire and Leicestershire. Garrendon, from whence the letter is dated, was an abbey in Leicestershire, founded in 1133 by Robert le Bossu earl of Leicester, for a colony of monks from Waverley. The last prior was Thomas Syeston *alias* Shepyshed. The priories mentioned in this letter were very small foundations. Bradley was founded in the reign of John: its last prior was John Arundell, appointed Jan. 18, 1509. Kirkby Beler was a small house in Leicestershire founded by Roger de Beler in the reign of Edward II.

LXII.

GEORGE GIFFARD TO CROMWELL.

[From MS. Cotton. Cleop. E. IV. p. 213.]

Ryght honorable sir, after myne humble recommendacions, thys shalbe tadvertyse youe that I have receyved your most comfortable letters, for the whiche in my right lowly wyse I rendre unto youe most hartie thankes; pleasithe itt your mastreship to be fferther advertised, that we have sirveyed the howse or priore of Brook, the certificathe wheroff I sent you by your ffermers sunn and my nephu Roger Carell this present, the xviij. day of June, the priorie of Bradley, thabbey of Wolneston, the priorie of Kirby Bellers, the priorie of Woulstropp, and now be att thabbey of Garadon. And, sir, forasmyche as of late my fellows and I dyd wright unto Mr. chauncellour of the awgmentacions in the favour of thabbey of Seynt James* and the nunrie of Catysby in Northampton shire, whiche letter he shewed unto the kynghis highnes in the favour of those howsez, where the kynghis highnes was displeased, as he seyd to my servant Thomas Harper, seyeng that itt was like that we had receyved rewardes, whiche caused us to wright as we dyd, whiche myght putt me in ffeare to write, nottwithstondyng the sure knowlege that I have had allwey in your indifference gyvethe

---

* The abbey of St. James in Northampton was founded by William Peverel, the natural son of king William the Conqueror, for black monks. The abbot with eight monks had subscribed to the king's supremacy. Between 1532 and the dissolution of this house it had two abbots—John Dasset and William Brockden.

me boldnes to wright to yowe in the ffavour of the howse of Wol-
s[troppe],* the governour wherof is a vere good husbond for the
howse, and welbeloved of all thenhabitantes therunto adjoynyng, a
right honest man, havyng viij. religious persons beyng prestes of
right good conversacion and lyvyng religiously, havyng such quali-
ties of vertu as we have nott ffownd the like in no place ; for ther ys
nott oon religious person thear butt that the can and dothe use eyther
inbrotheryng,† wrytyng bookes, with verey ffayre haund, makyng
ther own garnementes, karvyng, payntyng, or graffyng.‡ The
howse without any sclandre or evyll ffame, and stonds in a wast
grownde verey solitarie, kepyng suche hospitalite that except by
synguler good provision itt cowld natt be meynteyned with halfe
so muche landes more as they may spend, suche a nombre of the
poure inhabitantes nye therunto dayly relevyd, that we have nott
sene the like, havyng no more landes than they have, God be
evyn my juge, as I do wright unto youe the trothe, and non other
wyse to my knowlege, whiche vere petie alloon causithe me to
wright. The premyssez wheroff considered, in most humble wise
I beseche youe to be a meane unto the kynghis majestie for the
stondyng of the seid Wolstroppe, wherby his grace shall do a myche
gracious and a meritorius acte ffor the releff off his poure subjectes
their, and ye shalbe sure nott only to have the contynewall
prayour of those religious persons thear, butt also the hartie prayour
off all thenhabitantes withyn iiij. or v. myle abowt that howse. And
this ffor lack of wytt I am bold to wright unto youe the playnes
of my harte, as unto hym that of all lyvyng creatures I have most
assured and ffaythfull trust yn, so knowyth our lord God, who '
have you in his most mercyfull tuycion. From Garadon, the xix.
day off June.

Your bounden bedeman att comandement,
GEORGE GYFFARD.

---

* Woolstrope is about four miles from Grantham in Lincolnshire.
† i. e. embroidering.   ‡ i. e. engraving.

On the 9th of July in this year (1536), Cromwell was raised to the peerage as baron Cromwell of Okeham, and henceforward we shall always find him addressed by the title of *lord*. It is a distinction which has enabled me to fix the date of a letter in several instances where it had been previously mistaken.

Richard Southwell, the writer of the following letter, was one of the commissioners who were now visiting Norfolk and Cambridgeshire. It is hardly necessary to observe that Walsingham was one of the most famous places of pilgrimage in England. The discovery mentioned in the letter is a curious trait of the scientific pursuits of the monks.

LXIII.

RICHARD SOUTHWELL TO CROMWELL.

[From MS. Cotton. Cleop. E. iv. fol. 231.]

It maye please your good lordshipe to be advertised that sir Thomas Lestrange and Mr. Hoges, according unto the sequestratyon delegate unto them, have ben at Walsingham and ther sequestred all suche monney, plat, juelles, and stuff, as ther wasse inventyd and founde. Emoung other thinges the same sir Thomas Lestrange and Mr. Hoges dyd ther fynd a secrete prevye place within the howse, where no channon nor onnye other of the howse dyd ever enter, as they saye, in wiche there were instrewmentes, pottes, belowes, flyes of suche strange colers as the lick non of us had seene, with poysies, and other thinges to sorte, and denyd(?) gould and sylver, nothing ther wantinge that should belonge to the arte of multyplyeng. Off all wiche they desyred me by lettres to advertyse you, and alsoo that frome the Satredaye at night tyll the Sondaye next folowinge was offred * at ther now beinge c.xxxiij^s. iiij^d. over and besyd waxe. Of this moultiplyeng it maye please you to cawse hem to be examyned, and so to advertyse unto them your further pleasuer. Thus I

* i. e. offered by the pilgrims at the image of our Lady of Walsingham.

praye God send your good lordshipe hartye helthe. Frome my pore howse, this xxv. of Julii, a° xxviij°.

humblye yours to commande,

Ric. Southwell.

To the right honerable
and my synguler good
lord, my lord prevye
seale.

The Benedictine nunnery of Pollesworth in Warwickshire, of which the ruins are still considerable, owed its modern foundation and earliest endowments to the second Robert de Marmion, distinguished by his turbulence in the troublesome reign of king Stephen. Tradition, however, carries back the date of its original foundation to the time of the Saxons. The last abbess, Alicia Fitzherbert, was elected to that office in the first year of the reign of Henry VIII.

LXIV.

THE COMMISSIONERS TO CROMWELL.

[From MS. Cotton. Cleop. E. iv. fol. 210.*]

After oure dueties of humble recommendacion unto youre good lordship hade, it may please the same to be advertysed that we have surveyd the monasterye or nonnery of Pollesworth in the countye of Warwike, wherin ys an abbas namyd dame Alice Ffitzherbert, of the age of lx. yeres, a very sadde, discrete, and relygyous woman, and hath byn heed and governour their xxvij. yeres, and in the same howse under her rule ar xij. vertuous and religyous nonnes, and of good conversacion as farr as we can here or perceyve, as well by our examinacions as by the open ffame and report of all the countrey, and never one of the nonnes thar will leyve nor forsake therr habite and relygyon. Wherfore in our opyneons, yf it myght so stande with your lordships pleasure, ye mought doo a right good and meryetoryous dede to be a medyatour to the kinges highnes for the said house to stande and remayne unsuppressed; ffor, as we thinke, ye shall not speke in the preferment of a better nonnery nor of better women. And in the towne of Pollesworth ar xliiij. tenementes, and never a plough but one, the resydue be artifycers, laborers, and vitellers, and lyve in effect by the said house, and the repayre and resorte thar ys made to the gentylmens childern and sudjournentes that ther doo lif to the nombre sometyme of xxx^tie, and sometyme xl^tie and moo, that their be right vertuously brought upp. And the towne and non-nery standith in a harde soile and barren ground, and to our esty-macions, yf the nonnery be suppressed, the towne will shortely after falle to ruyne and dekaye, and the people therin to the nombre of vj. or vij. score persones are nott unlike to wander and to seke for their lyvyng, as our Lorde Gode beste knowith, who preserve youre lordshipe in good lif and longe, with encrease of honour. Wrytton at Maxstoke * beside Coventre, the xxviij. daye of July.

By the kinges commissioners, JOHN GREVYLL, SYMOND MOUNTFORT, THOMAS HOLTE, ROGER WYGSTON, GEORGE GYFFARD, ROBT. BURGOYN.

The following letter furnishes us with another instance of the eagerness with which the courtiers sought after their share in the spoils of the monasteries. Sir Thomas Elyot was a distinguished diplomatist, a man of great learning, and had been an inti-mate friend of Sir Thomas More.

LXV.

SIR THOMAS ELYOT TO CROMWELL.

[From MS. Cotton. Cleop. E. IV. fol. 220*.]

My moste speciall goode lorde, whereas, by your contynuell exercise in waighty affayres, allso frequent access of sutars unto your goode lordship, I could not fynde oportunity to gyve to your lordship due and convenyent thankes for your honorable and

* Maxtock, a parish in Warwickshire, near the town of Coleshill.

gentill report to the kinges majesty on Wenysday last passid in my favour, I am now constrayned to supply with my penne my sayde duety, offryng unto your lordship all harty love and servyce that a poure man may ow and beare to his goode lorde and approved frende, which allthowgh hability lakking in me, I can not expresse by any benefyte, your wisedom notwithstanding, which I have allway honoured and trustid, will I doubt not accept my goode intent, being, I thank Godd, ever syncere and withoute flatery or ill dissimulacion, I wisshing unto your lordship the honorable desyres of your hart, with the contynuall favor of Godd and of your prynce. My lorde, forasmoche as I suppose that the kinges moste gentill communicacion with me, and allso his moste comfortable report unto the lordes of me, procedid of your afore remembrid recommendacions, I am animate to importune your goode lordship with moste harty desyres to contynue my goode lorde in augmenting the kinges goode estimacion of me; whereof I promyse yow before Godd, your lordship shall never have cause to repent. And where I perceyve that ye suspect that I favour not truely Holy Scripture, I wold Godd that the king and you mowght see the most secrete thowghtes of my hart, surely ye shold then perceyve that, the ordre of charity savyd, I have in as moche detestacion as any man lyving all vayne supersticions, superfluouse ceremonyes, sklaunderouse jouglynges, countrefaite mirakles, arrogant usurpacions of men callid spirituall, and masking religions, and all other abusions of Christes holy doctrine and lawes. And as moche I injoy at the kinges godly proceding to the due reformacion of the sayde enormyties as any his graces poure subject lyving. I therefor beseeche your goode lordship now to lay apart the remembraunce of the amity betwene me and sir Thomas More, which was but *usque ad aras,* as is the proverb, consydering that I was never so moche addict unto hym as I was unto truthe and fidelity toward my soveraigne lorde, as Godd is my juge. And where my speciall trust and onely expectation is to be holpen by the meanes of your lordship, and naturall shamefastness more raigneth in me than is necessary, so that I wold not prese to the kinges majesty withoute your lordshippes assistence, unto whome I have sondry tymes declarid myn indigence, and whereof it hath hapned, I therefor moste humbly desyre you my speciall goode lorde, so to bryng me into the kinges most noble remembrance, that of his moste bounteouse liberality it may like his highnesse to reward me with some convenyent porcion of his suppressid landis, whereby I may be able to contynue my life according to that honest degree whereunto his grace hath callid me. And that your lordship forgete not, that neither of his grace nor of any other persone I have fee, office, pencion, or ferme, nor have any maner of lucre or advauntage, besydes the revenues of my poure land, which are but small, and no more than I may therewith mayntayne my poure house. And if by your lordshippes meanes I may achieve goode effect of my sute, your lordship shall not fynde me ingrate. And whatsoever porcion of land that I shall attayne by the kynges gift, I promyse to give to your lordship the first yeres frutes, with myn assured and faithfull hart and servyce. This lettre I have writen, bycause that I herd that your lordship went to the court; and as for my first sute, I shall at your lordshippes better laysour recontynue it, trusting allso in your lordshippes favour therin.

Writen at my house by Smythfeld, this Moneday.

Yours moste bounden,

TH. ELYOT, kt.

To my speciall goode lorde
my lorde pryvy seale.

The baths of Buxton, in the Peak of Derby, to which the next letter relates, were frequented as early as the times of the Britons and Romans. In popish times, these, in common with other wells and fountains, were regarded with a superstitious feeling, derived from the period of Saxon paganism, and preserved in many popular ceremonies to the present day. The wells at Buxton were dedicated to St. Anne, and the chief place for drinking the waters is still called St. Anne's Well. The abbey of Burton upon Trent, in Staffordshire, was celebrated as the resting place of the bones of St. Modwen. The image alluded to in the following letter probably stood over the well, still known by the name of Modwen's well.

LXVI.

SIR WILLIAM BASSETT TO CROMWELL.

[From MS. Cotton. Cleop. E. iv. fol. 238.]

Ryght honorabull my inesspeyciall gud lord, acordyng to my bownden dewte and the teynor of yowre lordschypys lettres lately to me dyrectyd, I have sende unto yowre gud lordschyp by thys beyrer, my brother, Francis Bassett, the ymages off sentt Anne off Buxtone and sentt Mudwen of Burtun apon Trentt, the wych ymages I dyd take frome the place where they dyd stande, and browght them to my owne howss within xlviij^e. howres after the contemplacion of yowre seyd lordschypis lettres, in as soober maner as my lyttull and rude wytt wollde serve me. And ffor that there schullde no more idollatre and supersticion be there usyd, I dyd nott only deface the tabernaculles and placis where they dyd stande, butt allso dyd take away cruchys, schertes, and schetes, with wax offeryd, being thynges thatt dyd alure and intyse the yngnorantt pepull to the seyd offeryng; allso gyffyng the kepers of bothe placis admonicion and charge thatt no more offeryng schulld be made in those placis tyll the kynges plesure and yowre lordschypis be ffurther knowen in that behallf. My lord, I have allso lokkyd upp and sealyd the bathys and welles at Buxtons, thatt non schall enter to wasche them, tyll yowre lordschypis plesure be ffurther knowne, whereof I besych yowre gud lordschyp that I may be acertanyd off agayn att yowre plesure, and I schall nott fayle to execute yowre lordschipis cummandmentt to the uttermust of my lyttull wytt and power. And, my lord, as concernyng the opynion off the pepull and the ffonde trust that they dyd putt in those ymages, and the vanyte of the thynges, thys beyrer my brother can telle yowre lordschyp much better att large then I can wryte, for he was with me att the doing of all, and in all placis, as knowyth Jhesu, whome ever have yowre gud lordschyp in hys blessyd kepyng. Wrytten att Langley,* with the rewde and sympyll hande of yowre assuryd and feythfull orator, and as on ever att yowre cummandmentt next unto the kyng to the uttermost of my lyttull power.

WILLIAM BASSETT, knyght.

The following letter relates to Bury St. Edmunds, one of the largest monastic foundations in England, which therefore did not come under the first act of suppression, but it was visited for the purpose of confiscating its superstitious relics, &c.

LXVII.

THE COMMISSIONERS TO CROMWELL.

[From MS. Cotton. Cleop. E. iv. fol. 229*.]

Pleasith it your lordship to be advertysed, that wee have ben at saynt Edmondes Bury, where we founde a riche shryne whiche was very comberous to deface. We have takyn in the seyd monastery in golde and sylver $m^l.m^l.m^l.m^l.m^l.$ markes, and above, over and besydes a well and riche crosse with emereddes, as also dyvers and sundry stones of great value, and yet we have lefte the churche, abbott, and covent very well ffurnesshed with plate of sylver necessary for the same. And forasmuche as we be creadably informyd that ther dyed of late ij. monkes at Ely, whether they dyed of the sykenes or no we knowe not as yet, and there hathe ben great death in the towne, notwithstondyng we entende to make further serche therein, so that if we fynde not the mater to muche daungerous, we wyll prosede, and els

* Langley Meynell, about four miles from Derby, was the estate and residence of Sir William Basset. It subsequently passed from the Bassets to the family of Cavendish.

not untyll your pleasure be knowyn therein. And this present day we departe from Bury towardes Ely, and we assure your lordship the abbott and convent be very well contented with every thyng that we have done there, as knowith God, woo preserve your lordshipp.

Your Lordeshipe moste bownden,

JOHN WILLIAMS.

RYCHARD POLLARD.

PHYLYP PARYS.

JOHN SMYTH.

The abbey of Woburn did not come within the Act of Parliament, but in the course of the visitation crimes appear to have been laid to the charge of the inmates that were sufficient to call for its dissolution. In the present letter, the abbot and convent attempt to defend themselves; but they were unsuccesful, for early in the year following (1537) the abbot and prior and the parson of Puddington (a parish in the neighbourhood) were executed at Bedford. Robert Hobs, the last abbot, is mentioned as holding that office as early as 1524.

Woburn abbey was founded in 1145 by Hugh de Bolebeck. The estate was given to John lord Russell in the first year of the reign of Edward VI., and the site of the abbey is now the seat of the duke of Bedford.

The following letter is not dated, but it must have been written in the latter part of the year 1536.

LXVIII.

THE ABBOT AND CONVENT OF WOBURN TO THE KING.

[From MS. Cotton. Cleop. E. iv. fol. 96.]

In most humble and obedient wise shewithe unto your most excellent highnes your contynuall orators and daily bedemen thabbot and covent of your monasterie of Woburn, that whereas we do apperceyve by the relation of your graces commissioners Mr. doctour Legh and Mr. Williams, that diverse and sondrye accusementes have ben made upon us unto your highnes and your

CAMD. SOC.
U

graces most honorable counsell, concernynge manyfolde crymes, enormites, and high treason to your excellent maiesty, we beynge inwardely stryken with sorowe and hevynes four that our desertes shulde be suche that any jote of dewe obedience unto your grace (whom under God we do aguise to be our supreme heed, our comfort and joye) shulde be notyd in us, seynge we be and ever have ben, as we trust in God, cleane frome any suche crymes and enormites, and therfor judging nothing to be so expedient and behovefull unto us as clerely to renounce all pretext of excuse or triall with your grace, by whiche we might percase in our default incurre your majesties high indignacion to our utter undoynge, do in moost humble wise and upon our knees with harte and mynde submytt owr selfes and our monasterye, with all the moveables and unmovables therof, unto your majesties accustomede grace and mercy, mekely desirynge the same to shewe your pitie and compassion upon us in suche godly wise that we maye deserve to contynewe (as we trust we have ben) your perpetuall orators and bedemen, and to contynewe utile membres of your commen wealthe, to the high lawde and praise of allmightie God, and perpetuall merite and renowne of your excellent majestie, whom almightie God of his infinite grace preserve longe to endure.

Your humble and most obedient oratours and dayly bedesmen,

Thabbot and convent of Woburn.

Richard Cromwell, the nephew of Lord Cromwell, was one of the commissioners employed to visit Cambridgeshire and the monastic houses in the Fen district. The following letter leaves him at Ramsey. The date of the month would seem to show that this letter was written in 1538, when the 15th of October would be on a Tuesday.

LXIX.

RICHARD CROMWELL TO LORD CROMWELL.

[From MS. Cotton. Cleop. E. iv. fol. 204*.]

I have me most humbly commendyd unto your lordshipp, I

rode one Sondaye to Cambrige to my bedd, and the next mornyng
was upe betymes, supposyng to have found at Elye Mr. Pollard
and Mr. Williams, but they were departyd bifore my commyng,
and so beyng at dynner at Somersham with the busshop of Elye
I overtoke theym, at which tyme I openyd your pleasure unto
them in every thyng. Your lordshipp, I thynke, shall shortely ap-
parseyve the pryour of Elye to be of a frowarde sorte, by evydent
tokens, as at our commyng home shalbe at large relatyde unto
youe. At the makyng herof we hadd done nothyng at Ramseye,
savyng that over nyght I commenyd with the abbot, whome I
found conformable to every thyng as shalbe at this tyme put in
ure, accordyng as your lordshipps will is. Assone as we have done
at Ramsey we go to Peterborough, and frome thense to my house,
and so home, the which I trust shalbe at the farthest one this
daye come sevyn days. Thus the blessyd Thrynytye preserve
your lordshipps helth. From Ramseye, on Tewysday in the mornyng, beyng the xvth of Octobre.

Your lordshipps most bounden nephewe,
Rich. Crumwell.

The two next letters are from Hugh Latimer, bishop of Worcester, and relate chiefly
to the religious matters and to the monastic houses towards the borders of Wales.
They bear no date of year, but they must belong to the last months of 1536.

LXX.

BISHOP LATYMER TO CROMWELL.
[From MS. Cotton. Cleop. E. iv. fol. 139.]

Ryght honorable, *salutem in Christo*, and, syr, when I was with
your lordshype laste you were desyrows to kno where you myght
have good monkes. I tellyd you of too with my lord of Westmyster, I colde natt then name them to you, butt now I can; the
won ys callyd Goorson, the other Clarke, both bachelars of divinite, well lernyd, of ryght jugment, and very honeste men. The

prior of Coventre,* as I here say, ys dede; the matter ys sum‑
whatt entyrd with the kynges grace and lyke to goo forward,
yf you putt thertoo your helpynge hande, I dowght natt butt my
brother abbott of Westmyster, as yll as he myght spare them,
yett wyll forgoo them for such a purpas, butt much the rather yf
he perceve your pleseur therin.

I wold have waytyd uppon your lordshyppe my selff, as my dewty
hade byn, butt sewrly, syr, I doo whatt I can to able my selff to
stande in the pulpytt uppon Tewsday. I am in a fayntt wery‑
nesse over all my boody, butt cheffly in the small of my backe,
butt I have a good nursshe, good mastress Pasham, wych,
seynge whatt casse I was in, hath fachyd me hoom to here owne
howsse, and doth pympur me upe with all dylygence, for I fere a
consumption, butt ytt makyth lytull matter for me. I pray God
preserve your lordshyppe longe in helth, to all such good purposes
as God hath ordenyd you too.

In master Pashames howsse,

H. LATYMER, Wigorn.

viij of Novemb.

Great Malvern was a celebrated priory, founded about the year 1083. At present
there are little remains, except the priory church, which was preserved for the use of
the parish, and is a very handsome building. The prior at this time was Thomas
Dereham, who was succeeded immediately before the dissolution by Richard Why‑
thorne *alias* Bedyl.

LXXI.

BISHOP LATIMER TO CROMWELL.

[From MS. Cotton. Cleop. E. iv. fol. 264.]

Right honorable, *salutem in Salvatore*, and, syr, I have to thanke
your good lordshype ffor many thynges, ande now a laitt ffor

---

* Thomas Wyfford, who was succeeded by Thomas Camswell, Camsele, or Kamps‑
well (the name appears differently written), so that bishop Latimer's recommendation
was not carried into effect.

your synguler goodnesse showyd (as I undyrstand) to master
Lucy, a right good gentilman, ande also toward master Acton,
another of the same sortt, butt of thys my dewtye moor att moor
leyser. And yett thus much now I wyll say, ande natt say it alone,
butt with many, that your lordshype won man have promotyd
many moo honeste men synyste God promotyd you, then hath
many men doon befoore your tyme thowgh in licke authorite
with you, *tamquam non tibi natus soli, sed multorum commodo :*
efficiat qui omnia facit ut in eundem finem diutissime vivat domi-
natio tua, ut sic inter nobiles nobilissimus evadas, quum quidem
nihil esse possit nobilius quam bonos viros evehere, malos autem re-
primere, id quod tibi hactenus usuvenit plus omnibus facere.

Butt now, syr, another thynge, that by your favour I myght
be a motionare unto you, at the reqweste of an honeste man, the
prior of Grett Malverne in my diocese, thowgh natt of my diocese, referrynge the success of the hooll matter to your ownly
approvyd wyssdoom and benynge goodnesse in every casse, ffor
I knoo that I doo play the ffowll, butt yett with my foolysshnesse
I sumwhatt qwyett an unqwyett man and mytygatt hys hevynesse,
which I am bold to doo with you, ffor that I kno by experience
your goodnesse, that you wyll bere with fowlles in ther freylnesse.
Thys man both heryth and feryth (as he sayth) the suppressione
of hys howsse, wich, thowgh he wyll be conformable in all
poynttes to the kynges hynesse plesewr, and youres, ons knoyn,
as both I advertysyd hym, ande also hys bownden dewtye ys to
be, yett neverthelesse yf he thowght hys interpryesse shuld natt
be mystake nor turne to ony displesewr, he wold be an humble
sewter to your lordshype, and by the same to the kynges good
grace, for the upstandynge of hys forsayd howsse, and contynuance of the same to many good purpasesse, natt in monkrye,
he maynyth natt soo, God forbyd, butt ony other ways as shuld
be thowght ande seyme good to the kynges majestye, as to
mayntayne techynge, prechynge, studye with prayynge, ande
(to the which he ys much gyvyne) good howskepynge, ffor to
the vertu of hospitalitye he hathe byn grettly inclynyd from hys

begynnynge, ande ys very much commendyd in thes partces for the same; so that if ccccc. markes to the kynges hynesse, with cc. markes to your selffe for your good wyll, myght occasione the promatione of hys intentt, att leste way for the tyme of hys lyffe, he dowbtyth natt to make hys frendes for the same, yf so lytull cold bringe soo much to passe. The man ys old, a good howskepere, fedyth many, and that dayly, for the contreth ys poore and full of penurye; ande, alas! my good lord, shall we nat see ij. or iij. in every shyre changyd to such remedye.

Thus too thys honeste man is importunyte hath browght me beyounde my dewtye, savynge for the confydence and truste that I have always in your beningnytye. As he hathe knolege froom you, soo he wyll prepare for you, ever obedyentt to your advertyessment. Syr Wylliam Kyngston can make re-portt of the man. God prospere you to the utterynge of all hoolow harttes. Blessyd be God of Englande that workyth all, hows instrumente you be! I herde you say wons aftur you hade sene that furyows invectyve of cardynall Pooll, that you wold make hym to ete hys owne hartt, which you have now, [I trow,] browght to passe, for he muste [nedes] now ette hys owne hartt, and be[cum as] hartlesse as he ys gracelesse.

H. L. Wigor.

13 Decemb. Hartl.*

The priory of Laund, in Leicestershire, was founded by Richard Basset and Maud his wife about 1125. The site of the priory of Laund, with all belonging to it, was granted by Henry VIII. to Lord Cromwell.

John Smith, the writer of the following letter, has already occurred as one of the commissioners in Norfolk. The letter was addressed to his brother-in-law Francis Cave, one of the king's commissioners for taking the surrender of the religious houses.

LXXII.

JOHN SMITH TO FRANCIS CAVE.

[From MS. Cotton. Cleop. E. iv. fol. 217.**]

My hartie recommendacions to yow premyssed, this is to adver-

* Hartlebury, the palace of the bishops of Worcester.

tyse yow that uppon Wenysday last I receyvyd your letter, and
syns the receyte therof I have indevored my selff to the best of
my power accordyng to theffecte therof; and as concernyng the
priory of Lawnd, I have caused too honest persons to vewe the
demaynes of the same, and wheras the seid demeynes withe
Whatbore* ffelde, were wont and accustemyed to kepe this tyme
of the yere too thowsande sheipe or very nere, ther be at thys
scant ffyve hunderde sheipe, of the wiche I suppose the one daye
halff of them be not the priores; and wheras the seid prior was
accustymed to kepe uppon his comynes in Loddyngton ffeld
ffyve hunderd sheipe, ther is at this daye not one sheipe; and
wheras the seid prior was accustymed to have uppon his comyns
in Frysby ffeld a fflocke of sheipe, ther is at this day non. And as
concernyng beys, all ffate beys, excepte a very ffewe for the howse,
be sold, and mych of the stuf of howshold is conveyd awey, wiche
sheipe, beyse, and howshold stuf was sold and coveyed beffore the
last geyng of the prior† to Londone, and in the tyme of his beyng
ther; but syns his comyng home I cane not lerne that he hathe
made awoye any catall, except certeyn of the best mylche kye he
hade and one bull, wiche I am informyd he cawsed to be conveyed the ffirst nyght that he came ffrom Londone to Loddyngton.
And as concernyng the plate, the prior told me that he hade made
hit awey a good whyll agoo, to the intent to have redemyd his
howse, if itt wold have bene, except the juelles and plate of
chirche, wiche I am informyd remayns stylle. And as for his
horsez, he told me that he had gyven to dyvers of hys servauntes
every of them a geldyng, and that I thyncke ther remaynd but a
ffewe good. And as concernyng leices, I thyncke ther be non
letten owt of the demeynes, except hit be tythis, wiche I thynk
were grauntyd, but uppon condicion, as I suppose the partyes, if
thei be well examyned, wyll conffesse. And as concernyng Loddyngton, I understand ther be dyvers leices graunted of certeyn
clowsez and of the mylles ther, wiche I thyncke weer lykwyse letten

* Whadborough is a hamlet in the parish of Lodington.

† John Lancaster. He surrendered the priory to the king in 1534, and had a
pension of £60 a year.

but uppon condicion, wiche leysez were grauntyd beffore the priores goyng to Londone, but, as I am informyd, thei weer not all delyverd tyll the priores comyng whom agayn.   Syns the priores retorn from Londone, I thyncke ther were no leyces sealed.   Notwithstandyng I have perffyt knowlege that the priore hathe bene sore in hand with his brether, syns his comyng whom, to have a leace sealyd of all his purchesed lond in Alstyd and other townez adjonyng, for on of his kynnesmen, wherunto his brether wyll not agree as yet, becawse hit is unresonable, as his brether report. This is all that I have seye at this tyme, but as I lerne so shall I certyffy yow.   I trust I shall lerne more agaynst the kynges comyssyoners comyng, as knoythe our Lorde, who kepe yow. From Withcoke,* the xxij. day of December.   By your lovyng brother,

JOHN SMYTHE.

It required little foresight to perceive that the larger abbeys must soon follow their weaker brethren, and we find the abbots and priors, in their consternation, attempting every means of conciliating and appeasing the government : the repression of the great insurrection in the north had left them more than ever exposed to the king's resentment.   In the following letter we see the abbot of the great monastic establishment in the fens of Lincolnshire (the early foundation of St. Guthlac) attempting to conciliate the good-will of the all-powerful minister by a present of fish.   The abbot of Croyland was John Welles *alias* Bridges.

LXXIII.

THE ABBOT OF CROYLAND TO CROMWELL.

[From. MS. Cotton. Cleop. E. iv. fol. 57.*]

With dew reverence I commaund me unto yowr honorable lordshipe, humblye asserteynyng the same that I sende yowr lordshipe by this berar parte of owr fenne fyshe, ryght mekely besechyng yowr lordship favorablye to accepte the same fyshe, and to be gud and favorable lorde unto me and my pore house, in suche cause as I heraftir shal have cause to sewe unto your gud lord-

---

* Withcote, co. Leicester.   It is on the edge of Rutlandshire.   John Smith was lord of Withcote.

ship, and I with my brethern shall daily pray to owre Lord God for the long contynuaunce of your good lordship in helth. At Croyland, the xxv^{te} day of Merche. By yowr dayly oratour.

JOHN, abbot.

In the earlier part of the year 1537, the two large Cistercian abbeys in Lancashire, Whalley and Furness, came into the king's hands. The former of these houses was first founded at Stanlaw in Cheshire, about A.D. 1172, whence it was removed to Whalley in 1296. The last abbot, John Pasleu, elected to that office in 1506, was executed on the 12th of March, 1537, at Whalley, having been concerned in the rebellion called the Pilgrimage of Grace. The abbey of Furness, now remarkable for its fine ruins, was quietly surrendered by the last abbot, Roger Pyle, and his brethren, as appears by the following document. Furness abbey was founded in 1127 by Stephen, then earl of Boulogne, but subsequently king of England.

LXXIV.

REPORT OF THE SURRENDER OF FURNESS ABBEY.

[From MS. Cotton. Cleop. E. iv. fol. 246.]

M^d. at Whalley abbay, the Thursday beyng the vth day off Aprill, in the xxviijth. yere of our soverand lord kyng Henrie viijth. that I, Roger abbot of the monasterie of Furnes, knawyng the mysorder and evyll liff both unto God and our prynce of the bredren of the said monasterie, in dischargyng of my conscience doo frely and hollie surrender, giff, and graunt unto the kynges highnes, and to his heyres and assignes for evermore, all suche interest and titill as I have had, have, or may have, of and in the said monasterie of Furnes, and of and in the landes, renttes, possessions, revenous, servyces both spirituall and temporall, and of and in all goodes and cattalles and all other thyng whatsoever it be, belongyng or in ony vise apperteynyng to the said monasterie and every part and parcell therof, in as large and ample maner and forme as ever I hade or aught to have of and in the same or ony part or parcell therof by ony maner of meanes, titill, interest, gift, graunt, or othervise, permittyng and byndeyng my selff by thes presentes that from hensfurth I shall at all tymes and in all places, whansooever I shalbe called uppon, be redye and glad to conferme, ratefie, and astabilishe this my deyd, purpos, mynd, and intent, as shalbe devised by the lerned counsell of the kynges said highnes, wiche commyth frely of my selff and without ony inforcement, in consideracion of the evyll dissposicion of the bredren of the said monasterie, as is aforesaid ; in wittynes wherof herunto I have subscribed my name, and writtyn this byll with myn awn [hand], the day, yere, and place beforsaid, in the presence of the right honorable lord my lord therle of Sussex, the kynges leuetenaunt within this countie of Lancaster, and also in the presence of sir Thomas Butteler, sir William Leyland, Mr. Johan Cladon, clerk, sir Johan Beron, and sir Antony Fitzherbert, one of the kynges justicis, beyng of the kynges counsell within the said countie, who hereunto have also put to theyr handes to testefie the same.

Per me, ROGERUM abbatem Furnesii.

ROBERTUS SUSSEX.

ANTONY FITZHERBERT.

WYLLIAM LEYLAND.

HENR. FARRYNGENK. (?)

JOHON CLAYDEN, prest.

The next letter relates to a small priory in Norfolk, Newbridge, of the history of which very little is known. The duke of Norfolk appears to have wished to protect it by giving up voluntarily to the minister a share in the patronage.

LXXV.

THE DUKE OF NORFOLK TO CROMWELL.

[From MS. Cotton. Cleop. E. IV. fol. 41.*]

My veray goode lorde, after my herty commendations unto your good lordship, thiese shalbe tadvertise the same that it is comme unto my knowleage, by the relation of the berers hereof, that the priour of the house of Newburgh, beyng of my fundation, is lately departed this world; and albeit of many yeres heretofore it hath not ben seen contrary but the religiouse persones of the same in such like cases have ever furst repaired unto me and myne auncetours for our consent as patrone of the same, and theruppon to tharchebushoppe of Yourke for their confirmation, yet nowe, forasmoche as they knowe not howe to use themselffes (considering the kinges highnes hath *plenariam potestatem* in such cases) any further than as I shall directe them, I have therfore thought convenient at this present to sende them to your good lordshippe, requiring the same to take such good order with them therin as by your great wisdome shalbe thought most expedient, and in such sorte as the same be not to the hurt or prejudice of any my right and title in the saide house, wherunto I doubte not but ye woll have good respecte accordingly. My good lord, considering as well that the said house is far indebted and behynde hande by the great mysorder and negligence of the saide late priour there, as also that none of that house is mete to be rewler therof, beyng of such sorte as not lik of long tyme tamende and restore the same to his pristine estate, I require you therfore, my good lorde, to handle them by all the policie ye can, that they at their retourne from you may frelye put the matier of ther election in compromission to us twoo, to thentent that we boothe conjoinctly togeyther may so order the matier as to us shalbe thought most convenient; and of your procedinges with them herein I require you of advertisement. And thus most hertily fare ye well. From Kenyngale, the xij[th] daie of Aprill.

Yours assewredly, T. NORFFOLK.

My lord, if ye shall fynde any diffyculte in them to consent to compromytt this mater to us ij., I requyre you to retorne them to me hither, trustyng to reforme their folies, little gode discrecion being in any of them, as I thynk.

In the summer of this year (1537) began the second great visitation of the monasteries, preparatory to the final measure of suppression.   Layton and Legh, who in the following letter solicit their commission, were from begining to end two of the most active agents of the court.   It was during this visitation, which continued through the year 1538, that so many houses were persuaded or compelled to a voluntary surrender.

LXXVI.

DR. LAYTON TO CROMWELL.

[From MS. Cotton. Cleop. E. iv. fol. 10.]

Pleasit yowe to understonde, that whereas ye intende shortly to visite, and be lyke shall have many sutters unto yowe for the same to be your commissares, if hit myght stonde with your pleasure that doctor Lee and I myght have committyde unto us the north contre, and to begyn in Lincolne dioces northwardes here from London, Chester dioces, Yorke, and so furthe to the borders of Scotlande, to ryde downe one syde and to cum up the other, ye shalbe well and faste assuryde that ye shall nother fynde monke, chanone, frear, prior, abbott, or any other of what degree so ever he be, that shall do the kynges hyghnes so goode servys in this matter for thos partties, nether be so trusty, trewe, and faithfull to yowe in the same, doyng all thynges so diligently for your purpos and your discharge.   And forasmuche as the kynges hyghnes hath put his onely truste in yowe for the reformacion of his clergie, gyvyng yowe therunto onely auctoritie and power, ye muste have suche as ye may trust evyn as well as your owne self, wiche muste be unto yowe as *alter ego*.   Doctor Lee and I have onely bene preferryde to the kynges servys by yowe, *et te solum ab eo tempore in huncusque diem habuimus Mœcenatem et unicum patronum, nec alium unquam habituri*.   Owre desier is, therfor, nowe to declare unto yowe owre trewe herttes and faithfull mynde, owre faste and unfaynede servys that we bere towardes yowe, and owe unto yowe, as ye have of ryght bownde us.   Ther ys nother monasterie, selle, priorie, nor any other religiouse howse in the north; but other doctor Lee or I have familier acqwayntance within x. or xij. mylles of hit, so that no knaverie can be hyde from us in that contre, nor ther we cannot be over fayssede nor suffer any maner injurie. We knowe and have experiens bothe of the fassion off the contre and the rudenes of the pepull, owre frendes and kynsfookes be dispersyde in thos parties in evere place redy to assyste us if any stoborne or sturdy carle myght perchaunce be fownde a rebellous. If ye hade leisure to overlooke the booke of articles that I made for your visitacion this tyme xij. monethes, and to marke evere sondrie interrogatorie therin wryttyn, dowtles ther is matter sufficient to detecte and opyn all coloryde sanctitie, all supersticiouse rewlles of pretensyde religion, and other abusys detestable of all sorttes, hether[to] clokyde and coloryde by the reformitors (so namede) of evere religion wiche ever, by frendeshipe, tyll this day hath founde craffty meanys to be ther owne visiters, therby no reformacion intendyng nother goode religion (if any be) to incresse, but onely to kepe secrete all matters of mischeffe, with muche privey murmuryng emong them selffes, sellyng ther jewelles and plate to take half the valew for redy money, with gret rewyne and dekay of ther howsis, wiche muste nedes yet continewe and indure dayly more and more with incresse, unleste ye nowe sett to yowr helpyng hande, and with expedicion spedy and efftsones tendre the premisses. Moste humble desieryng yowe to take no displeasure with this my rude and playne letter, thus boldely utteryng unto yowe my intire mynde and consayte, referryng all to your wisdom and goodnes. This Friday, the iiij[th] day of June, by the hasty hande of your moste assuryde poir preste,

RYCHARDE LAYTON.

The large and celebrated abbey of Jervaulx, Jervaux, or Jorvalles, in Yorkshire, was also forfeited by the attainder of its abbot, who was brought to the scaffold for the part he had taken in the Pilgrimage of Grace. Sallay or Sawley Abbey, in Craven, in the West Riding of Yorkshire, was founded by William de Percy in 1146 or 1147. The last abbot, William Trafford, was hanged at Lancaster for his opposition to the measures of the court. The site of Sallay was given to Sir Arthur Darcy, the writer of the following letter, who was the second son of Sir Thomas Darcy, created baron Darcy of Darcy, on the accession of Henry VIII. who had been involved also in the Pilgrimage of Grace, and delivered up Pontefract Castle to the rebels. Sir Arthur Darcy appears on the present occasion to have been sent to the North to aid in pacifying the country after the suppression of the rebellion.

LXXVII.

SIR ARTHUR DARCY TO CROMWELL.

[Cott. MS. Cleop. E. iv. p. 240.]

Yt schall lyke your honourabyll lordschypp to be advertyssyd, that I was with my lorde lewtenant att the suppressyon off Gervayes, whyche howes within the gatt ys coveryd wholly with leadd, and ther is oon off the ffayrest chyrches that I have sseen, ffayr medooze, and the ryver runnyng by ytt, and a grett demayne. The kynges hyenes is att greatt charge with hys sstoodes off mares, att Thornbery and other placys, whyche arr ffyne growndes, and I thynke thatt att Gervayes and in the grangyes incydent, with the hellp off ther grett large commones, the kynges hyenes by good oversseers scholld have ther the most best pasture thatt scholld be in Yngland, hard and sownd off kynd; ffor ssurly the breed off Gervayes ffor horses was the tryed breed in the northe, the stallones and marees well ssoortyd, I thynke in no reallme scholld be ffownd the lykes to them, ffor ther is large and hye growndes ffor the ssomer, and in wynter wooddes and low growndes to serve them. My lord, by my lord lewtenant I have restytucyon off a grett part off my goodes att Coverham. From Gervayes I went to Sallay, wher I inqueryd owtt a chalyce thatt was brybbed ffrome the kyng affor the ssuppressyon off the howes, and allso I have ffownd a booke off dettes belongyng to the howes, and ther is a barkhawes stoord with leddyr. I requyre yowr lordschypp to send to me your pleassure whatt I schall doo therin.

My good lord, I requyre yow to gett me lycenes ffor xiiij. dayes to cum upp to dysspache me off dettes thatt I ow. Off my ffaythe, I never brake so muche credence as I have lattly doon. I have dessyrd Mr. Jolymentt to remember yowr lordschypp ffor my cawssys. Off trewthe, my lord, I doo wast the kynges money here att Pomffrett; ffor off a trewthe the contreyes in the northe was never in a moore dredeffull and trew obbeysance.

My lord, I bessyche ȝow be good lord to me : ytt is schewd to me thatt the kynges hyenes wolld ageyn survey my landes, and fferther Mr. chanssler dyd send to me thatt ytt was thoght thatt I had dysseyvyd the kyng. My lord, ye know thatt I myght have hadd seynt Lenardes, whiche is better by iij^c markes then my landes in the ffyrst survey. I dyd reffuze thatt; and on my ffaythe I never knew whatt Salley was, tyll ytt was grauntyd. M. Fermer and M. Montagew wolld have gyffyn syx c. markes yerly ffor Grenessnorton ; and in consyderacyon theroff, and with my wyffe in maryage, the kynges hyenes gave me my landes wn-ssurveyd. Yff ytt be the kynges pleasure to have my rentalles, appon my lyff I schall not lye, butt bryng them my sellfe, and hys grace schall have all thynges att hys conssyence and pleasure, as know-ythe God, who ever presserve ȝow with myche honorr. The viij. day off Juyn.

ȝowrs humbly till comandment,

ARTHUR DARCY.

A great stumbling block with King Henry VIII. was the question of the marriage of the clergy. He appears to have been always strongly opposed to the marriage of priests (a sentiment in which his daughter Elizabeth also partook) ; but having at one time given some reason for thinking that he was not averse to such marriages, many of the clergy acted accordingly, and became thereby involved in considerable embarrassment. The date of the two following letters is somewhat doubtful, but they appear to belong to the present year. The vicar of Mendlesham in Suffolk, and John Foster, present instances of priests who ventured to contract marriages ; and the precipitancy with which the latter put away his partner on learning his mistake, is extremely amusing.

LXXVIII.

THOMAS TYRELL TO CROMWELL.

[From MS. Cotton. Cleop. E. iv. fol. 124*.]

With moste humble recommendacions, plese it your grace, my lord, to be advertysed, that the vicar off Mendyllsham, my neybour, hath nowe at the feste off Penticoste laste passyd browght home hys woman and chyldern into hys vicarage, opynly declaryng how he is mared wnto her, and sche is hys lawfull wyff. Thys acte by hym done is in thys countre a monster, and many do growge at it. But for that he reportyth that the kynges grace doth know he is maryd, men do refrayne to do that theyre harttes wold serve theym to do; and as to our ordynary, he dare do no thyng. I moste lowly beseche your grace that I may know your plesure whatte is beste to be done for the reformacion off hys opyn cryme, whyche is abomynable in the jugement off the laye peopell; and hys ensample wnponnyched shall be occacion for other carnall evyll dysposed prestes to do in lyke maner, whyche God defend, and preserve your grace in helth, with long prosperus lyffe, the joye future trustyd apon not therby in any wyse minysched. Wrytyn the xij[th] day off June.

Your humble dayly bedysman,

powre THOMAS TYRELL.

LXXIX.

JOHN FOSTER TO CROMWELL.

[From MS. Cotton. Cleop. E. iv. fol. 116*.]

In my moste humblyst wyse, I beyng not so bold as to appere before youre lordschyp untyll your plesure is knowyn, feere sett appartt, nede compellythe me to wrytt. Thys last Lentt I dyd no lesse then wrytt, and also to your presence I dyd approche, suyng for your lordschyppys gracyous servyce; but now my sute ys muche other, for my dysfortune hathe byn to have conceyvyd untruly Goddys worde, and not only with yntellectyon to have thought yt, but exteryally and really I have fulfyllyd the same. For I as then beyng a presste have accompleschyd maryage, nothyng pretendyng but as an obedyentt subyect; for yf the kyngys grace could have founde yt laufull that prestys mught have byn maryd, they wold have byn to the crowne dubbyll and dubbyll faythefull; furste yn love, secondly for fere that the byschoppe of Rome schuld sette yn hys powre unto ther desolacyon. But now by the noyse of the peopull I perseyve I have dunne amysce, which saythe that the kyngys erudyte yugementt with all hys cowncell temperall and spyrytuall hathe stableschyd a contrary order, that all prestys schalbe separat by a day; with which order I have contentyd my selfe, and as sone as I herde yt to be tru I sentt the woman to her frendys iij. score mylys from me, and spedely and with all celeryte I have resortyd hether to desyre the kynges hyghtnes of hys favour and absolucyon for my amysce doyng, prayng and besechyng your lordschypps gracyous cumfort for the optaynyng of hys gracyous pardon, and I schalbe your bounden servauntt yn hartt and also yn contynuall servyce, yf yt schall please your gracyous lordschypp to accept yt, duryng my lyfe. Wryttyn the xviij. day of June.

Youre bounden for ever,
JOHN FOSTER.

The next letter relates to the monks of the Charter House in London, who continued still in the king's displeasure. One or two letters on the same subject have already been given in the earlier part of the present volume.

LXXX.

BEDYLL TO CROMWELL.

[From MS. Cotton. Cleop. E. IV. fol. 217.]

My very good lord, after my moost hertie commendations, it shall pleace your lordship to understand that the monkes of the Charterhouse here at Londone, whiche were committed to Newgate for thaire traitorus behavor long tyme continued against the kinges grace, be almoost dispeched by thand of God, as it may appere to you by this byll inclosed, whereof, considering thaire behavor and the hole mater, I am not sory, but wold that al suche as love not the kinges hignes and his wordly honor were in like caas. My lord (as ye may) I desire you in the wey of charite, and none other wise, to be good lord to the priour of the said Charterhouse, whiche is as honest a man as ever was in that habite (or els I am muche deceyved), and is one whiche never offended the kinges grace by disobedience of his lawes, but hath labored very sore continually for the reformation of his brethern. And now at the last, at myn exhortation and instigation, constantly moved, and finally persuaded his brethern to surrender thaire house, landes, and goodes into the kinges handes, and to trust only to his mercy and grace. I beseche you, my lord, that the said priour may be so entreated by your help, that he be not sory and repent that he hath fered and folowed your sore wordes and my gentil exhortation made unto him to surrender his said house, and thinke that he might have kept the same, if your lordship and I had not led him to the said surrender. But suerly (I beleve) that I knowe the man so well, that howsoever he be order he wolbe contented without grudge; he is a man of suche charite as I have not seen the like. As towching the house of the Charterhouse, I pray Good, if it shal pleace the king to alter it, that it may be turned into a better use (seing it is in the face of our werls), (?) and muche communication wol run thereof throughout this realme ; ffor Londone is the common countrey of al England, from whiche is derived to al partes of this realme al good and yll occurrent here.

From Londone, the xiiijth day of Juny.

By your lordships at commandement,

THOMAS BEDYLL.

The following letter is one of many which will subsequently occur relating to the manner in which the minor articles of monastic property were disposed of. The monastery of Leicester alluded to, was that of St. Mary de Pratis, near the town, founded in 1143 by Robert le Bossu, earl of Leicester.

LXXXI.

FRANCIS CAVE TO CROMWELL.

[From MS. Cotton. Cleop. E. iv. fol. 215.*]

My most bownden dutye rememberyd, this is to advertis yower good lordshippe of the hole estate of the late monastery of Leycester, in the wiche we have taken the surrender and feyne of thabbott an convent, and the wrytinges therof be in my custodye. By yower lordshippes goodnes towardes me I now ame in the possession of the house and all the demeynes wiche was unlet at the tyme of owre repare thether. We also fownde the house indettyd to dyvers creditors in iiij^c.xj^{li}. x^s. over and besydes certen summes of money the house was indettyd to the kynges heyghnes, wherof we make no reconinge of; and for the discharge therof, we have made sale of the stoke and store, withe the housholdstuffe and ornamenttes of the churche, wiche amounte unto ccxxviij^{li}. The plate is onsolde, wiche maister Freman takithe the charge of, and is valuyd at by weyght c.iiij^{xx}x^{li}. The leade by estymation is valuyd at m^{li}. ; the belles at iiij^{xx}viij^{li}. For the dischargeynge of thabbott, conventt, and servanttes of the

seyde monastery, there haithe beyne payde, as dothe apere more
particularly by the bouke we send yower lordshippe, cxlix^{li}.; and
forasmoche as thabbott haithe nott receyvyd of hus in redy
money butt xx^{li}, he haithe requyerde me to desyer yower lordshippe to be so good lorde unto hym he may have xx^{li}. or twentie
markes more.   The churche and house remenythe as yet unde-
facede; and in the chirche be meny thynges to be maide sale of,
for the wiche yt may plese yower lordshippe to lett me knawe
yower pleysure, as well for the farther sale to be made as for the
defasinge of the chirche and other superfluus byldinges wiche be
abowte the monastery.   A hundrithe markes yerly will not sus-
teyne the charges in reparyng this house, yf all byldinges be lett
stande, as yower lordshippe shall knowe more hereafter.   Thus I
pray Jhesus longe to preserve yow in helthe withe muche honore.
Wrytten at the late monastery of Leycester, the xxixth day of
Auguste, by yower lordshipes most bownden servantt,

FRAUNCIS CAVE.

The following letter relates to a similar subject to that spoken of in the preceding,
the demolition of the monasteries of Jervaux and Bridlington. Bridlington priory
(already mentioned) came into the king's hand by the attainder of the prior, who was
active in the rebellion of 1536.

LXXXII.

RICHARD BELLASYS TO CROMWELL.

[From MS. Cotton. Cleop. E. IV. fol. 241.]

Pleashithe your good lordship to be advertysed, I have taken
down all the leade of Jarvaxe, and maid it in pecys of half foders,
whyche leade amowntythe to the nombre of eghten skore and fyve
foders, wythe thryttye and ffowre foders and a half that were
there byfore; and the said leade can not be conveit nor caryed
unto the next sombre, for the ways in that cowntre are so foule

and deape that no caryage can passe in wyntre. And as concerninge the rasing and takyn down the howse, if it be your lordships
pleasour, I ame myndet to let it staunde to the sprynge of the yere,
by reason the days ar now so short, it wolde be doble charges to
doo it now. And as concerninge the sellyng of the belles, I can
not sell them above xv^s. the howndrethe, wherin I wolde gladly
knowe your lordships pleasour whether I shuld sell them after that
pryce, or send them up to London; and if they be sent up,
surely the caryage wolbe costly frome that place to the water.
And as for Byrdlington, I have doyn nothing there as yet, but
sparythe it to Marche next, bycause the days now are so short;
and frome suche tyme as I begyn, I trust shortlye to dyspache it,
after suche fashon, that when all is fynished, I trust your lordship
shall think that I have ben no evyll howsband in all suche
thinges as your lordship haithe appoynted me to doo. And thus
the Holye Gost ever preserve your lordship in honour. At Yorke,
this xiiijth daye of Novembre, by your most bounden beademan,

RICHARD BELLYCYS.

The following letter gives a brief account of the dissolution of a number of monastic
houses of the north of England.

The Benedictine abbey of Burton-on-Trent, in Staffordshire, was of Saxon origin,
having been founded about the year 1002 by Wulfric Spott. In ancient times it was
often called Modwennestow, because the relics of St. Modwen were enshrined there.
William Edys was the last abbot : the date of the surrender given in the last edition
of the Monasticon, 1539, must be wrong, and appears to have originated from a mistake of the date of the present letter.

The alien priory of Pontefract in Yorkshire was founded by Robert de Lacy in the
reign of William Rufus, and was made dependent on the foreign house of La Charité
sur Loire, whence the first monks of the English house were brought. The last prior
was James Thwayts.

The Cistercian abbey of Fountains, the magnificent ruins of which still excite the
admiration of visitors, was founded in 1132 by a colony of monks from St. Mary's at
York. The last abbot was Marmaduke Brodelay, or Bradley, suffragan bishop of Hull.

St. Mary's abbey at York has been mentioned on a former page.

Nun-Appleton was a nunnery near Tadcaster, in the West Riding of Yorkshire,
founded by Alice de St. Quintin in the latter part of the reign of Stephen. The last
prioress was Anne Langton.

The rich mitred-abbey of Selby in Yorkshire, was founded by William the Conqueror in 1069. The last abbot was Robert Selby or Rogers. The fine abbey church is still entire.

The hospital of St. Leonard at York is said to have been first endowed by king Athelstan, and to have been refounded by William Rufus.

It may be observed that the dates of the surrender of nearly all these houses appear to be wrongly given in the Monasticon.

LXXXIII.

THE COMMISSIONERS OF THE NORTH TO CROMWELL.

[From MS. Cotton. Cleop. E. iv. fol. 242.]

After meest humble commendacions to your good lordship, pleaseth it the same be advertiesed, that we have altered Burton-upon-Trent; and accordinge to the kinges highnes commission and instruccions we have dissolved the howses of Hampole, Sancte Oswaldes, Pountefracte, Fontaunce, Sancte Maries in Yourke, Nonappleton, and Selbye, and also altered the howse of Sancte Leonerdes in Yourke, after suche ordre and fassion as we trust shall appeir to your lordship to be to the kinges honour and contentacion. Albeit, we could natt maike dispeche in parte of the said places withoute some difficultie, as your lordship shall perceyve at our repayer to Londone, ffurther certifienge your lordship that we have takyn the shrynes in all such places as we have yett hetherto repayrede unto the kinges use; and forasmoche as we have no commission in that behalf, we beseiche youe that we may have a commission for that purpouse, beringe date of the other commissions, to shewe if neede shall requier. And thus our Lorde ever preserve your goode lordship in moche honour.

At Selbie, the viij[th] day of Decembre.

Yours at commandement,

WALTERE HENDLE.
RICHARDE LAYTON.
THOMAS LEGH.
RYCHARD BELASSYS.
RICHARD WATKYNS.

The following letter contains a continuation of the proceedings of the commissioners in Yorkshire.

The priory of Monk-Bretton, or Lund, two miles from Barnsley, was founded early in the reign of Henry II. and made dependent upon the monastery of Pontefract. The last prior appears to have been William Browne.

The priory of St. Andrew at York, sometimes called St. Andrew in Fishergate, was founded about the year 1200, for twelve canons of the order of Sempringham.

Byland abbey (Bella Landa) was founded in 1143 by Roger de Mowbray. This and St. Andrew's at York had been preserved from the wreck of the smaller monasteries, to which, by the smallness of their revenues, they belonged. The last abbot of Byland was John Ledes, *alias* Alanbrigg.

The priory of Austin canons at Kirkham was founded by Walter Espec and his wife in 1121. The last prior was John Kilwik.

Elreton, or Ellerton priory, situate on the Derwent in Spaldingmore, was founded before 1212, by William Fitz Peter, for canons of the order of Saupringham. The last prior of this house was John Golding. A portion of the priory church now forms the parish church.

There was a house of friars at Tickhill, which is mentioned by Leland, but so little is known of its history, that it is even uncertain to what order it belonged.

The "Friars" at Doncaster is known chiefly by the note in Leland. "There was a house of Gray Freres here, at the north ende of the bridge, comunely caullid the Freres Bridge."

At Pontefract there was a house of Black Friars, and another of White Friars. The latter was founded by Edmund de Lacy, earl of Lincoln, before 1257.

At York there were numerous houses of Friars, belonging to the different orders.

Bolton Abbey is now the beautiful seat of the duke of Devonshire. It was founded in 1120 by William de Meschines.

LXXXIV.

THE COMMISSIONERS OF THE NORTH TO CROMWELL.

[From MS. Cotton. Cleop. E. iv. fol. 242*.]

Owre moste singulere good lorde, owre bowndon dewties lowlie premysede, pleas yt youre honorable lordeshippe too be advertisede, we have laytlye receyvede youre letters conteiginge the kinges majesties pleasure anempsce the ordere of leed and belles apperteanynge to suche howses off religeon conteanyde in the kinges graces letters commissionall to us addressed, wherof we have allredye commytte the salve custodie to substanciall honeste persons liable too answer therefoore, and have not solde ne intended to sell anye percell thereof. We have qwyetlye takine the surrenders and dissolvyd the monasteries off Wyeresoppe, Monckebreton, Sancte Androos at Yorke, Byland, Ryvaille, Kyrkeham, and Ellerton, the ffreers at Tykhill, Doncastere, Pontefracte, and the citie off Yorke, where we perceyved no murmure ore gruge in anye behalfe, bot were thanckefullye receyvede, as we shall within vj. dayes more playnlie certefye your lordeshippe. And wheere yt haithe pleasyd youre lordeshippe too wryte fore reservinge of leed and belles at Bolton, in chauns ther ys as yet noo suche commission cummyne to owre handes, as Jhesus knowethe, whoo preserve your lordeshippe in helthe and honour. At Yorke, the xv^{the} daye of Decembere,

> Youre lordshippes humble boundon orators,
>> GEORGE LAWSON.
>> RYCHERD BELASSEZ.
>> WILLM. BLITHMAN.
>> JAMES ROKEBY.

The next letter relates to the suppression of the monastery of St. Andrew at Northampton, of which a short account has been given on a former page.

LXXXV.

THE COMMISSIONERS TO CROMWELL.

[From MS. Cotton. Cleop. E. iv. fol. 207.]

Hit may please your lordshipe to be advertissede, that this seconde day of Marche we have taken a realesse and a deade of feofftement of the monasterie of Saint Androse in Northehamptone to the kinges use, and an humble submission of the prior and covent, as we suppos, to the kinges honoure and contentation, refferryng our diligence and doynges therin to your jugement.

We have also compowndede with the hoole covent for ther pensions, excepte the prior and supprior, wiche desierithe to abyde your order in thassyngnement of theires: here inclosede your lordeshipe may persave our order taken with the reste of the covent, haveyng a respecte therin to the age, qualitie, and discretion of the persons; and by yowre lordeshippes better advice we thynk hit expedient the saide pensions to be payede by the hondes of the particuler recever of the suppressede londes of this countie of Northamton, and ther pensions payable at our Ladys day next insewyng; and for that cause we have dispachede them with lesse money in honde. We have also assignede a vicarage of vij^{li}. nowe at this tyme vacant, to one of the covent for his pension, wiche moste humblie desierithe to have remission of the firste fruites therof, wiche we juge necessaire to be grauntede by the kinges highnes, leste the pore man shulde bege in the mean tyme, the thyng beyng of so smale valew that evere of them haveyng his pension shalbe in better case then he. The halle chambers seillede with the beste parte of the edifices is covered with leade; whether the kinges pleasure is we shall discover* the same or not, we be desierouse to be certifiede by this bringer. For the survey of the londes we shall do therin what we may. We fynde many leasses grauntede oute by the olde prior, muche unthrifftelye, with muche tangullyng and besines, wiche we shall declare unto yowre lordeshipe at our cumyng. Thus our Lorde sende yowe longe lyffe with increase of honoure. Frome Northehamptone, by your lordeshippes moste assurede to commaunde,

WYLLIAM PARRE.

Your servant, RICHARD LAYTON, preste.

Your pore and most bonden old servaunt,

ROBERT SOWTHWELL.

Your humble and obedyent servaunt,

THOMAS MYLDEMAY.

* i. e. uncover.

An ordre taken the secunde daie of Marche, the xxix. yeare of the reign of our soveraign lorde kyng Herry the Eyght, by his highnes commyssioners, with the religious of the late monastery of saint Andrews thappostell in Northampton, for their annuall pencions yeven unto them onely of his graces charyte duryng the terme of their naturall lyves, to begynne at the ffeast of thannunciacion of our Lady nexte ensewing, as on his graces behalfe is to them promysed by the saide commyssioners.

First, Fraunces Leycetour, late priour, and Thomas Bettes, suppriour of the saide late monastery, ben by the saide commyssioners respyted uppon certen consyderacions, tyll my lorde prevy sealys pleasure therein be knowne   .   .   .

Thomas Smyth of thage of lij. yeares for his yerely pencion .   .   .   .   .   .   iiij^{li}.

Thomas Cowlestone of thage of ffyftye yearys for his yerely pencion   .   .   .   .   iiij^{li}.

Robert Marten of thage of xlj. yeares for his yerely pencion .   .   .   .   .   .   iiij^{li}.

James Hopkyns of thage of lij. yeares for his yerely pencion .   .   .   .   .   .   iiij^{li}.

Richarde Bunbery of thage of xl. yeares for his pencion yerely   .   .   .   .   .   iiij^{li}.

John Rote of thage of xxxvj. yeares is assigned by the saide commyssioners to the vycarage of Saint Gyles in Northampton, being of the yerely valew of vij^{li}. and of the gyfte of the saide monastery, in recompence of his yerely pencion.

Jhon Harolde of thage of xxxij. yeares for his yerely pencion .   .   .   .   .   .   lxvj^{s}.   viij^{d}.

Thomas Barbor of thage of xxxj. yeares for his yerely pencion .   .   .   .   .   .   lxvj^{s}.   viij^{d}.

Wylliam Warde of thage of xxix^{ti}. yeares for his
yerely pencion . . . . . liij^s. iiij^d.
Thomas Atbury of thage of xxvij. yeares for his
yerely pencion . . . . . liij^s. iiij^d.
Wylliam Sowthecote of thage of xxxj. yeares for his
yerely pencion . . . . . liij^s. iiij^d.

WYLLIAM PARRE.
RIC. LAYTON, preste.
ROBERT SOWTHWELL.
THOMAS MYLDEMAYE.

The following letter also relates to the dissolution of the monastery of St. Andrew
at Northampton. The priory of Westacre in Norfolk, founded about the reign of
William Rufus as a cell to the abbey of Lewes in Sussex, had been surrendered on the
14th of January in the present year. Boxley in Kent was a Cistercian abbey, founded
in 1144 by William de Ipre earl of Kent. It was surrendered, according to the
Monasticon, " Jan. 29, 1537, 29 Hen. VIII." which must of course mean Jan. 29,
1538. The last abbot of Boxley was John Dobbs.

LXXXVI.

ROBERT SOUTHWELL TO CROMWELL.

[From MS. Cotton. Cleop. E. iv. fol. 218.]

Although, my very good lorde, that there wanted here summe
parte of the occasions comprehendyd in the submyssion of the late
monastery of Westacre, as concerning the clere alienacion of the
possessions belonging to the same, with suche lieke, yett fownde
we here of other (that as I suppose ben in the more parte of the
resydew that at this daie stonden) sufficient inowgh for the full-
fyllyng of the submyssion that now we sende your lordeshipp in
the place of the other that wanted, so as by the variete of occasions this booke in the more parte or all is alteryd from the other
in matter, as by the perusing therof your lordeshipp shall wele

perseyve, which I humbly beseche you that it may lieke you to do. And although it shall seme tedyous, or the over reding onworthie, yet shall I eftsons humbly beseche you to accepte it in good parte, and for a perfight demonstracion of my good will to have made the bettyr, in case my knowlege had extended therto. The ernest employture neverthelesse of my pore and symple wytt shall at no time wante to serve to the very best and uttermost force therof. Sir, theis pore men have nat spared to confesse the treweth, as ye shall wele perceyve, wherby in my pore mynde they deserve the more favour, and I dare saie in their hartes thinke them selffes rather to have meryted perdon by their ignorance than prayse or lawde for their forme of lyving. Whether ther was cawse why that Boxley shulde recognyce as moche or more, it may please you to judge, whom it also pleased to shewe me the idolle that stode there, in myne opynyon a very monstruows sight. Here was also of late in this monastery a pece of saint Andrews fynger, covered with an unce of sylver or there aboughte (as I conjecture), a very precyows juell in the estimacion of many, and now leyde to pledge by the monastery to one of the towne for xl^{li}., which we intende nat to redeme of the pryce, excepte we be commaunded so to do. Levyng this matter, it maie lieke you farther to undrestande, that in perusing the olde accomptes of the monastery we fownde the yerely revenews of the same to have extended in times past to sevyn hundreth markes, and by the bookes of the tenth nat to fower hundreth markes, and yett no parte of the possessions clerely alienate from the monastery, but decressed by the receyte of the rentes afore hande by the pre-decessours to this priour of suche as be fermours to them for many yeares. There have growne no decay by this priour that we can lerne, but surely his predecessours plesured moche in odoryferous savours, as it shulde seme by their converting the rentes of their monastery, that were wonte to be paide in coyne and grayne, into gelofer flowers and roses. Wherto the valew of the lande will uppon this survey amounte, I can nat as yett advertyce your lorde-

shypp, but the monastery in moveables is very pore, moche in-
detted, and in ledd, as I conjecture, worth fower or fyve hundreth
powndes. Sir, we have practysed with the pore men for their
pencions as easely to the kynges charge and as moche to his graces
honour, as we cowde devyce. The boke wherof we do sende unto
your lordeshypp, with the names and summes for the makyng of
their patentes, which being sent unto us to be delyvered to the
parties afore our departure, shalbe moche to their contentacion,
and no lesse to the kynges honour, to imparte with somewhat of
his gracyous charyte towarde the maintenaunce of their pore
lyvyng. My lorde, if it myght so stande with your pleasure, I
wolde humbly beseche you to have in your good lordeshippes remembraunce my ffathers sute consernyng Mallyng : I made your
lordeshipp (as my synguler good lorde) prevy to the onely consideracion that moved me to use this importunyte with you, as
God shall judge me, whom I most hertyly beseche to send your
lordeshipp long liffe with moche incresse of honour. At Northampton, the 3 of Merche, by the handes of your pore and most
bounden old servaunt,

ROBERT SOWTHWELL.

The Carthusian priory mentioned in the following letter, was situated near Eppe-
worth, in the isle of Axeholm in Lincolnshire, and was styled *the priory in the wood.*
It was founded by Thomas Mowbray, (then earl of Nottingham, but afterwards created
duke of Norfolk) in the nineteenth year of Richard II.

LXXXVII.

ARCHBISHOP CRANMER TO CROMWELL.

[From MS. Cotton. Cleop. E. iv. fol. 211.*]

After most hartie commendacions to your lordeshype, fforas-
moch as I am enformed that your lordshype entendeth to depose
the priour of the Charterhowse within the ile of Axholme, theis
shalbe to desyre you to permytt the saide priour styll to contynew in

hys rome, for I am abowte throwe the helpe of suche ffreyndes as I have in thoyse parties to procure that the saide priour shall wyllinglye resygne the same into the kynges hondes. Thus almyghtie God preserve your lordshype. Frome Fourde, the vijth daie of March.

Your own assured ever,

T. CANTUARIEN.

The following letter is placed here somewhat out of its place, on account of its immediate connection with the preceding.

LXXXVIII.

LETTER FROM THE BRETHREN OF THE CHARTER HOUSE IN AXHOLM TO THE PRIOR OF SHENE.

[From MS. Cotton. Cleop. E. iv. fol. 97.]

Humly shewyth and complanyth unto your faderhede your poor oratours and chyldren of obediens, nott knowyng whome we may make our complant and shewe our dolorus grefes, but only unto your worshypfull faderhede, that our fader prior hath done and dayly doth in convayng our goodes owt of our howse. As sone as he was comme home fro London, he sayd that he had gyfyne up hys offyce, the howse and the landes, but not the goodes. At hys goyng up to London he left us in monye nother golde nor sylver, but only iij^{li}. for to kepe our howse withall, and it is not a lytyll that he hath receyvyd of our baly * syns Myghylmes, and yet he dyd report to mayster doctor Layton that he had devydyd the same monye in porcions and gyfyne it to his brethren, whych thyng is not trwe. Butt when prior Awstyn†️ was dead, this man was vicar, and mych of that that we had that

---

* Bailiff.

† This prior is not mentioned in the Monasticon, where the last prior is stated to have been Michael Makeness.

tyme he delyvered it to us in porcions; and as sone as he was prior, he cald it in agane; but now at thys tyme for our comforth we can nothyng gett of hym. He hath convayde owt of hys celle wax worth xl^s., and pewtyr vessell to the nowmbyr of iij. score, or ther abowte, and iij. pecys of lyne cloth, and ij. pecys of wolan cloth, and a great qwantyte of spyce, with other moo thynges. Our chese and fysshe is greatly wastyd, sych as we shuld lyve withall; and all our rydyng horses is gone, and none left in the howse but our cartte horses, with certen other catell and movable goodes that dyd belong to the howse, whych werre to long to wryte every thyng. His prevy caryers dyd convay thys by nyght, and thys they dyd so long at last they were takyn with our awne servans, and such thynges were broght in agayne. Also our fader hath presumyde, after he had gyfyn up the howse and landes, he wold have lettyn a certen fermhold by the covent seale to one of hys kynsmen, but parte of the covent wolde nott consent therto, and therfore he is sore grevyde with some of them. Also he hath lett my lord of Darbyis offyser take copyes owt of our copes that we holde of my lord of Darby, whych we feare shall turne us to hurt and trobull; and as sone as he had them he dyschargde us of them and of our fyshyng waters, whych thynges were the most profytt that longde unto us. Also we fere convayng of our evydence, and he receyvyth renttes as he dyd before, whych we thynke shall be but lytyll profytt to our howse. We dyd desyre hym to have a key with hym in the kepyng of our covent seale, but he wyll grawntt us none, and we fere of more hurt and dyspleaser shall cum to us therby. For but late we were certifyed that mayster Stokwith sayd to our fader, " yf that the visitors of your religion cum to visitt, abyde hym not, but convey your selfe with the covent seale, and tarry nott hys commyng." And Henry Stokwith dyd say to the same man, if that that he had done wolde not serve, then he wold take another way. And, as we be informyd, our fader is myndyd to send hym to London very shortly, and we

fere he shall have the covent seayle with hym for to do the worst
to the howse that he can. Also mayster Henry Stokwith was at
London at the feast of All Santes, or there abowte, and he had
with hym of our monye xx^{li}. to labor for our fader, that he shuld
not preche when he comme home : he sayd that my lord pryvy
seale had grawntyd hym that he shuld not preche, nor he shuld
not be put owt of his office, and for that promys my lord had on
hym xx. markes. But we, that ar the poor covent, can not thynke
that my lord had it, but that M. Stokwith dyd kepe it hym
selfe, and so doth report of my lord. Also, after the tyme that
M. Stokwith comme home, our fader wold asyne no man to preche
accordyng to your commawnment. And when our fader is any
thyng movyd or troblyd with us, hewyll send for M. Stokwith
for to reforme us, as he hath done many tymes. Of what autoryte
he do take it upon hym, we pray you, fader, that it may be
knowne. Also M. Stockwith doth sclawnder the covent, and
sayth our howse is noght els *nisi spelunca latronum*, nor he caryth
not what he doth say, so that his wordes may make for his purpas.
Also, our husbandrye is not lokyd upon, our lond is not tylde,
muke is not led, our corne lyth in the barn, sum is threshte, and
[sum is husbo]ndyd, and mych is yit to threshe, and taketh hur[t]
with vermyn ; and as sone as our fader comme home, he shewede
our servandes that he had gyven up the [howse, and] bad them
shyfte for them selfe, and so at Ester they went many of them away.
And shortly hay tyme shall cum, and when it shuld be sped,
other thynges shalbe to do. And for we can se none other by
all his actes and dedes, but that he goth abowte to undo the
howse ; and for fere that an other man shuld have hys offyce, he
intendyth to leave hym lytyll or noght to kepe howse withall. Also
he and his carnall frendes detrackyth us, sayng that all the troble
that the howse is in commyth nothyng of hym selfe, but by us,
with letters that we have wrytyn op to my lord of the prevy
seale. Now, worshypfull fader, for the love [of] God, helpe us at

gret nede, and send us sum conforthable cowncell, and our lord
Jhesu rewarde you in hevyn, and evermore kepe you and all your
devoute brederen.   Amen.

By your beadmen and chyldren of obediens,

Dan BRYAN LEE, vicar.

Dayn THOMAS ALRED.

Brother THOMAS CONVERE.

The great Benedictine abbey of Evesham, in Worcestershire, was founded by Egwin
bishop of Worcester, at the beginning of the eighth century.   The last superior of this
house but one was abbot Litchfield, who built the noble gateway-tower still standing ;
he was persuaded to resign, and was succeeded by Philip Hawford, *alias* Ballard, who
surrendered the abbey to the king's commissioners.

LXXXIX.

WILLIAM PETRE TO CROMWELL.

[From MS. Cotton. Cleop. E. IV. fol. 255.]

My duete most humbly remembryd, it may please your lordeshipp to bee advertised, thatt according to yower commawndment I
have byn at Evesham, and ther receyvyd the resignation of
thabbott, whiche he was contentyd to mak immediatly uppon the
sight of your lordeshippes letters, saving thatt he desiryd me very
instantly thatt I wolde nott open the same during the tyme of
my being here, bicause (as he sayd) it wold bee notydd thatt he
was compellyd to resigne for fear of deprivation.   As touching his
pension, and the assurance therof, he hath made certayn requestes, submitting hym self to bee ordred in all thinges as to your
lordeshipp shall be thought mete.   Wee have taken the surrendar
of this priorye* with as moche quyetnes as might be desiryd, and
prepare our self four the dispeche of all other thinges as diligently
as we may, which finisshed wee shall wayte on your lordeshipp,

* Lantony : see the end of the letter.   The Austin priory of Lanthony, near Gloucester, (generally called Lanthony secunda) was founded by King Henry I. in 1136.
The last prior was Richard Hemsted or Hart.

and certefye the same of all thinges at large. This berar can certefye your lordeshipp whow farre wee have procedyd hitherto, by whom wee have send the names of the chanons for the making of ther capacites. And so allmighte God have your lordeshipp in his blessed keping. From Lanthonye, the xvij[th] of Marche.

Your lordeshippes most bownden beadesman and servant,

WILLIAM PETRE.

The abbey of Peterborough was a foundation of great antiquity, dating from the middle of the seventh century. It was originally named Medeshamstede, but was afterwards called Peterborough, from the name of its patron saint. Its abbot in later times wore the mitre, and had a seat in parliament. At the dissolution, it was converted into a bishop's see by the king. The last abbot was John Chambers, who became the first bishop, being consecrated on the the 23rd October, 1541.

XC.

WILLIAM PARRE TO CROMWELL.

[From MS. Cott. Cleop. E. IV. fol. 205.]

Pleasethe your lordship to bee advertised, that according to the tenour of my last lettre sente unto your lordship by this berer, I have bene at Peterbourgh, where the abbot, upon the rumour that was spred abrode of the commyng downe of the visitours, and not upon any occasion geven or mynistred to hym either in worde or dede by doctor Layton, shewed hymself to bee affrayed, insomoche as at my furst commyng thiddir he required me of myne advise and favour what was best for hym to doo, and perceiving by hym amongis other commynicacion that speciallie he tendred the contynuaunce and standing of his monastery, I declared that I had no auctorite ner commyssion to treate or comon with hym concernyng any poynt, cause, or purpos, touching either the standing or the dissolucion of his hous, and that my commyng thiddir was for no other matier but bicause he sent for me, advising hym to put all doubtes awaye, onles he knewe other matier thene I did. Nevertheles this coude not satisfie his myende, but ffering that some thing shulde bee done contraire to his myende, he sent sir Thomas Tresham, the marshall of his hall, and Johan Layne of Kettring to me, who alledged on his behalf that he was contente upon condicion that he mought bide in suertie that his hous shulde stande to give the kinges highnes on hoole yeres rent of all the landes apperteynyng to the monastery, whiche I thinke amountethe nigh upon two thousaunde and five hundred merkes. And over that to gratifie your lordship to bee good lorde to hym, with the some, as I suppose, of thre hundred poundes. Notwithstanding therein I gave hym directe aunswere, that I coude not determyne any such poyntes with hym more thene I had alredie before shewed hym, untill suche tyme as I had knowleige of your lordshippes pleasure, wherewith and at that same tyme there arrived this said berer with letters from your lordship. And aftre he had knowelege howe good lorde ye were unto hym, by the reaporte of on that came from the court, he digressed apartelie from his ffurst commynicacion, and said that in his suetes towardes the kinges highnes and your lordship he wolde bee ordred as Mr. comptroller and myself wold advise hym, and in this state I left hym, without any ferther prouf or treatie bitwene hym and me. Howebeit if [it] shall pleas your lordship to commaunde me with any ferther service in thapproving hym eftesones in his matier, I shall most humble ensue the same, supposing that small treatie wolde moeve hym to accomplishe his furst offre.

It maye pleas your lordship to bee soo goode lorde to me as to have the bill of Kendall for the pore inhabitauntes of the same in your remembrance, wherebie your lordship shall not onlie, in my judgement, doo as good a dede as ever was done and acquire all the comons there for ever to bee your perpetuell bedmen, but alsoo suche rest, quietnes, and suertie against the kinges ennemyes shall therebie procede, that it shalbee to the comforte and rewise of all that parties, whiche nowe by the crueltie and senistre pollicie of on or two privat persones is in maner clerelie subverted. The pore men hathe no other meane but dailie either on nombre or other to labour hiddir to shewe theire grieffes, in trust that for theym all I shulde bee a sueter unto your lordship to releasse theym of theire extreme oppressons and bondage, whiche most humblie I beseche your lordship amonges other your weightie busynes to considre. And thus the hoolie Trenytie evermore have you, my singler good lorde, in his hoolie governaunce. At Horton, the xviijth. daye of Merche.

Your lordshippis assurred most boundon,

WYLLIAM PARRE.

The great priory of Lewes in Sussex was founded by William earl of Warren in 1077 or 1078. The priors were mitred and sat in parliament. Robert Crowham was the last prior. The site of this house was granted to Cromwell. The date of the surrender given in the last edition of the Monasticon, 6 Nov. 1538, must be incorrect. March 1537, is, of course, 153⅞. The following letter gives a singular picture of the devastations made in many of the dissolved houses.

XCI.

JOHN PORTINARI* TO CROMWELL.

[From MS. Cotton. Cleop. E. iv. p. 232.]

My lord, I humbly commend my selfe unto your lordshyp, the laste I wrote unto your lordshyp was the xxth daye of thys present monith by the handes of Mr. Wyliamson, by the whych I advertised your lordshyp of the lengthe and greatenes of thys churche, and how we had begon to pull the hole down to the ground, and what maner and fashion they used in pulling it down. I told your lordshyp of a vaute on the ryghte syde of the hyghe altare, that was borne up with fower great pillars, having abowt it v. chappelles, whych be compased in with the walles lxx. stokes (?) of length, that is, fete ccx. All thys is down a Thursday and Fryday last. Now we ar pluckyng down an hygher vaute, borne up by fower

* Perhaps this is a disguised name, as the letter appears to be in the hand-writing of Richard Moryson.

thicke and grose pillars, xiiij. fote fro syde to syde, abowt in circumference xlv. fote. Thys shall downe for our second worke. As it goth forward I woll advise your lordshyp from tyme to tyme, and that your lordshyp may knowe with how many men we have don thys, we browght from London xvij. persons, 3 carpentars, 2 smythes, 2 plummars, and on that kepith the fornace. Every of these attendith to hys own office: x. of them hewed the walles abowte, amonge the whych ther were 3 carpentars: thiese made proctes to undersette wher the other cutte away, thother brake and cutte the waules. Thiese ar men exercised moch better then the men that we fynd here in the contrey. Wherfor we must both have mo men, and other thinges also, that we have nede of, all the whych I woll within thys ij. or thre dayes tell your lordshyp by mouthe. A Tuesday they began to cast the ledde, and it shalbe don with such diligence and savyng as may be, so that our trust is your lordshyp shall be moch satisfied with that we do, unto whom I most humbly commend my self, moch desiringe God to mainteyn your helth, your honour, your hartes ease. At Lewes, the xxiiij. of March, 1537.

Your lordshyps servant,
JOHAN PORTINARI.

Undernethe here your lordshyp shall see a juste mesure of the hole abbey.

The churche is in lengthe cl. fote.

The heygthe, lxiij. fote.

The circumference abowte it, M.D.lviij. fote.

The wall of the fore fronte, thicke x fote.

The thyckenes of the stepil wall, x fote.

The thickenes of the waules *interno*, v. fote.

Ther be in the churche xxxij. pillars, standyng equally from the walles.

An hygh roufe made for the belles.

Eyght pillars verry bygge, thicke xiiij. fote, abowte xlv. fo.

Thother xxiij. ar for the moste parte x fote thicke, and xxv. abowght.

The heygthe of the greater sorte is xlij. fo.; of thother xviij. fote.

The heygthe of the roufe before the hyghe altare is lxxxxiij. fote.

In the middes of the church, where the belles dyd hange, ar cv. fote.

The heygthe of the stepil at the fronte is lxxxx. fote.

Binham and Beeston, mentioned in the following letter, were two priories in Norfolk. The first was a cell to St. Albans, although the writer of this letter states the contrary. It is said to have been as old as the time of the conqueror: the last prior appears to have been John Albon. Beeston was founded about the beginning of the reign of Hen. III.; its last prior was Richard Hudson or Hodgeson.

XCII.

SIR RICHARD RICHE TO CROMWELL.

[From MS. Harl. No. 604, fol. 67.]

Aftur my harty recommendacions, thes shalbe to render to yowe my most harty thankes for your good expedycion of my matter of Syon, for the wyche, on my faith, ye have and shall bynde me; for this and many other pleasures and gratuytes to me shewyd, I reken my selff most bownden to owe to yowe my pore servyce (next to the king) duryng my lyff. My lorde, I entend to suppresse Bynham before my retorne, which pretendyth hit selff to be a sell to Seynt Albonys, yf ye advertyse me not to the conterary. I have fynez and other matters of record levyed by them not namyng the abbott of Saynt Albanys. Also contynually they make leasez under ther owne seale, not namyng the abbott. Also I entend to suppresse Beeston, which pretend them selffez to be ffryers, which ys not true, but they ar chanons, and so apparellid, knowen, and taken. They consume the goodes and cattalles. I and other have sent to yowe a generall lettur of our procedynges in thes partyes.

And thus I beseche Jhesu preserve yowe in honor and helth. Frome Wood Rysing, this present xxixth daye of Marche.

Your owne assurydly,
RYCHARD RYCHE.

To his ryght honerable
and singuler good lorde
the lorde privy seale.

The next letter is from William Barlow, then bishop of St. David's, and (with others which follow) gives a curious picture of the state of Wales at the time of the dissolution of the monastic houses. An immense number of superstitious images and relics were during the present year confiscated and destroyed in all parts of the kingdom.

XCIII.

BISHOP BARLOW TO CROMWELL.

[From MS. Cotton. Cleop. E. IV. fol. 117.]

After my right humble commendacions, the benevolente goodnes of your lordship towarde me, apperceaved both by your lordships lettres and by relacion of M. doctour Barnes concernyng soch sommes of moneye as I am yndetted to the kynges highnes favorably to be respited, though I can not in this nor in other your manyfold benefites condigly make recompensacion, yet the litle that I maye to the uttermost of my pore possibilitye my unfayned endevour shall not fayle faythfully to perfourme. Concernynge your lordships lettres addressed for the taper of Haverforde West, yer the receyte of them I had done refourmacion and openly detected the abuse therof, all parties which before tyme repugned penitently reconcyled. But sythen I chaunced apon another taper of moch greater credyte and of more shamefull detestacion, called our ladyes taper of Cardigan,* which I have sente here to your lordship with convenyent instructyons of that develish

---

* There was at Cardigan a small priory of Benedictine monks, dependent on the abbey of Chertsey in Surrey, founded before 1291; the last prior was Thomas Hore.

delusyon.   Forthermore, where I admonished the canons of
Sainte Davids accordinge to the kynges injunctions in no wyse to
set forth fayned reliques for to allure people to supersticion,
nether to advaunce the vayne observacion of unnecessary holy
dayes abrogated by the kynges supreme authoritye, on sainte
Davids daye the people wilfully solemnysinge the feest, certen
reliques were set forth which I caused to be sequestred and taken
awaye, detaynynge them in my custody untill I maye be advertised of your lordships pleasour.   The parcels of the reliques are
these : two heedes of sylver plate enclosinge two rotten skulles
stuffed with putrified clowtes; Item, two arme bones, and a
worme eaten boke covered with sylver plate.   Off the canons
slombringe necligence towarde the prefermente of Gods worde,
and what an ungodly disguysed sermone was preached in the cathedrall church in the feest of Ynnocentes last passed, they beinge
presente with an auditory of iij. or iiij. hundred persons, this
bearer, a mynister of the same church, shall forder declare, havynge
parte of the said sermone in wrytinge apparente to be showed.
Forthermore, though I myght seme more presumptuous then
neadeth to mocion any sute for the translacion of the see from
St. Davyds to Kermerddyn, yet, my good lorde, the just
equytye therof and expedyente utilytie enforceth me so to presume, consyderinge that a better deade for the comen wealth and
dew reformacion of the whole mysordered dyocesse can not be
purposed, as well for the preferremente of Gods worde, as for the
abolyshinge of all antichristian supersticion, and therin the kynges
supreme majestie to be amplyfied with the unyversall commoditye
of hys graces subjectes there reseaunte, annoyenge none with
discommoditye, excepte perchaunce foure or fyve persons will
surmyse their pryvate pleasour to be anoyed yn profetinge the
comon wealth.   And the cause partlye that moveth me thus
with importune instaunce to be urgente in my sute, ys the over
sumptuous expenses that the canons have interprysed in reedi-
fyenge the body of theyr cathedrall church, which yer it be

fully fyneshed will utterly consume the small resydew of the church treasure remayninge in their custody, without any profytable effecte, savinge to norysh clatteringe conventycles of barbarous rurall persons, the deformed habitacions of the pore collegyans in soch beggerly ruyne and so wrechedly decayed that honestye will abhorre to beholde them.   Which to remedy, pleaseth the kynges highnes of his gracyous bountye to graunte the Grey Freres place at Kermerddyn,* where his most noble progenytour and graundefather lyeth honorably entiered, lycensynge the see thydder to be translated, which (his graces pleasour condescendinge) maye be perfourmed withoute any chargeable difficultie, and not only the pore collegyans but also the canons resydentearyes myght be there pleasantly enhabited, with haboundant provision of all necessarye commoditees, contynually havinge oportune occasion to profite the kynges subjectes.   Whereas at S. Davids, lurkynge in a desolate corner, they that be best mynded can do veraye litle good in case they wold, savynge to them selves.   And concernynge the ffreres, that they nether shuld be agreed with any prejudice, I dowte not but under the kynges highnes favour of soch preferrementes as I have of his grace sufficiently to provyde for every one of them that shalbe founde an able mynister of Christes church in competente lernynge and honest conversacion.   Moreover the sayed towne of Kermerddyn beinge the most frequented place and indifferently sytuate in the myddle of the dyocesse, I myght there (and God willinge so I wolde) settle my contynuall consistory, assisted with lerned persons, maynteynynge a ffre grammer scole, with a dayly lecture of holy scripture, whereby Gods honour princypally preferred; the Welsh rudenes decreasynge, Christian cyvilitye maye be in-

* This was probably the priory at Caermarthen, of which there are still considerable remains. This letter seems to contradict the common opinion that Edmond Tudor, first earl of Richmond, the father of King Henry VII. was buried in the cathedral of St. David's. His remains were perhaps removed thither on the suppression of the priory.

troduced to the famous renowne of the kynges supremytye, whose princely majestye almightye Jesu preserve with your good lordship. From Kermerddyn, the last daye of Merch.

Your lordeshyppes to commaund,

W. MENEVEN.

To the right honorable
and my synguler good
lorde my lorde privey
seale.

[Inclosed with the foregoing letter.]

Thexaminacion of Thomas Hore, prior of Cardigan, donatyve of the late monasterye of Chersey, concernynge the pretensed taper of our Lady there.

Inprimis, the said pryour sayeth that he hath be prior there the space of fyve yeres.

Item, that he never saw the taper of our Lady within but at the neder ende, where it appered wood unto his judgement.

Item, that he estemed the same to be a holy relyque to his judgemente, accordinge to the fame of the cuntrey, unto the tyme that he saw it opened. And then he confesseth hym selfe to have be deceaved therin.

Item, that the image now situate in the church of Cardigan, which ys used for a greate pilgremage to this presente daye, was founde standinge apon the ryver of Tyve, beinge an arme of the see, and her sonne apon her lappe, and the same taper bernynge in her hande.

Item, that the said ymage was caryed from thens unto Christes church of Cardigan, and the sayd ymage wold not tarry there, but was founde thre or fowre tymes in the place where now ys buylded the church of our Lady, and the taper brunnynge in her hande, which contynued styll burnynge the space of nyne yeres, without wastinge, untill the tyme that one forsware hymselfe theron, and then it extincted, and never burned after.

Item, that sence the ceasinge of burnynge of the sayd taper, it was enclosed and taken for a greate relyque, and so worshipped and kyssed of pylgremes, and used of men to sweare by in difficill and harde matters,[*] wherof the advauntage admounted to greate sommes of money in tymes passed, payenge yerely of the same xx^{ti} nobles for a pencion unto thabbot of Chersey.

Thexaminacion of syr † Morgan Meredeth, vicar of our Lady church there.

Inprimis, he sayeth that he hath be vicar there xxj^{ti}. yeres.

---

[*] We might imagine, by the number of holy relics which the Welsh had to swear by, that they were constantly in the habit of false-swearing, and did not believe one another. Other instances will be found in Giraldus Cambrensis, &c.

† *Sir*, applied to a priest, was a scholastic title, the translation of *dominus*, given to a person who had taken his first degree in the university. We meet with other instances in the course of these letters.

Item, that prior Johan Frodsam* tolde hym, that because the people toke the wax awaye, he put the tree beneth, that the people shuld not dyminesh the substance of the taper, otherwise he assenteth and agreeth in all thinges with the priour.

Injunctiones dictis priori et vicario facte et injuncte, decimo sexto die mensis Mercij, auctoritate regia mediante.

Inprimis, that the sayd prior and vicare *alternis vicibus* shall preach and declare the gospell or the epistle reade apon that daye in the mother tongue, exponynge the same syncerly as ferre as their lernynge will extende, openynge to the people the abhominable idolatri and disceatfull jugglinge of their predicessours there in worshippinge and causinge to be worshipped a pece of old rotten tymber, puttinge the people in belefe the same to be a holy relique, and a taper which had burned without consumynge or wast, &c.

Item, the sayd pryour and vicar shall so preach every Sondaye and holyday betwixte this and *dominica in albis.*

Item, the sayd prior and vicare shall do awaye or cause to be done awaye all maner of clothes, fygured wax, delusyons of myracles, shrowdes, and other entysementes of the ignorante people to pilgremage and ydolatry.

Item, that they shall take an ynventory of all and every soch clothes, wax, shrowdes, and other entysementes, and the same shall converte into the use of pore people, or otherwise to some other good use, makynge therof a recknynge in writinge, declaringe the trewe bestowynge and usinge of the same.

Item, that all and synguler these injunctyons shalbe inviolablye observed in payne of contempte.

XCIV.

BISHOP BARLOW TO CROMWELL.

[From MS. Cotton. Cleop. E. iv. fol. 262.]

After moste humble recommendacions, pleasith your lordeshippe to be advertysede, that immedyatly upon the receyte of your honorable lettres, I made delyvery of soche goodes of the chauntours of Seynte Davydes as remayned in my custodye; and where itt was suggestyde that I vysetede his howse and toke awaye all his

* Probably Hore's predecessor in the office.

goodes and catalle, to sertefye your lordeshippe unfayndly of the treweth, I causyde nothinge to be removede thence butt certeyne chestes, wherein was perceyvede to be his plate and money, whiche after his voluntary submyssion I dyd upon consyderacyons, bycause parte of the contrie was ryotously raysid uppe by his ffrendes, and for the manacynge rumoures of Mr. Rychard Devourax hyther commynge, as this barer my brother can ferder enforme your lordeshippe with the hole circumstance of the chauntres ferre abusyde demeanour and intollerable fassheon. Wherein doinge my dutie, though I have nott excedyd equyte and conscience, yett is ther soche valyant baringe, contrarye to all justice, that onles your good lordeshippe be my favorable defence in right, I shall not escape confusyon. For, whatt by moche money and many myghty ffrendes, my adversaries, as they make theyr advaunte, dubt nothinge to prevayle. And of this partyall baringe the pryncypall procurers are two of my rycheste cannons (other lawde I can nott geve theym), sworne chaplaynes to my lorde Ferreis, Mr. Gryffith ap Owen and Mr. John Lewes, treasorer of Seynte Davydes, who upon dyspleasure causeles in this mater to hynder my fame and to elevate my hatred, have sythen absentyd theyme selff, contrarye to the kynges actes, ydelly sojournynge in Carmerdyne, and nowe fully porposide withowte occasyon of greyff to be playntyffe agaynste me, whom I never agrevyde in no case, excepte they acounte it for a greif, bycause in the late sedytyous season, havynge notycion that certeyn of the rebellyous lettres were amongest the cannons, sever[ally] examynynge theym I tryede owte that the treasorer had a copye, whiche I requyringe hime to delyver, he made excuse that he hade loste it, whereof I wrote to my brother then beinge att London to certefie your lordeshippe, whiche cam nott to his handes, butt as I am enformede were syns delyvered to Mr. William Popley. Concerninge the other, Mr. Lewes Gryffyth ap Owen, in my late vysytacion itt was presentyde and founde that he hade kepte a certeyn woman, havinge dyvers chyldren by her, and causyde

(as she affirmith, forced) her to contracte matrymony with a ser-
vante of his owen, and sythen by the space of ij. yeres hath suf-
frede her dayly frequentynge his howse to acompany another canon,
one of his nexte neyghboures (by whome she hath. hade one
chylde, and is redy to be delyverede of another) ; whiche with lyke
necessarie maters of reformatyon I charytably layde to theyr
charge.   And as for any other causes of greiff, I knowe none that
they can lawfully allege agaynste me, excepte they be agrevyde
with my contynuall prechinge and syncere settynge forthe of the
kynges gracyous artycles to the reproche of ungodly superstycyon
and abhomynable idolatry, whiche with horryble blasphemy agaynste
God, and detestable delusyon of the kynges subgettes, have bene
here shamfully supportyd, as by apparente evydens att your lordeshippes pleasour redy to be showed, shall manyfestly apere.   And
yet in all thiese thinges, natwithstandynge their obstynate repug-
nance, I have usyde soche attempred moderacion, that yf they can
justly convynce me of any rasshe inordynate extremyte, I wyll
never desire to be favored of your lordeshippe, whiche as I have
allwayes largely founde withowte any demeryte, so I truste never
by noo mysdemeanour to lose ; as knowith Criste, who have your
good lordeshippe in his kepynge.   Frome Seynte Davydes, the vth
daye of Apryll.

Your lordeshyppes to commaunde,

W. Meneven.

The image of Darvel Gatheren, mentioned in the following letter, which appears to
have been an object of great reverence in Wales, was subsequently transported to
London, and in May was publicly burnt in Smithfield, along with friar Forest of
Greenwich, who had been condemned for high treason in denying and opposing the
king's supremacy.   The burning of this image with the friar appears to have created
considerable sensation at the time, and is mentioned by most of the chroniclers.   Hall,
after telling the story of friar Forest, says—" A little before the execution, a huge and
great image was brought to the gallows, which image was brought out of Wales, and of

Welshmen much sought and worshipped. This image was called Darvell Gatheren, and the Welshmen had a prophecy that this image should set a whole Forest a fire, which prophecy now took effect, for he set this friar Forest on fire and consumed him to nothing . . . . . . Upon the gallows that he died on was set up in great letters these verses following :

> " David Darvell Gatheren,
>   As saith the Welshmen,
>   Fetched outlawes out of hell.
>   Now is he come with spere and shilde
>   In harnes to burn in Smithfelde,
>   For in Wales he may not dwell.
>   And Forest the frier,
>   That obstinate lyer,
>   That wilfully shalbe dead,
>   In his contumacie
>   The Gospell doth deny,
>   The kyng to be supreme head."

It would seem by these verses that the image represented a man in armour, or at least armed. Bishop Latimer preached a sermon on this occasion.

XCV.

ELIS PRICE TO CROMWELL.

[From MS. Cotton. Cleop. E. iv. fol. 55*.]

Ryghte honorable and my syngular goode lorde and mayster, all circumstauncys and thankes sett aside, pleasithe yt youre good lordeshipe to be advertisid that where I was constitute and made by youre honorable desire and commaundmente commissarie generall of the dyosese of Saynte Assaph, I have done my dylygens and dutie for the expulsinge and takynge awaye of certen abusions, supersticions, and ipocryses usid within the saide diosece of Saynte Assaph, acordynge to the kynges honorable actes and injunctions therin made. That notwithstondinge, there ys an image of Darvellgadarn within the saide diosece, in whome the people have so greate confidence, hope, and truste, that they cumme daylye a pillgramage unto hym, somme withe kyne, other with oxen or horsis, and the reste withe money, insomuche that there was fyve

or syxe hundrethe pillgrames to a mans estimacion that offered
to the saide image the fifte daie of this presente monethe of Aprill.
The innocente people hathe ben sore aluryd and entisid to worshipe the saide image, insomuche that there is a commyn sayinge
as yet amongist them that whosoever will offer anie thinge to the
saide image of Darvellgadarn, he hathe power to fatche hym or
them that so offers oute of hell when they be dampned.   Therfore, for the reformacion and amendmente of the premisses, I
wolde gladlie knowe by this berer youre honorable pleasure and
will, as knowithe God, who ever preserve your lordeshipe longe
in welthe and honor.   Writen in Northe Wales, the vj. daye of
this presente Aprill.

   Youre bedman and dayelye oratour by dutie,

             ELIS PRICE.

A party of commissioners were, about this time, dispatched towards Wales, who appear to have been chiefly directed against the houses of the different orders of friars,
many of them small establishments, which had been allowed to escape the first act of
suppression.   One of the most active of these commissioners was Richard (suffragan)
bishop of Dover,* and we will break through the strict chronological order of the letters during the present year (1538) in order to follow him, and afterwards a different
party of commissioners, in their several progresses.

XCVI.

RICHARD BISHOP OF DOVER* TO CROMWELL.

[From MS. Cotton. Cleop. E. iv. fol. 212.]

My synguler good lorde, in my umbyll maner pleseyht yt yower

* He signs his name *Richard Doverensis* or *Dovorencis;* and in an authentic document printed at p. 202 of the present volume he is called *Rychard byschop of Dowor*,
and on another occasion (p. 228) by Dr. London *my lord of Dover.*   In the catalogue
of the Cottonian MSS. he is always called *Richard Devereux*, but the *Mr. Rychard
Devourax* mentioned by bishop Barlow (p. 188) must either be another person, or a
mistake of the bishop's.

                *

good lordeschyp to understand, that accordeyng to my dewte at yower commandement I have receyveyd to the kynges heynes use the iiij. howseys off ffreyrs in Boston,* very pore howseys and pore persons, and accordeyng to yower letter I have delyveryd the same howses to master Taverner and master Johnys, servanttes to the kynges grace, with all the pore implementtes for hys money. In my way thederwarde I fonde a howse of Austen ffreyrs in Huntteyngton,† very pore, the which also I receyveyd, and dely-veryd the same to one Phelyp Clampe, one of the kynges ser-vanttes, accordeyng to the kynges plesur as master chanseleres letter of the agmentacyon sygnyfyyd to me. They howseys be all metely ledeyd; I thynke in Hunteyngton abowte viij. foder, and in Boston I thynke in the iiij. howses abowte iiij. schor foder or more. I now am in Lyncolne, where that also I have receyveyde iiij. pore howseys,‡ non thyng lefte but stonys and pore glasse, but metely ledeyd. All the led and bellys I leve to the kynges use; and as for plate allso I save, the which ys very lytyll. Yf that I fynde xij. unc. in a howse, yt ys well; fore the more parte vij. or viij. unc. ys the most. In Lyncolne, in the Grey Freyrs ys a godely condyte, for the which the meyar and the aldermen was with me to make sute to have the condythe into the cete. I kowde nott satysfy them tyll that I promyseyd them to wryght in ther behalfe to yower lordschyp for the same, and so they have a letter of me to yower lordschyp, besecheyng yow to be good lord to them; they orderyd me very jentylly ther. I trosteyd to a made an ende of the vesytacyon: but I am certefyyd that yet ther be stondeyng in the north parte above xx. placeys of freyrs, as in Grantham, in Newarke, in Grymsseby, in Hull, in Beverley, in Scharborow, in Carlehyll, in Lancaster, and in dyverse placeys more, for the which howseys I well serge so that I trost to leve but fewe in Ynglond

* The Monasticon contains accounts of only three houses of friars at Boston in Lin-colnshire, namely, the Black Friars, Grey Friars, and White Friars.

† The priory of Austin canons at Huntingdon is said to have been founded originally in the tenth century. The last prior was Hugh Olives, alias Whitewick.

‡ There were houses of black, grey, white, and Austin friars, in Lincoln, besides a house of friars de Sacco, all which are described in the Monasticon.

before Ester, and I thyngke yt woll be ner Ester or that I can make an ende, besecheyng yower lordschyp to be good lorde for the pore ffreyrs capacytes; they be very pore and can have lytyll serves withowtt ther capacytes. The byschoyppys and curettes be very hard to them, withowtt they have ther capacytes. And, my good lord, I harttely beseche yow be good lord to me for my leveyng in Langley, as all my trost ys in yower lordschyp, and in non oder, and I evar att yower commandemente to the uttermost of my lytyll powre, be goddes grace, hoo evar preserve yower lordschyp to hys hey honor. Wretyn in Lyncolne, thys fyrste Sonday of Lentt, by yower pore servantt and orator,

RICHARD DOVORENC.

To my syngular good
lorde Crumwell lorde
prevy seale thys delyver.

In the next letter we find the Bishop of Dover already on the Welsh border, having probably received new directions from the court.

XCVII.

RICHARD BISHOP OF DOVER TO CROMWELL.

[From MS. Cotton. Cleop. E. IV. p. 250.]

My singular good lorde, in my humely maner plesith yt your good lordechipe to understande, that I have ben at Norhthampton, at Coventre, at Aderstone, at Warwike, at Thelford, at Draytewich, at Wisitor,* and now am at Gloscetur intendyng toward Bristowe. In every place ys povertey and moche schiffte made with suche as theie had before, as yewellys selling, and other schiffte by leasys. But in all thes placys I have sett steys by indenturys making, and the common sealys sequestering, so that

* Worcester.

now thei have no schiffte to make, so that I thinke before the yere be owt ther schall be very fewe howsis abill to lyve, but schall be glade to giffe up their howseis and provide for them selvys otherwise, for their thei schall have no living. As for Gloscetor, wher that now I am, I thinke their be ij. howseis that will give up their howsies, for thei have no living. I schall order them so well as I can, and at my next letter I schall certefey your lordeschipe of them. The cause of my writing now ys for ij. howseis specially; that ys for Aderston,* an howse of Austen freeres, x. mile from. Coventre, and for Wheych. For thes ij. howseis your lordechipe may at your plesure adpoynte to helpe sum to them. At Aderstone, I have adpoynteid the prior to se good serveyd till that I knowe further off your plesure; but all ys gon, so that thei war not abill to make schiffte to paye for my costis, nor to giffe me on peny of the contribucyon to their visitor accustomeyd. That howse ys a propar howse, and certeyne londe longing to yt lieing rownde abowte yt to the valure, as yt ys laten owt by lease, of iiij. markys by yere. All the stuffe ys not worthe xlˢ. beside a chales and a bell, and leade ys non ther. And towcheing Wheych, the which ys the principall cause of my writing, yt ys not abill to contynue a howse of religion to kepe above on freer, for all ys solld. He that was prior, by whom at Hester yow senthe your letters to the balys their to se all their stuffe delyveryd ageyne into the howse, he hathe in lesse than on ʒere that he hathe be prior ther fellyd and solld vij. score good elmys, a chales of gillt of iijˣˣ. unc. and x. unc., a senser of xxxvj. unc., ij. gret brasse pottys eche abull to sethe an holl oxe as men sey, spetys, pannys, and other, so that in the howse ys not left on bede, on schete, on plater or dische, nor for all the promes that be made to your

---

* At Atherstone, in Warwickshire, there was a small priory of friars eremites of the order of St. Augustine, founded in 1375, by Ralph, lord Basset of Draiton. It is stated in the Monasticon that this house was dissolved in the 27 Hen. VIII., which must be an error.

lordeschipe he ys not abill to bring home eny thing ageyne, nor
yet to make a trewe accowntes wher this ys spent by xx. markys
truly. And in his cofer I fowne xj. bullys of the bischopis of Rome,
and above an hunderyd letters of pardons, and in all the bokys in
the quere the bischope of Rome still standing as he did xx. yerys
past. I have chargid the balys that he schall be forthe cumming;
and for the howse I have sett a pore freer to kepe masse ther, and
I have providyd for his borde and leveyng to be payde xvj. a
weke, till your further plesure be knowen in yt. Their be iij.
labur for yt, that ys sir John Russell, schreyve of Wisitor schere,
he ys cum to London to sewe for yt; Mr. Pye; and Mr. Newell,
servant with my lorde of Wisitor, ffor whom at the desyar of my
lorde of Wisitor I spake to your lordescipe, for and excepte he
have yt I thinke he schall lese a mariage of xl. markys by yere.
Your lordeschipe may do your plesure. This ys the substans of
yt. The howse ys mete for no man to dwelle in, withowte gret
costis don on yt. Yt standith in a good ayer, and yt hathe so
many tenauntreys and closeis abowte yt as be laten for v^{li}. by ʒere.
Their be ij. good bellys, a chales, and a fewe vestmentes of litill
valure; the stuffe beside ys not worthe xl^s. Leade ther ys non,
except in ij. gutteres, the which the prior hathe conveyd into the
towne, but yt ys suar. Yt ys metely wodeyd in hege rowys. Here
ys all, beseching your lordeschipe to knowe your plesure, yff eny
thing I schall do in theis ii. howseis. I schall cum within x. mile
of them in my progresse, but what soever yow order for them I
pray yow be so good lorde that my chargis their may be payde off
the stuffe and the dewteis of the howseis, and that I may be dischargid of the borde and wagis for the freer at Wheich, for I had
neither peny nor penyworthe in eny off them. Also, my lorde, I
beseche yow to sende me your plesure yff that I schall medill with
the howse of wheite freeres in Winchester.* I here that their be
no freeres, and whether eny ordenans be made by the kingis grace

---

* At Winchester there was a priory of Carmelite or white friars, founded in 1278,
which stood opposite the church of St. Michael, but of which very little is known.

or yow I knowe not. Your plesure in theis, my lorde, I hartely beseche yow, and I ever at your commandment by Goddis grace, hoo preserve yow to heis hei honor. This xxiij. day of Maye. From Gloscetur, by your servant and orator,

RICHARD DOVORENS.

It seems by the date of the following letter that the bishop remained several weeks occupied between Gloucester and Bristol. It appears, however, that during this period he had visited Marlborough and Winchester, and perhaps also some other places in that part of the country.

XCVIII.

RICHARD BISHOP OF DOVER TO CROMWELL.

[From MS. Cotton. Cleop. E. iv. fol. 251.]

My synguler good lorde, my dewte presupposyd, pleseythe yt yower good lordeschype to understande, that before I receyvyd yower letter by my servantt, I had beyn in Brystowe at the Whyte Fryers,* and also in ij. howsys of Glowsetur, and ther for the gret clamor that was for dettes ther, I had men assyngneyd by the mayeres of bothe towneys to prise suche as was in thoys iij. howsys, and solde all and payd the dettes, as by my accounttes yt shall appere, and the howsys put in saffe custody tyll the kynges plesur be forther knowyn. The substans in the more parte of the howsys ys very small; in dyverse placeys lytyll more than the dettes; and the clamor of pore men to whom the monye ys oweynge ys to tedyus. Wherfor thys order I toke tyll yower letter cam specyally, where that the dettes were moche. But nowe that I knowe your forther plesur, I shall folowe yower commandement so nere as I can, and accordeynge to yt I have begon with the Grey Fryers in Glowsetur.† And because I am in dowte off

---

* The priory of the Carmelites or White Friars in Gloucester, a small house, was founded in the latter part of the reign of Henry III.

† There was in Gloucester a house of Grey or Franciscan Friars, or Friars Minors, which existed as early as the year 1268, but the date of its foundation is uncertain.

my returne to London, I sende to yow here the copys off every
indenter off the inventorys off every howse that hathe gyffyn up into
the kynges hondes, because yf that yt shall forten in the tyme any
howse by the kynges grace or yow to be set any order for yt, that ye
maye knowe the order and substans off that howse by theys copys.
And where that yt hathe pleseyd yower lordeschype to wryght
to me, as ye juge, that thowgh I have changeyd my habet, I have
not changeyd my fryeres hartt, goode my lorde, juge me not so,
for God shall be my juge, my fryers hart was gone ij. yeres befor
my habet, saveynge only my leveynge; but the favor that I have
schewyd hathe not be for my fryers hartt, but to brynge all
thynges with the moste quiet to passe; and also tyll now that
yower honorabull letter cam to me, I never koulde perseyve any
thynge of yower plesur, but ever fereyd that yf I wer to quike,
that I shulde offende yower lordeschype, the whyche I wolde not by
my wyll for all that I am abull to make in the worlde. But yff
that I myght know that I shulde not offende the kynges grace
nor yower lordeschype, I koulde by juste and fayer menys, and do
no wronge, dyspache a gret parte off the fryeres in Ynglonde, or
my yere off vysytacyon was endeyd, so that I myght have sum
lyberte to lycens them to change ther habettes after ther howsys
were gyffyn up. For off trewthe ther harttes be clene from the
relygyon the more parte, so they myght change ther cotes, the
whyche they be not abull to paye for, for they have no thenge. I
harttely beseche yower lordeschype be good lorde to theys pore
men that have gyffyn up ther howsys that they may have sum
dyscharge. I sende ther namys here incloseyd. And where yower
lordschype noteythe that I shulde sum thinge wryght in commen-
dacyon of the fryers, and suffer sum to tery at mennys desyer, the
trewthe ys, I have so don because that I wolde not be taken to
schewe them extremyte, but rather favor. But in my besynes
amonge them, ther appereythe lytyll favor, for where that I fynde
them fawte, I declare ther fawttes after suche facyon that they
rather woll gyffe up the howsys, than I shulde declare ther deme-

nors, as by that menys I have receyvyd iij. howsys sythe that I wroght laste to yower lordeschype, the whyche I thynke wolde not a lytyll a moveyd yower lordschype, yff ye had knowen the order off them; sum stekeynge faste in wyndowys nakeyd goynge to drabbes, so that the peler was fayne to be sawyde to have hym owte; sum beynge plucked from under drabbes beddes; sum feytynge so that the knyffe hathe stoken in the bone; wythe suche other praty besynes, off the whyche I have to moche. But on I thynke ye shulde doo a goode dede to wryght to the mayer of Marleburthe, that he sumwhat loke on a fryer ther that ys in prison for a mayde chylde off x. or xi. yeres of age, whom he useyd nowtely; they wolde that I shulde a delyveryd hym at my beynge ther, but master Yorke and I spake with the chylde and here fryndes, so that the mater appereyd so that I wolde not medell with the fryer. As for the Blacke Fryers of Wynchester,* I lefte yt with all the stuffe in a seculer mannys handdes, and gave but lycens to the prior to say masse ther tyll that I sent hym my letter ageyn, the whyche nowe I have senth to advoyde hym thense.

Sythe that I last wroght to yower lordschype I have receyvyd iiij. howsys into the kynges handdes. The Whyte Fryeres in Brystowe,† the whyche all that was in yt ys lytyll more than payd the dettes. Yt ys a goodly howse in byldeynge, mete for a gret man, no renttes but ther gardens. Ther ys a chapell and an yle off the chyrche, and dyverse gutteres, spowtes, and condytes, lede; the reste all tylle and slate. A goodly laver and condyte cumynge to yt. Thys howse was in dett above xvj^{li}. of the whyche payd viij^{li}., the rest dyschargeyd by plegeys. In Glowsetur I have dyschargeyd iij. howseys, as by the mayer and aldermennys handes

---

* The house of Black or Dominican Friars in Winchester, was founded by Peter de Rupibus, or Derroches, bishop of Winchester, in 1221.

† I find no account of this house in the Monasticon. It was against the order of the friars to possess lands; but the gardens, which they let out on leases, were allowed to pass by a quibble.

ye may perseyve. The Blacke Fryers * ys a proper lytyll howse; lytyll led but on yle; no renttes, but ther gardens, the whyche master Bell the alderman hathe in lese under ther convente sell for many yeres, and I harttely desyer yow be good lorde to hym that he also may have that howse. He dothe moche goode in that towne amonge the pore pepull, setteynge many on worke, above iij. hunderyd dayly; and I am moche bownde to hym for heys gret comfort in all my besynes ther at bothe tymys, and for the more parte I have beyn at borde with hym. I beseche youe be good lorde to hym. The Grey Fryers ys a goodly howse, moche off yt new byldeyd, specyally the chyrche, quere, and dorter; the rest small logeynges; dyverse leseys owt for yeres off logeynges and gardens; no led but a condyte and small gutturs. The Whyte Fryeres but a small howse, and in decay, and sum howseys taken downe and solde; no renttes but xx^s. by yere, and that ys taken for xx. yeres befor, off the wyche ix. or x. yere to cum. Yonge Thomas Bell hathe parte off the gardens off yt for yeres. I wold he myght have that howse, yf yt pleseyd the kynges grace and yower lordschype. My singuler goode lorde, I mekely beseche yow pardon me of my rude and longe wrytynge, and yff yt plese yow to be good lorde to me to sende the dyscharge for the fryeres and yower forther plesur by thys brynger, he shall sende yt to me to Ludlowe or Harforde † thys nexte weke, and I ever yower orator to Jhesu, whom I hartely beseche to gyve me that grace to do that thynge that shall be to hys hey honor, to the kynges graceys plesur and yowers, to the whyche I woll appley my selfe to the uttermost of my pore.

Yowr servantt and orator,
RICHARD DOVORENS.

My gude lorde, if that ȝe wold be so gode lord to me to send to

---

* The house of the black or Dominican friars in Gloucester was founded about 1239. The last prior was John Raynolds.

† Hereford.

me a hunderyd worans for the delyverans of a hunderyd ffreeres
that schall gyff up ther howseys in thys progresse, and leve a
space for ther nameys, I woll brynge ʒow the nameys and place
at my returne.   And, gode my lord, I beseche ʒou thynke noht
that I am any feynour to ʒow, for I insuer ʒow I am noʒt, but am
and woll be as trew and as secrete to ʒow as any servantt that ʒe
have, and as glad to do that thyng that schuld plese God specyally
and the kynges grace and ʒow.   I wolde do all thynges with so
moche quiet and withowt any clamor so ner as I know; if that I
knew ʒower plesur, ther schall no parte be left undon so ner as I
may.   My commyscyon gyffyht me no auctoryte to put any owte
withowte they gyff up ther howseys; but if that I knew ʒower
plesur, I may fynde causeys suffycyent to put them owte of many
placeys, for ther mysleveyng and for disobeyyng the instruccyons
and the kynges actes.

[At] Winchelse, accordeyng to ʒower commandement, I have
sold the stuff; the howse is at the kynges commandement and
yowres.

To my synguler goode lorde
Crumwell, lorde prevy seale,
be thys delyveryd with
honor.

(Inclosure.)

TO MY SYNGULER GOODE LORD CRUMWELL, LORDE PREVY SEALE.

I beseche yower lordeschype to have dyscharge for theys fryers to change ther
apparell.

The Blacke Fryers of Glosseter.

Fryer Johan Raynoldes, bachyler in dyvynyte, <i>prior nuper.</i>
Fryer Johan Howper.
Fryer Rychard Bylond.
Fryer Wyllyam Swan.
Fryer Wyllyam Walton.
Fryer Raffe Howell.
Fryer Thomas Meykyns.

The Whyte of Gloseter.

Fryer Thomas Knyght.
Fryer Wyllyam Plesans.
Fryer Henry Byschewode.

The Grey Fryers off Gloseter.

Fryer Wyllyam Lyghtfote.
Fryer Johan Barclaye.
Fryer Henry Jaket.
Fryer George Coper.
Fryer Johan Rebull.

The Whyte Fryers of Brystowe.

Fryer Thomas Wraxall.
Fryer Thomas Clyfton.
Fryer Symon Vagan.
Fryer Johan Hoper.

The Whyte Fryeres of Marlysborowe.*

Fryer Thomas Goldysborowe.
Fryer Crystofer Hyll.
Fryer Martyn Brasy.
Fryer Austen More.
Fryer Johan Arnolde.

The Grey Fryers off Wynchester. *

Fryer Thomas Parys.
Fryer Wyllyam Kenett.
Fryer Rycharde Forde.

The Austen Fryers off Wynchester.†

Fryer Johan Wyhtt.

The Blacke Fryers off Wynchester.

Fryer Rycharde Chessam, doctor of dyvynyte, prior.
Fryer Robarde Browne.
Fryer Johan George.
Fryer Nycholas Barker.
Fryer Johan Ynggylbye.
Fryer Robarde Haynys.

* The house of the white friars in Marlborough was founded by two merchants in 1316.

I wante iij. or iiij. freeres nameys of the Austen and Wheyte Freeres of Winchester.
I lefte the boke at hom. If ye wold be so gode to send to me iij. or iiij. waranttes
with a space for ther namys, I wer bonde to yow.

My lorde, I intende, God willing, your plesure not knowen to the contrary, to ride
now to Bristow, to Winchester, to Chichester, to Arrondell, to Sowthamton, to Salis-
bery, and so all the west contre within xvj. mile of the Mownthe, and so returne into
Walys, and cum ageyne to Ludlowe and to Schrewisbery, and so to Denbith and to
Bangar, and so to Westchester and to Lancaster, and so all the northe abowthe or
I returne. In all placeys wher as yet I have ben I have made inventory indenteid,
and seleyd up their common sealys so that thei shall sell or alienate nomore of their
jewellys nor other stuffe, wherfor I am suar that within a yere the more parte shall be
fayne to giffe up their howseis for povertey. I beseche your lordechipe that my
servant may knowe your plesure whether he shall adwaythe for a letter from your
lordeschipe or no.

XCIX.

REPORT OF THE SURRENDER OF THE FRIARS GLOUCESTER.

[From MS. Cotton. Cleop. E. iv. fol. 252.*]

Memorandum, thys xxviij. day of Julii, in the xxx. yer of ower
most dred soveren lord kyng Henry the viij^{te}, Rychard byschop of
Dowor and vesytor under the lord prevy selle for the kynges grace
was in Glowsetur, and ther befor the meyar and aldermen in the
howseys of freeres ther at ij. tymeys in ij. days putt the seyd freeres
att ther lyberteys, whether they vold contynew in ther howseys and
kepe ther relygyon and injuxcyons accordeyng to the same, or ellys
gyff ther howseys into the kynges handdes. The injuxcyons he
ther declareyd among them, the whyche war thowthe by the seyd
meyar and aldermen to be good and resonabyll, and also the seyd
freeres seyd that they war accordeyng to ther rewlys, yet as the

* The convent of the Grey Friars at Winchester is said to have been founded by
Edward III.

† This house stood outside the town : the Austin friars settled here in the time of
Edward I.

warlde ys nowe they war nott abull to kepe them and leffe in ther howseys, wherfore voluntaryly they gaffe ther howseys into the vesytores handes to the kynges use. The vesytor seyd to them, " thynke not, nor hereafter reportt nott, that ye be suppresseyd, for I have noo suche auctoryte to suppresse yow, but only to reforme yow, wherfor yf ye woll be reformeyd accordeyng to good order, ye may contynew for all me." They seyd they war nott abull to contynew. Wherfor the vesytor toke ther howseys, and charytabully delyveryd them, and gaff them letteres to vesyte ther fryndes, and so to goo to oder howseys, with the whyche they war wery well contentt, and soo departeyd. Thys whe the seyd meyar and aldermen testyfy by ower handes subscrybeyd.

Maister WYLLYAM HASARD, meyr.

Master WYLYAM MATHEW, aldermon.

Mr. THOMAS BELL the elder, alderman.

THOMAS PAYNE, alderman.

The next letter traces the visitors in their progress to Shrewsbury, where they were preparing to enter Wales.

C.

RICHARD BISHOP OF DOVER TO CROMWELL.

[From MS. Cotton. Cleop. E. IV. fol. 248.]

My synguler good lord, in my humble maner pleseythe yt yower lordschype to understande, that sythe I wroght to yow from Glosetur I have taken into the kynges handdes ij. conventes in Worsetur,* on in Brygenorthe,† on in Atherston, and on in Lechefyld,‡

---

* Leland speaks of a house of black friars at Worcester. He also mentions the Grey Friars, "without St. Martin's Gate," founded by the earls of Warwick in the thirteenth century. In the 31 Hen. VIII. the site of the latter house was granted to the bailiffs and citizens.

† There was in Bridgenorth a house of grey friars founded in the reign of Henry VI. by John Talbot earl of Shrewsbury.

‡ At Litchfield there was a house of grey friars founded about the year 1229.

of the whyche I wroght to yower lordschype by yower servant Holt
from Lechefylde. Sythe I have taken into the kynges handdes
ij. conventes in Stafforde,* on in Newcastell Underlyne,† and ij.
in Schrewysbery, and ther on standeytht styll; the occasyon of it
standeynge is because that I alwaye have declaryd that I had no
commyssyon to suppresse no howse, nor non I dede suppresse, but
suche as was not abull to lyve. Yff they gave ther howseys into
the kynges handdes for poverte, I receyveyd them, and elles
non. Now for that howse in Schrewysbery that standeyth, yt
ys of the blacke fryeres,‡ and I cowde fynde no gret cause in
them to cause them to gyve up. And also yt schall declare that I
do not suppresse the howsys, but suche as gyve up, seynge that
sum stande, and not all put downe. To wryght to yower lordschype
the copys of all the howsys and the inventorys of the same I have
no leyser, and I am lothe to sende them withowte yt war be my
servant, that I myght have sum answer of yower plesur agayn,
and my servanttes be seke, so that I have non to sende; but I
trust to se yower lordschype within a veke, and be that tyme I
trust to make an ende in all Walys. Sumwhat to certyfye yower
lordeschype of the state off suche as I have receyveyd sythe that I
wrote to yow towcheynge Stafforde, the Austen Fryeres ther ys a
pore howse, with small implementes, no jwelles but on lytyll
chales, no led in the howse, in rentes by yere ljs. viijd. The Graye
Fryeres ther, halfe the quere ledeyd and a chapell, small implementes, no plate but a chales and vj. small sponys, in renttes
xxvjs. iiijd. The Blacke Fryeres in Newecastell Underlyne, all
in ruyne, and a pore howse, the quere ledeyd and the cloeyster

---

* A house of grey or Franciscan friars existed at Stafford early in the reign of
Edward I. There was also a house of Austin friars, founded about 1344, in the south
suburb called Forbrugge.

† Leland, speaking of Newcastle-under-Line, says " there was an house of black
friars in the south end of the town."

‡ The Black Friars in Shrewsbury appears to have been founded about the sixth
year of the reign of Henry III.

led redy to fall downe, the reste slate and schyngyll; in fermys
by yere xl^s.   On master Broke hathe of late fownde the menys
with the prior to gett of hym the more parte of they howseys and
grownde ther by iij. leseys, and that for lytyll money; he wolde
a gyve me golde to a grantteyd to hys leseys, but I toke no peny
of hym nor of non other, nor non woll.   Yff he have thoys leseys,
ther ys lytyll besyde, for he hathe lyberte allmost in all.   Ther
ys a proper wode, but] he hathe all in lese.   No sylver above xiij.
ounce.   In Schrewysbery be iij. howsys.   The Blacke Fryeres
stande, as before I have wrytyn.   The graye fryeres* had conveyd all, and made a grett rumor in the towne, for the whyche
they war glade to gyve up all into the kynges handdes; that ys a
proper howse, small implementtes, no jwelles but a plate crosse
sylver, and on lytyll chales of lytyll valur; no renttes but ther
howse and abowte iij. or iiij. acores of eryabull londe lyeynge to
yt.   The Austen Fryeres, † a howse all in ruyne, and the more
parte falleynge downe; no thynge in that howse, not in all to the
valur off iiij. nobylles, in vestementes, copys, brasse, pewter, and
all other stuffe; no chales to sey masse, nor non wolde trust
the prior to lende hym any; no fryeres ther but the prior, a man
leke to be in a fransey,‡ and ij. Erysche§ men.   I have dyschargeyd
the prior of heys offys, and sent the ij. Erysche men into ther
owyn contre, and so take the howse into the kynges handdes.
The rentes be iiij. markes by yere.

Thys ys the holl state of all the conventes that as yet I have
receyveyd, of the whyche at more large and clerenes I shall schewe
to yow at my cumynge.   I ryde thys day toward Westechester,
and so into Walys.   My synguler good lorde, I beseche youe

---

* The Grey Friars in Shrewsbury was standing in the earliest half of the thirteenth
century, but its history is very obscure.   It was the burial place of the lady Hawisia
wife of John de Charlton first earl of Powis, and he, having probably been a benefactor,
came at a later period to be looked on as the founder.

† Leland says that the Austin Friars in Shrewsbury was a foundation " of the
Staffordes."

‡ Frenzy.   § Irish.

pardon me of my rude wrytynge, and yf that I do not my dewte as that I owte to do, I beseche youe pardon me, for my hart and intente ys to do that thynge that shulde specyally plese God, the kynges grace, and yower lordschype, accordeynge to my dewte; also besechynge yower lordschype, that yf before my cumynge ther be any order taken for Newecastell Underlyne, that ye wolde be good lorde to on master Johan Bothe, a servant of the kynges graces, the whyche ys a grett bylder in theys partes, that he myght for money have the slate and schyngyll ther; for ther ys no other to be don with the more parte of that howse, but save the lede and slate, and take the profete of the grownde. That master Bothe for yower sake scheuyd me many plesures, and gave me venyson; wherefor I may no lesse do but wryght to yower lordeschype, besecheynge yow to be good lorde to hym, an I ever yower orator to Jhesu, who preserve yower lordschype. Thys xiij[th] day of August. From Schrewysbery. By yower bedeman and servantt,

RICHARD DOVORENC.

I receyvyd non word from ȝower lordschyp sythe that I receyvyd ȝower letter by my servanth, wretyn in Petworth, the xxviij. day of Julii. I make promes to the freeres that gyff up ther how-seys that I shall send to them waranttes ffor ther abettes befor Myhelmas, and in the tyme I gyff them letters to vesyte ther frynddes.

While the visitors were entering Wales, we meet with another letter from bishop Barlow, which is interesting as picturing the state of the country at that time.

CI.

BISHOP BARLOW TO CROMWELL.

[From MS. Cotton. Cleop. E. iv. fol. 260.]

After my right humble commendacions, I considere my dutie

tadvertise your lordship, that accordinge to the purporte of your
lettres latly receaved, signifienge the kynges highnes pleasour for
the removynge of ydolotrous abused ymages, wherewith this contrey horribly dyd abounde, in satisfyenge of the same I have diligently done myne endevour, and that quyetly every where withyn
my diocesse unresisted, without tumulte, commotion, or disturb-
ance, with no frustrate expectacion (as I trust) of forther effectuall
redresse, yn all causes of Christen religyon and godly purposes of
the kynges most honorable and no lesse profitable proceadinges.
The people now sensibly seinge the longe obscured veryte manyfestly to display her brightnesse, wherby their inveterate accustomed supersticion apparantly detected, all popish delusions shall
sone be defaced, so that erudityon, the parente of vertue and un-
fallible foundacion of all ordynate pollecye, which by the kynges
most renowmed fortherance beawtyfully florisheth yn all other his
royall domynions, might also be planted here in his graces principa-
lyte of Wales, where knowlege utterly unknowen, scyence ys litle
regarded, barberouse ignorance pyteously pleatinge in possession,
notwithstandinge wolde easely be redressed, without hyndraunce
of the kynges advauntage, yee with notable augmentacion of his
most worthy honour, small expences therto requysite of any partie,
with moch commodytie of many, to the incommoditie of none
that preferre an unyversall weale before a private sensuall pleasure. In case my peticion thorow your good lordships medyacion
maye be attayned of the kynges highnes, for the translacion of the
see to Kermerddyn, and transposinge of Abergwilly college to
Brecknok, the princypall townes of Sowthwales, where provision
had for lernynge as well yn gramer as yn other scyences and knowlege of Scripture, the Welsch rudenesse wolde sone be framed to
English cyvilitie, and their corrupte capacyties easely reformed
with godly intelligens, which moveth me to be so instante a suter
and a contynuall peticyoner, especyally for the translacion of the
see, beinge sytuated in soch a desolate angle and in so rare a
frequented place (excepte of vacabounde pilgremes), that evill

disposed persons, unwillinge to do good, maye lurke there at lybertye in secrete withowt restraynte, and they that wolde fayne do well can have no convenyente oportunyte profitablie to utter their well doinge to the commodytie of the comon weale. Which, yf there were no nother causes, as ther be ynfinyte more reasonable then maye be justly disalowed, and so evydente that they can not be shadowed, yet yt mighte seme sufficient necessarylie to persuade a translacion of the see. But forthermoare, yt hath be allwayes estemed a delycate doughter of Rome, naturally resemblinge her mother in shamelesse confucion, and lyke qualified with other perverse properties of execrable malignitie, as ungodly ymage service, abhomynable ydolatrye, and lycentiouse lybertie of dishonest lyvinge, popish pilgremages, disceatefull pardons, and fayned indulgences, in whose lawde yt ys written,

Roma semel quantum dat bis Menevia tantum.

And as the bisshop of Rome crepte up by policye, and rayninge by tyranny was more then man, little lesse then God, whose authorytie never knowen was contynually obeyed, no reason admitted to aske why, but as he wold so did yt avayle, even thus hath our Welsh David byn avaunced to be patrone of Wales, as he that had signiory not only in erth, by lawles pryveleged exempcions, but power also in heven to geve it whom he wold, to discharge hell, to emptie purgatory, to pardon synne, to release payne, yee to save his beneficiall frendes, to curse and kyll his unfavorable adversaries, whose legende ys so uncerten of trueth, and certenly full of lyes, that not only his sayntly holynesse ys to be suspected, but rather to be dowted whether any soch person was ever bisshop there, as ys surmysed, experyence in semblable cases latly tryed owte by Dervelgadern,* Conoch, and soch other Welsch godes, antique gargels of ydolatry. And verely, yf credence ought to be geven to the most auntyente writinges that can

---

* See before, p. 190, of the present volume.

be exhibited, wherof I have certen pamflettes testifyeng antiquitie,
both in barbarouse letters and incongrue Latyne, agreable to the
maners of that season, also mencyonynge soch enormyous fas-
chion, that scarsly Rome myght be comparable with saynte Davids
terrytorye concernynge presumptuous usurpacyon apon their
princes, crafty yncrochinge of possessions, subtyle defeatinge of
enherytances, extorcion, brybery, symonye, heresie, ydolatrye,
supersticion, etc.   Wherfore, consideringe that where Rome with
all her popish pageantes (praysed be God!) thorow the kynges
most prudente provysyon ys exiled forth of England, the unfayned
fydelitie of myne allegeaunce enforseth me to wysh all memoryall
monymentes of her popetry yn lyke maner to be banyshed owt of
Wales, which hytherto remaynynge yn the terrytory of S. David,
unneth maye be extincte without translacion of the see.   For
excepte the manyfolde occasions of ydolatrous infidelytie and
papisticall practyses (notwithstandynge compulsory inhibycions
and tongue professions) be clerely abolyshed, shall allwayes reno-
vate new fangled ymaginacions to contrefayte the olde exercysed
wickednes.   Wherin reducynge to remembraunce the prysed
memoryes and perpetuall renowned factes of the famouse princes
of Israel, which did not only abarre ydolatrye and other ungodly-
nesse, but utterly abolished all occasyons of the same, lykewise
notifyenge their terreble reproches and aggravated punyshmentes
that were neglygent, I dowte not but that my supplyante sute
shall seme reasonable.   And though peraventure some will objecte the contrarye, the causes not prepensed, which partly I have
uttered yn these and other my former letters, omittinge the resydew, lest I shuld molest your lordship; yet havinge the kynges
most benynge and gracyous favour with your assistente supportacion, I trust so to justifie the equytie of my peticion that no adver-
sarye shalbe able to emblemish yt.   And yf urgente ymportunytie
of hasty sute shall neade excuse in this behalfe, I have sufficiently
to allege the importable charge and costly exspences of a sumptuous buyldynge (a comorthe latlye graunted for the same), which

bestowed yn Kermerddyn or some other frequented place, myght be pleasante, profitable, and commodyous for the kynges subjectes, whereas other wyse yt shalbe wasted yn vayne and unprofitably perysh in a barbarous desolate corner, as knoweth our Lorde, who have you in his tuicion. From Lantfey,* the xvjth daye of August.

Your lordeshyppes to commaund,

W. MENEVEN.

CII.

RICHARD BISHOP OF DOVER TO CROMWELL.

[From MS. Cotton. Cleop. E. iv. fol. 263.]

My synguler goode lorde, my dewte presupposeyd, pleseyth yt yower good lordschype to understond, that sythe I departyd from yow I have receyveyd to the kynges use xxviij^{ti}. conventes, as by a byll here incloseyd yt dothe appere, of the whyche before I have wrytyn to yower lordschype. The copys of the inventores of dyverse conventes, and also the testymonyalles of ther relesseys, subscrybyd with the handes of the wyttenesseys, of the rest that yet I have not sent to youe before I sende here now, noteyd on the backes of the inventores of ther value yerly so ner as I can knowe. Goode my lorde, I praye yow be good lorde to me, that the waranttes for ther habettes maye be had accordeynge to my promes, for they may not be sufferyd to saye masse abrode in chyrchys tyll they have ther exempcyons. I have wreten to dyverse of the byschoppes, and with dyverse I have spokyn, to lycens them tyll after Mychelmas, and at that tyme I have promyseyd to sende ther lycens to certen placeys wher they shall have them fre, for the more parte of them have no peny to paye

---

* Llanfey castle, in Pembrokeshire, was one of the residences of the bishops of St. David's.

for the charge of them. In many placeys ther ys moche clamor for dettes of conventtes, so that withowte ye be goode lorde to pore men, many shall lese moche moneye by the fryeres, the whyche woll make a grett clamor amonge the pepull, for now I have moche besynes to satysfye the pepull for dettes. They say that yt ys not the kynges plesur that pore men shulde lose ther monye, with manye worddes; but by feyer menys I satysfye them; sum I make schyfte and pay, sum I satysfye with worddes, for in dyverse placeys all the stuffe in the howseys ys not abull to pay the dettes. I wroght to yower lordschype for ij. howseys in Schrewysbery. The Blacke Fryeres yet standeythe, and for the contynewans of that shall be made moche labour to yow. I praye yow grauntt nott but as I shall order that accordeynge to my commyssyon, for the standeynge of that makeythe me to have more besynes in dyverse placeys than I schulde have. Also ther ys a howse of Austen fryers, that I dyschargeyd the prior, and sent the ij. Yeryschemen into ther owyn contreys; ther war no more at hom ther, and all was gone, and all the more parte of the howseys in falleynge downe, and non chales to say masse, nor no man wolde trust them to lende them any. By ther inventory ye shall see ther substans. I here that the prior ys cum to London, to sew for hys howse agayne; yt wer pety that he shulde spede. Theys ij. sutes I wolde gladly have recysteyd. Also ther be iij. conventes yt in Brystowe; as for the Blacke be redy to gyve up, but the other ij. be styffe and bere them sore be gret favor. The Gray Fryeres, by reson that the warden ys warden of Reche-monde and ys in favor by reson of that, yet for all hys grett port I thynke hym xx. merke in dett, and not abull to paye yt. The Austen fryer, by reson of a grantt that he hathe of the kynges grace for terme of hys lyffe, by the whyche he thynkeyht that he may sell the howse and all, for the plate ys all solde and allso the tymber that grewe abowte the howse, so that he hathe within iij. yeres taken above a hunderyd markes of plate and tymber and other implementes, so that almost all ys gon. Yf yt wolde

plese yow to sende yower plesur by thys bryngar of theys ij. conventes in Brystowe, in my cumynge home I shall cum within x.
myle of Brystowe, and so I wolde thether to fynysche all thoys
partes; and so I wolde to Salysbury, and other ther, yf that I
knewe yow[er] plesur.   In many placeys I fynde but on lytyll
chales, and also in many placeys the substans in plege.   Suche
small chales and suche plegeys as be better than they ley for, I
pay the money, and receyve the pleges to the kynges use, and
suche I brynge with me.   I have chales bothe of tynne and coper,
plate in sum placeys I fynde non.   Goode my lorde, I beseche
yow be so goode lorde to me to sende me sum byll of yower plesur.
I had no worde from yow thys v. wekes.   I wold sende to yow dyverse relykes, but they wer to comeres to cary.   I have Malkows
ere that Peter stroke of, as yt ys wrytyn, and a м. as trewe as
that, but the holyest relyke in all Northe Walys I sende to yow
here ; ther may no man kysse that but he muste knele so sone as
he se yt, thowgh yt war in the fowleest place in all the contre,
and he must kys every stone, for in eche ys gret pardon.   After
that he hathe kyssyd yt he must pay a met of corne, or a chese
of a grote, or iiij^d. for yt.   Yt was worthe to the fryeres in
Bangor,* with another image, the whyche I also have closeyd up,
xx. markes by yere in corne, chese, catell, and money.   Yf that
I shulde wryght of all suche ymages at that ydolatre hathe be
useyd, that wold take a schete of paper, the whyche I have
avoydeyd.   I am now in Harford-est, wher that I have be thys
iij. days, and have had moche besynes to brynge my purpose to
passe, by reson of the Graye Fryeres.   With hom in every place
I have moche besynes, and also with an ancar in that howse; but
at the last I have my purpose, as by ther relesseys ye may perseyve, the whyche I send here, besechyng yower lordschype to be
good lorde to the mayeres and balys of suche cetes and towneys
as I have be in.   I have fownde them very goode, and dylygent

---

* There was a house of black friars at Bangor, founded at the beginning of the fourteenth century.

to do suche thynges as I have desyeryd them. And also I praye you be good lorde to yower servant master Holt, and to master . . . ; they have moche comforteyd me. I also am desyeryd be many other of the kynges servanttes to wryght for them; and dyverse be so inportune on me to wryght, that I can not voyde them, tyll that I promyse to wryght. Sum woll gyve me xx. nobylls, sum more, but I have taken no peny of any, nor non I woll take. On Johan Turner, the man of the garde at Ludlowe, sore laboryd to me to wryght. And thys daye I ryde to Brekenocke, and so to Carmarden and to Harforde-west, and so over to Sent Myhelles Mownte, and so brynge all Cornewall and Denschyar with me. Besechynge yower lordschype to sende me yower pleser of Brystowe, Sowthehampton, Salysbury, and other, and I ever yower orator to Jhesu, who preserve yow. Thys xxvij. daye of August. Wreten from Harforde-est, by yower servantt,

RICHARD DOVORENC.

I sende the namys of them that schuld have warantes for ther apparell.

We now leave the bishop of Dover, to follow the commissioners who during the summer and autumn of this year visited the monastic houses in the southern and south-western counties, among whom one of the most active was Dr. John London. He appears also to have begun his progress in the midland counties, but we find him first at Oxford.

CIII.

DR. LONDON TO CROMWELL.

[From MS. Cotton. Cleop. E. iv. fol. 237.]

My most humble dewtye observyd unto your gudde lordeshippe, with my assurede prayer and faithfull service during my liff. I

have taken the surrendres of Kyme,* Noncotton,† Irforthe,‡
Fosse,§ and Hevenynges.‖ Altho universally in every place re-
ligiose persons makith ther hondes, as they have done lardgely in
every oon of thees howses, yit have I lefte thees howsys clerly
owt of dett, have rewardyd them honestly towardes ther apparell,
payd all servantes wages, with rewardes convenyent, left the
howsys undefacyd, bellys and ledde reservyd to the kinges majestie
thorowly, and yet have I all that litill plate was lefte with som
monye above all costes and chardges, wiche I shall dispache my
hondes of as sone as I may convenyently send it with the plate to
Mr. Thackre. Mr. Johan Hennage, Mr. Wisman, and M. Cotton
wer with me at every of these howsys, and we have commytt the
custodyes of thes howsys with the evydenses perteynyng unto the
same, as we wer commaundyd by your lordeships letters ; Hevenynges, wher moche wast ys made in the woddes, to Mr. Johan
Hennage, depute for sir Thomas Hennage ; Noncotton to M.
Skipwith ; Kyme to the bayliff ther, for my lord Talbos ; Irforde
to M. Turwhyte ; and Fosse, a beggerly power ruynose howse, to
M. Philippe Hobye. Many of thes nonnys wer professyd at x.
and xij. yeres of age, as they do reportt, and after they knew the
frayltie of ther bodies, and com to rypar age, lyvide in unperfytt
chastitie, and now be wonderfull gladde of thys late ordinance it
pleasyd the kinges majestie to mak in hys high cowrt of parlyament, declaring suche as wer professyd befor the age of xxj. to be
at lybertie to marye if they will, and do pray right hartely for the

    * Kyme, in Lincolnshire, a priory founded by Philip de Kyme, in the reign of
Henry II. The last prior was Ralph Fairfax.

    † Nun Coton, or Cotham, in Lincolnshire, was a small house of Cistercian nuns,
founded in the first half of the twelfth century.

    ‡ The Premonstratensian nunnery of Irford in Lincolnshire, was founded by Robert
de Albini in the time of Henry II. The surrender in the Augmentation Office is dated
July 8.

    § The nunnery of Fosse, near Torkesey in Lincolnshire, was founded by the towns-
men of Torkesey, in the reign of king John. The last prioress was Agnes Marr.

    ‖ Hevenynge, or Heyninges, was a small nunnery in the parish of Lea in Lincoln-
shire, founded about A.D. 1180. The site was granted in the 31 Hen. VIII.

kinges majestie. I perceyve many of the other sortt, monkes and chanons, wiche be yonge lustie men, all ways fatt fedde, lyving in ydelnes and at rest, be sore perplexide that now being prestes they may nott retorn and marye. Most partt of them be no thing lernyd, nor apte therto, and therby in moche warsse case. I have geven as well to sondrie of them, as to ther masters, suche power counsell as I myȝt do, and have advisede them that wher they be nother lernyd nor apte unto the same, to torne som of ther seremonyns of ydilnes unto som bodely exercise, and nott to sytt all day lurking in the cloister ydellye. After I hadde don with those v. places in Lincoln shyer, Mr. Freman browȝt me a commission for the Charterhowse in Notingam shyer callyd Bow-vale,* and for a howse of chanons callyd Newstede.† Of Bow-vale, sir Johan Hussey hathe the custodi, and sir Johan Beryn of Newstede. We founde the prior of the Charterhowse in hys shortt gowen and velvytt cappe, redy befor our commyng, and the proctor of that howse in lyke apparell the next day following. I think it were harde to geve so manye ageu into these howseys I have be att as I have dispacchyd, ffor in every howse, as well of men as of wemen, they be in maner all gon that nyȝt I have taken ther surrendre, and streightway in new apparell. Now I have done in all those howsys acording to the kinges highnes commis-sions, and shalbe at all owors redy to the best of my litell power to do suche farther service as may lye in me, acording to my most bounden dewtie, by the helpe of almyȝtie Jhesus, who with increse of moche honour long preserve your gudde lorde-shyppe. Oxon., xxvij. Julii.

Your most bounden oratour and servant,
JOHAN LONDON.

* The priory of Beauvale, in Nottinghamshire, or as it was called in Latin, *de Pulchra Valle in parco de Gresseley*, was founded by Nicholas de Cantelupe, in 1342. The last prior was Thomas Woodcock.

† The abbey or priory of Newstead in Sherwood, since the picturesque seat of the Byrons, was founded about A.D. 1170. The last prior was John Blake. The site was granted to Sir John Byron, mentioned in the letter, and from whom the poet Byron was a lineal descendant.

The ' visitor of the friars' mentioned in the following letter, was probably Richard bishop of Dover. Little is known of the two houses of friars in Salisbury. The Grey Friers was founded by Richard, bishop of Salisbury, in the reign of Henry III. The Black Friars, of which house we do not even know the founder, stood in the west suburb of the town, near Fisherton Bridge.

CIV.

JOHN FITZWARREN TO CROMWELL.

[From MS. Cotton. Cleop. E. iv. fol. 146.]

After my most hartie recommendations unto your honorable lordeshipe, plese it the same to be advertised, that syns I receyved your lovyng and hartie lettres by your servaunte Mr. Goodale, with the warrant for a stagg in Purbeke, for the wiche I render to your honorable lordeshipe my most hartie thankes, he mayntenauntly declared unto me the pryvie operation of certayn prystes within the cyte of Sarum, in ther confessions concernyng forbyddyng of whytmeates in Lent, the redyng of the New Testament in Englisshe, and the cumpany of such as be of the new lernyng. Whom I have not only examyned, but also have examyned certayne witnes agenst them, the ponesshement wherof I have stayed untyll your lordesheps pleaser be further therin knowen. And, my good lord, wher that I am enformed that the vysytour of the fryers shortly will repayre to the cyte of Sarum to dissolve and make sale of all such thynges as he at his last beyng ther dyd take an inventory of, I most hartely desyer your good lordeshepes lovyng letters unto the saied vysytour in my favour, that I may have the stuff of the Black Fryers for my money befor any other with the place to dwell in for my rent. And if it may stond with your lordeships pleaser, I desyer your good lordeshipe to wrytt your lyke lettres unto the saied visytour in the favour of your servaunte Mr. Goodale for the Gray Fryers, who dwellith next unto hit, and who also taketh so much paynes for the comen wele, and in helpyng and furtheryng poore mennys matiers, as I knew never bayliff to doo lyke in my tyme. And thus most hartely fare your lordeshipe well. Frome Dorneford, the xx^{ti} day of August.

Youer lordships faythfully assured,

JOHAN FYTZWAREN.

In the following letter we find Dr. London still at Oxford, which seems to have been the centre of his operations.

CV.

DR. LONDON TO CROMWELL.

[From MS. Cotton. Cleop. E. iv. fol. 227.]

In my most humble maner I have me commendyd unto your gudde lordeschippe, with my assured prayer and service duringe my lyff. I have causyd all our fower ordre of fryers to chaunge ther cotes, and have dispacchide them as well as I can till they may receyve ther capacities, for the wiche I have now agen sent uppe thys berar doctor Baskerfelde, to whom I do humblie besek your lordeschippe to stonde gudde lorde. He ys an honest man, and causyd all hys howse to surrendre the same and to chaunge ther papistical garmentes. I wrote to your lordeschippe specially for hym to have in hys capacytie an expresse licens to dwell in Oxford, altho he wer benefycyd; and your lordeschipp then wrote that yt wasse your pleasur he and all other shulde have ther capacities acording to ther desyer, and for that thys man ys now an humble sutar unto your lordeschippe. He hath be a visitar of dyvers places wiche they do call custodies, and knowith many thinges as well in London as otherwise, wiche he hath promised me to declare unto your lordeschippe, if it be your pleasur he schall so do. And a frynde of myne, the warden of the Grey Fryers in Reding,* hathe

---

* The priory of the Grey Friars, in Reading, was founded in 1233. The deed of surrender of this house, printed in " Coates' History of Reading," p. 303, is dated Sept. 13, 30 Hen. VIII. i. e. 1538.

also desyred me to be an humble sutar for hym and hys brothern, that they may with your lordeschips favour also chaunge ther gar-mentes with ther papisticall maner of lyvinges. The most partt of them be very agede men, and be nott of strength to go moch abrode for ther lyvinges, wherfor ther desyer ys that yt myght please your lordeschippe to be a mediator unto the kinges grace for them that they myȝt during ther lyves enjoy ther chambres and orcharde, and they wolde assuredly pray unto almiȝtie Godde long to preserve the kinges grace and your lordeshipp to hys most blessyd pleasure. Oxon, ultimo Augusti.

At Merston Mr. Johan Schorn stondith blessing a bote, where-unto they do say he conveyd the devill. He ys moch sowȝt for the agow. If it be your lordeschips pleasur, I schall sett that botyd ymage in a nother place, and so do with other in other parties wher lyke seking ys.

Your most bounden oratour and servant,
JOHAN LONDON.

Richard Pollard, another of the commissioners, was occupied partly on the same ground as Dr. London. In the following letter we find him at Winchester; it is with-out date, but probably belongs to the earlier part of the September of this year.

CVI.

POLLARD AND OTHERS TO CRUMWELL.

[From the State Papers, vol. i. p. 621.]

Pleasith your lordship to be advertised, that this Saturdaye, in the mornyng, aboutes thre of the clok, we made an ende of the shryne here at Wynchestre. There was in it no pece of gold, ne oon ring, or true stone, but al greate counterfaictes. Nevertheles we thinke the sylver alone thereof woll amounte nere to twoo thousande markes. We have also receyved into our possession the crosse of emeraudes, the crosse called Hierusalem, an other

crosse of gold, 2 chalices of gold, with some sylver plate, parcel of
the portion of the vestrye; but thold prior made the plate of the
house soo thynne, that we can diminish non of it and leave the
prior any thing furnished.   We found the prior, and all the convent, very conformable; having assistentes with us, at the open-
yng of our charge to the same, the mayre, with 8 or 9 of the best of
his brethern, the bisshops chauncelour, Mr. doctour Craiforde,
with a good apparaunce of honest personages besides; who, with
oon voyce, most hartely gave lawde and prayse to God and to
the kinges majestye, thinking verily that they doo all as moch
rejoise of his majestes godly and most christian purpose herin as
canne be devised.   We have also this mornyng, going to our
beddes warde, vieued thaulter, whiche we purpose to bring with us.
It wol be worthe the taking downe, and nothing therof seen; but
suche a pece of work it is, that we thinke we shal not rid it, doing
our best, befor Monday night, or Tuesdaye mornyng, which doon
we entende, both at Hide* and St. Maryes, to swepe awaye all the
roten bones that be called reliques; which we may not omytt,
lest it shuld be thought we cam more for the treasure thenne for
avoiding of thabomynation of ydolatry.   Other thinges, as ferre
as we canne lerne, there be none for us in those places, whiche
thinges doon, and our thinges set out-warde, we shall attende
uppon your lordship with diligence.

I, Thomas Wriothesley† humbly beseche your good lordship to
pardon the rudenes of this letter, writen in hast in the churche
whenne I was wery; and, in like maner, I beseche your lordship
to be good lorde to the poore man the berer of this letter.   It is
the same of whom I told your lordship concernyng the ferme

---

* The monastery of Hyde, without the walls of Winchester, was the same abbey
which, founded by King Alfred, was in Saxon times called the New Minster; but it
then stood adjacent to the cathedral or Old Minster, from whence it was removed to
Hyde in the reign of Henry I.   There are still some remains.   The last abbot was
John Sulcot, or Saltcot, *alias* Capon, who for his subserviency to the court was made
bishop of Bangor, and afterwards of Salisbury.   The abbey of St. Mary was the nunnery founded in this city by king Alfred.   The last abbess was Elizabeth Shelley.

† Sir Thomas Wryothesley, afterwards earl of Southampton.

whiche sir William Kempe wold have from him.   He affirmethe
constantly that he is utterly undon if he shuld forgo either thole,
or that half that Mr. Kempe wold have.   Forty acres of his best
lande he wold be content to let him have, at reasonable rent, for
his favour; which, in my poore opinion, is more thenne reasonable.   Thus having certain affiance that your lordships goodnes
woll pardon this my boldnes, we shall pray to God to kepe your
lordship in healthe.   From St. Swythines in Winchestre, this Saturdaye mornyng.

Your lordshippes most bounden,

Rychard Pollard.
Thomas Wriothesley.
John Williams.

To the right honorable and
our singular good lord,
my lorde privye seale.

If the date of the preceding letter be right, Pollard seems to have gone from Winchester to Reading, where he would act in conjunction with Dr. London. The following letter must refer to the priory, and not to the abbey, in this town.

CVII.

RICHARD POLLARD TO CROMWELL.

[From MS. Cotton. Cleop. E. IV. fol. 224.*]

Pleasyth youre lordshyp to be advertysed, that att my comyng to
Readyng I dyd dyspatche Mr. Wrytheslys servaunt wyth every
thyng accordyng to youre commaundement, wyche amountythe to
the some of cxxxj^{li}. ix^s. viij^d., as appeyrythe by the partyculers
herein inclosyd, and parte of the stuffe reservyd for the kynges
majestyes use, wyth the whole house and churche undefasyd.   I
and my fellowes have lefte hytt by indenture in the custody
of Mr. Penyson, and as for the plate, vestementes, copys, and
hangynges, wyche we have reservyd also to the use of the

kynges majestye, we have lefte hytt in the custody of Mr. Vachell * by indenture, wych shalbe conveyd to London ageynste my comyng thyther; and, thangkes be to God! every thyng ys well ffynysshyd there, and every man well contentyd and gyvythe humble thankes to the kynges grace. I wythe my ffel-lowes intend on Tewsday next, God wyllyng, to take oure journey frome Readyng, as knowythe God, who ever preserve youre good lordshyp. Frome Readyng, the xv. daye of Septembre.

Your owan assuryd to command,

RYCHARD POLLARD.

The three following letters from Dr. London, all relating to the suppression of the priory of Reading, are almost counterparts of one another. The two first were cer-tainly not addressed to the same person—the second was probably sent to the chan-celler of the augmentations.

CVIII.

DR. LONDON TO CROMWELL.

[From MS. Cotton. Cleop. E. iv. fol. 225.]

In my most humble maner I have me commendyd unto yower gude lordeschippe, acertenyng the same that I have pullyd down the image of our ladye at Caversham, wherunto wasse great pilgre-mage.† The image ys platyd over with sylver, and I have putt yt in a cheste fast lockyd and naylyd uppe, and by the next bardge that comythe from Reding to London yt shall be browght to your lordeschippe. I have also pullyd down the place sche stode in, with all other ceremonyes, as lightes, schrowdes, crowchys, and imagies of wex, hangyng abowt the chapell, and have defacyd the same

---

* Cromwell was high steward of Reading, and Thomas Vachell, Esq. who repre-sented the town in parliament, acted as his deputy-steward.

† Caversham is about a mile and a half to the north of Reading.

thorowly in exchuyng of any farther resortt thedyr. Thys chapell dydde belong to Notley abbey,* and ther always wasse a chanon of that monastery wiche wasse callyd the warden of Caversham, and he songe in thys chapell, and hadde the offeringes for hys lyving. He wasse acostomyd to shew many pretty relykes, among the wiche wer (as he made reportt) the holy dager that kylled kinge Henry,† and the holy knyfe that kylled seynt Edwarde.‡ All thees, with many other, with the cotes of thys image, her cappe and here, my servant shall bring unto your lordeschippe thys wek, with the surrendre of the Freers under the covent seale, and ther seale also. I have sent the chanon home agen to Notleye, and have made fast the doores of the chapell ; wiche ys thorowly well coverd with ledde ; and if it be your lordeschips pleasure, I schall se yt made suer to the kinges graces use. And, if it be nott so orderyd, the chapell standith so wildely that the ledde will be stolyn by ny3t, as I wasse servyd at the Fryers ; ffor as soon as I hadde taken the Fryers surrendre, the multytude of the poverty of the town resortyd thedyr, and all thinge that my3t be hadde they stole away, insomyche that they hadde convayd the very clapers of the bellys. And saving that Mr. Fachell, wiche made me great chere at hys howse, and the mayer dydde assist me, they wolde have made no litill spoyle. In thys I have don as moche as I cowde do to save every thing to the kinges graces use, as shall apper to your lordeschippe at the begynnyng of the terme, Godde willinge, who with increse of moche honour long preserve your gudde lordeschippe. At Redinge, xvij° Septembris.

At Caversham ys a propre lodginge, wher the chanon lay, with a

* Notley, or Nutley Abbey, in Buckinghamshire, of which there are still considerable remains, was founded in 1162, for Austin canons, by Walter Gyffard, second earl of Buckingham. The last abbot was Richard Ridge.

† Henry VI. This is curious, as showing the established belief that the king had been murdered.

‡ Edward the martyr, the son and successor of king Edgar.

fayer garden and an orcherd, mete to be bestowyd upon som frynde of your lordeschips in thes parties, ffor the chanon hadde no thing to do ther butt to kepe the chapell and receyve the offringes.

I besek your gudde lordeschippe to admytt me a power sutar for thees honest men of Redinge. They have a fayer towne and many gudde occupiers in ytt, butt they lacke that howse necessary, of the wiche, for the mynystracion of justice, they have most nede of. Ther towne hall ys a very small howse, and stondith upon the ryver, wher ys the commyn wassching place of the most partt of the towne, and in the cession dayes and other cowrt dayes ther ys such betyng with batildores as oon man can nott here another nor the quest here the chardg gevyng. The body of the church of the Grey Fryers, wiche ys solyd with lath and lyme, wold be a very commodiose rowme for them. And now I have rydde all the fasschen of that church in parcleses, ymages, and awlters, it wolde mak a gudly towne hall. The mayer of that towne, Mr. Richard Turner,* is a very honest gentill person, with many other honest men, hathe expressyd unto me ther gref in thys behalf, and have desyred me to be an humble sutar unto your lordeschippe for the same, if it shulde be solde. The wallys besyd the coyne stonys be butt chalk and flynt, and the coveryng butt tile. And if it please the kinges grace to bestow that howse upon any of hys servantes, he may spare the body of the churche, wiche stondith next the strete, very well, and yit have rowme sufficient for a great man.

Your most bounden oratour and servant,

JOHN LONDON.

---

* Richard Turner was mayor of Reading from September 19, 1537, to Sept. 1538, and was succeeded by Thomas Mirthe, (mayor from 1538 to 1539), and Richard Justice (from 1539 to Sept. 1540.) See Coates' History of Reading. The petition of the townsmen for the priory church to be converted into a town hall was granted.

CIX.

DR. LONDON TO SIR RICHARD RICH (?).

[From MS. Cotton. Cleop. E. IV. fol. 226.]

Right worshipfull, in my most hartie maner I have me commendyd unto yow, I have pullyd down the image of your lady at Caversham, with all trynkettes abowt the same, as schrowdes, candels, images of wexe, crowches, and brochys, and have thorowly defacyd that chapell in exchuyng of any farther resortt, ffor even at my being ther com in nott so few as a dosyn with imagies of wexe. The image ys thorowly platyd over with sylver. I have putt her in a chest fast lockyd and naylede, and by the next bardge that comythe uppe it schall be browȝt to my lorde, with her cootes, cappe, and here, with dyvers relykes, as the blessyd knyfe that kylled seynt Edward, the dagger that kyllyd kinge Henry, schethe and all; and I myssed no thing here butt oonly a peece of the holy halter Judas wasse hangyd withall. Here song a chanon of Notley, wiche hadde conveyd home to hys master as great a relik as any of thees befor I com; butt I wyll have hym, and schall send yt to my lorde. And thys wek folowing I will send uppe Mr. Johan Schorn, and so as many as I fynde. I have occasion for my colledg besynes to go by Aylisbery and Bedford thys next wek, and as I suppose by Northampton. In all thees places be howsys of ffryers. If it be my lordes pleasur I will dispache them quyckly, ffor seying they wold fayne be abrode yt wer pytie to stay them. And in dyvers of thees howsys moche ydolytrie have be usyd, and the people sore abusyd. I besek yow remembre Mr. Knyȝtes mater I have movyd yow in; and if by your gudnes it be browȝt to passe, I know well yow will herafter moche rejoyse yow dydd ytt. My servant schall be with yow thys wek to bringe uppe the Fryers surrendre, with the relykes of Caversham, and schall also bring yow a tokyn in parchement undre

the covent seale from the abbott and covent here.* He desy-
rethe oonly your favour, and no other thinge; and I know so
moche that my lord schall fynde hym as conformable a man as
any in thys realme, as more at lardg I will tell yow at the begynnyng of the terme, by the grace of Godd, who with increse of
moche worschippe longe preserve yow. At Reding, xvij° Septembris.

Your most bounden oratour,
JOHAN LONDON.

CX.

DR. LONDON TO CROMWELL.
[From MS. Cotton. Cleop. E. iv. fol. 223.]

In my most humble maner I have me commendyd unto your
gudde lordeschippe, with my assured prayer and service, I have
sent upp to your lordeschippe the surrender of the Grey Fryers of
Reding, with ther plate, suche as yt ys.   I have inwardly defacyd
the churche and dorter; the resydew of the howse I have left hole
till I know your farther pleasur, and clerly dispacchyd all the
fryers owt of the doores in ther seculer apparell, and have geven to
every oon of theym mony in ther purcys, and have clerly payd
ther dettes. Thys ys a towne of moch power people, and they
fell to steling so fast in every corner of the howse, that I have be
fayne to tary a hole wek here to sett every thing in dew ordre,
and have and schall receyve to the kinges grace use I trust
above xl^li. The mansion holy reservyd. I have sent uppe the
principall relik of idolytrie within thys realme, an aungell with
oon wyng that brow3t to Caversham the spere hedde that percyd
our Saviour is syde upon the crosse. It wasse conveyd home to

---

* Reading Abbey was not dissolved till the year following, when the abbot was
hanged.

Notley, butt I sent my servant purposley for ytt. I have sent also iij. cotes of the image, with such thinges as I fownde upon them, with the dagger that they say slew king Henry the vj. and the knyff that kylled seynt Edward, with many other lyk holy thinges. I have defacyd that chapell inward, and have sent home the chanon to hys master to Notley. I have requyred of my lord abbott the relykes of hys howse, wich he schewyd unto me with gudde will. I have taken an inventary of them, and have lokkyd them upp behynde ther high awlter, and have the key in my keping, and they be always redy at your lordeships commaunde-ment. They have a gudde lecture in scripture dayly redde in ther chapitour howse, bothe in Inglysche and Laten, to the wich ys gudde resortt, and the abbott ys at yt hym self. In any other thing I can do your lordeschipp service I am and always schalbe redy, Godde willyng, who with increse of moche honour, long preserve your gudde lordeschippe. Att Reding, xviijᵒ Septembris.

Your most bounden oratour and servant,
JOHAN LONDON.

THE INVENTORYE OFF THE RELYQUES OFF THE HOWSSE OFF REDYNG.

Inprimis, twoo peces off the holye crosse.

Item, saynt James hande.

Item, saynt Phelype stolle.

Item, a bone off Marye Magdelene, with other moo.

Item, saynt Anastasius is hande, with other moo.

Item, a pece off saynte Pancrates arme.

Item, a bone off saynt Quyntyns arme.

Item, a bone off saynt Davyde is arme.

Item, a bone off Marye Salomes arme.

Item, a bone off saynt Edwarde the Martyre is arme.

Item, a bone of saynt Hierome, with other moo.

Item, bones off saynt Stephyn, with other moo.

Item, a bone off saynte Blase, with other moo.

Item, a bone of saynt Osmonde, with other moo.

Item, a pece off saynt Ursula stole.

Item, a chowbone of saynt Ethelmold.

Item, bones off saynt Leodigarye and of S. Herenei.

Item, bones off saynt Margarett.

Item, bones off saynt Arnal.

Item, a bone off saynt Agas, with other moo.

Item, a bone off S. Androwe, and ij. peces of his crosse.

Item, a bone off S. Fredyswyde.

Item, a bone off saynt Anne.

Withe many othere.

Ther be a multitude of small bonys, laces, stonys, and ermys, wiche wolde occupie iiij. schetes of papyr to make particularly an inventary of every part therof. They be all at your lordeschips commaundement.

The nunnery of Godstow, in Oxfordshire, founded in the time of Henry I., is chiefly celebrated as the place of burial of Fair Rosamond, the mistress of Henry II. The last abbess was Catherine Bulkeley, *alias* Bewmaris, who in a subsequent letter complains that Dr. London was actuated by personal resentment towards her. As, however, we have here the visitor's private letter to Cromwell concerning the abbey, where he speaks with leniency, it appears that the abbess was mistaken. Her letter has been frequently quoted as a proof of the harsh and unjust treatment of the nuns and their superiors, but the fact was overlooked that on the dissolution Catherine Bulkeley received the extremely large pension of fifty pounds a year.

CXI.

DR. LONDON TO CROMWELL.

[From MS. Cotton. Cleop. E. iv. fol. 227*.]

In my most humble maner I have me commendyd unto your

gudde lordeschippe, acertenyng the same that I am now at Godstow to execute the kinges highnes commission, wher I perceyve
my ladye do tak my commynge som thinge penciflye, and hathe
desyred me to spare herre determynate answer untill suche tyme
sche may with convenyent spede know the kinges hignes determynate and resolute pleasure in that behalf. And in the mean tyme
I schall som thing rype my self in knowledg of the state of the
howse bothe inwardely and utterward, and if the kinges grace
pleasur be notwithstonding herre desyer for suche considerations
as movith his grace for the reformation of suche abuses to tak the
howse by surrendre, then I besek your lordeschipp to admytt me
an humble sutar for my lady and herre sisters and the late abbasse
and suche as have covent seales for lyvinges in that howse, that
they may be favorably orderyd, specially my lady, wiche lately
payd herre fyrst fruytes, and wasse indaungeryd therfor unto
herre fryndes. Many of the mynchys(?) be also agyd, and as I perceyve few of the other have any fryndes, wherfor I besek your
lordeschipp to be gudd lord unto them. In dyvers of the fryers
suppressyd they hadde no covent sealys, ffor my lord of Dover
tok them away, as they saye, and badd them lyve upon ther stock
and plate, and so dydd they, as apperithe. I have taken, wher the
kinges grace ys nott founder, a feofement also (besyd the surrendre) made to me to the kinges use. I dydd it by my lord
Bawdwyns counsell at Aylisbery. I have sent uppe all the plate,
wyche commythe, with the plate I delyverd to M. Gostwik, to
xviij^c. viij. unc. *et di.* Thys ys besyd the plate of Oxforde and the
Fryers of Redinge, wiche wasse befor delyverd to M. Thacker,
whom I have desyred to know your lordeschips pleasur in certen
articles necessary abowt my besynes. Oon of your lordeschips
injunctions geven in the kinges name ys that no ffryar schalbe
admytted to serve any cure. Now they be dimissed owt of ther
howses, no man will admytt any of them to be curattes, unlesse
they do bring ther capacyties ; wherfor I besek your lordeschippe
we may have them with spede, ffor in the mean tyme the power

men be withowt lyvinges, and now I have sett many abrode. I have sold no maner of thyng at Tollissop Crosfryers besyd Warwik,* for the howse stondith alone, and if I hadde begon any sale, all the howse wold have be spoylyd or I hadde com agen. I have left all in safe custodye till my retornyng. In thausten ffryers at Northampton,† a lytill befor my commyng, the prior devydyd xxxli. of plate money amonge hys brothern. In that I wold fayne know your lordeschips pleasure : ffor that and other lyk maters, I left the prior in prison, and I have xls. of that money agen. As your lordeschips pleasur schall farther be in all the premisses, I schall in that and all other do my best diligens, by the grace of almyʒtie Godd, who with increse of moch honour long preserve yower gudde lordeschipp. At Godstow, vjº. Novembris.

Thys mornyng my lady holy referrithe her self to your lordeschips pleasur ; wherfor I besek your lordeschippe of your favorable letters to herre, and also for your favour to herre and herre sisters for ther lyvinges. When I am at the Chartre Howse of Coventry, Colme‡ ys within iij. myles.

Your most bounden oratour and servant,

JOHAN LONDON.

CXII.

THE ABBESS OF GODSTOW TO CROMWELL.

[From MS. Cotton. Cleop. E. iv. fol. 228.]

Pleasithe hit your honour with my moste humble dewtye to be advertised, that where it hathe pleasyd your lordeship to be the

* I find no mention of this house in the Monasticon.

† The small house of the Austin friars at Northampton (founded in 1322) had been surrendered on the 28th of October. The prior was John Goodwyn.

‡ Combe abbey.

verie meane to the kinges majestie for my preferment most un-
worthie to be abbes of this the kynges monasterie of Godystowe,
in the whiche offyce I truste I have done the beste in my power
to the mayntenance of Godes trewe honour, withe all treuthe and
obedience to the kynges magestie, and was never movyd nor
desired by any creature in the kynges behalfe or in your lordeships name to surrender and gyve upe the howse, nor was never
myndyd nor intendyd so to do otherwise then at the kinges
gratius commawndement or yours, to the whiche I do and have
ever done and will submyt my selfe most humblie and obedientlie,
and I truste to God that I have never offendyd Godes lawes,
nother the kynges, wherebie that this poore monasterie ought to
be suppressyd, and this notwithstondyng, my good lorde, so it
is that doctor Londone, whiche, as your lordeship dothe well
knowe, was ageynste my promotyon, and hathe ever sence borne
me greate malys and grudge, like my mortall enmye, is sodenlie
cummyd unto me withe a greate rowte withe him, and here dothe
threten me and my susters, sayeng that he hathe the kynges commyssyon to suppres the house spyte of my tethe. And when he
sawe that I was contente that he shulde do all thinges accordyng
to his commyssyon, and shewyd him playne that I wolde never
surrender to his hande, beyng my awncyent enemye, now he be-
gynes to intreate me and to invegle my susters one by one otherwise than ever I harde tell that any of the kynges subgectes hathe
bene handelyd, and here tarieth and contynueth to my grete coste
and charge, and will not taike my answere that I will not surrender
till I knowe the kynges gratious commawndement or youre good
lordeshipes. Therefore I do moste humblie beseche you to contynewe my good lorde, as you ever have bene, and to directe your honorable lettres to remove him hens; and whensoever the kinges gratius
commawndement or youres shall cum unto me, you shall fynde
me moste reddie and obedyent to foloe the same. And notwithe-
stondyng that doctour Londone, like a untrewe man, hathe informyd

your lordeship that I am a spoiler and a waster, youre good
lordeshipe shall knowe that the contrarie is trewe, ffor I have
not alienatyd one halporthe of the goodes of this monasterie,
movable or unmovable, but have rather increasyd the same, nor
never made lease of any farme or pece of grownde belongyng to
this house other than hathe bene in tymes paste allwaies set
under covent seale for the wealthe of the house.   And, therefore,
my verie truste is that I shall fynde the kynge as gratius lorde
unto me as he is to all other his subgectes, seyng I have not
offendyd, and am and wilbe most obedyent to his moste gratious
commawndement at all tymes, withe the grace of allmighty Jesus,
who ever preserve you in honour longe to indeure to his pleasure.
Amen.   At Godistow, the vth daie of November.

Your moste bownden bedeswoman,
Katherine Bulkeley, abbes there.

From Godstow, we trace Dr. London to the priory of Twynham or Christ's Church,
in Hampshire, the church of which still remains a most interesting monument of
early ecclesiastical architecture.   This house was originally founded in the reign of
Edward the Confessor.   The last prior was John Draper.

CXIII.

THE COMMISSIONERS TO CROMWELL.

[From MS. Cotton. Cleop. E. iv. fol. 267*.]

Ower humble dewties observyd unto your gudde lordeshippe, it
may lyk the same to be advertised that we have taken the surrendre of the late priorye of Christechurche Twynham, wher we
founde the prior a very honest conformable person, and the howse
well furnysschide with juellys and plate, wherof some be mete for
the kinges majestie is use, as a litill chalys of golde, a gudly lardge
crosse doble gylt with the foote garnysschyd with stone and
perle, two gudly basons doble gylt having the kinges' armys well
inamylyd, a gudly greet pyxe for the sacrament doble gylt; and

ther be also other thinges of sylver right honest and of gudde
valewer, as well for the churche use as for the table, reservyd and
kept to the kinges use.   In thys churche we founde a chaple and
monument curiosly made of Cane stone, preparyd by the late
mother of Raynolde Pole* for herre buriall, wiche we have
causyd to be defacyd and all the armys and badgis clerly to be
delete.   The surveyng of the demaynys of thys howse, wiche be
lardge and baryn, and som partt therof xx^{ti}. mylys from the monastery, wiche we also do survey and mesure, hathe causyd usse
to mak longer abode at thys place then we intendyd.   And now
we be in jorney towardes Amysbery, wher we schall use like diligens for the accomplisshing of the kinges highnes commission,
and as sone as we have don ther we schall farther certifie your
lordeschippe of our doinges.   And thus we beseke almyȝtie Jhesus
longe to preserve your gudde lordeschippe with increse of moche
honour.   At Christchurche, ij° Decembris.

Your lordschipes humbly to comand,

Robt. Sowthwell.
Edward Carne.
Jhon London.
Rychard Poulet.
William Berners.

It appears by the following that Dr. London had been to Coventry and Northampton,
as he intimated his intention in a former letter.   He is now returned to Oxford, where
we found him at the beginning of his correspondence.

CXIV.

DR. LONDON TO CROMWELL.

[From MS. Cotton. Cleop. E. iv. fol. 208.]

In my most humble maner I have me commendyd unto your

---

* Cardinal Pole.   His mother was severely persecuted by the crown.

gudd lordeschippe, with my assurede prayer and servys during my lyf, I have sent unto your gudde lordeschippe a power tokyn, beseking almy3tie Godde most hartelye nott oonly to graunt unto yow thys new yere prosperose, butt many moo also, to the hyghe pleasure of Godde and the great comfortt of your lordeschipp and all your boundon oratours.* I have also sent with the same power tokyn the half-yere fee it pleasithe yow to accept of me and my power howse. Godde willing, I schall now with all diligens applie the execution of the commission I hadde of your lordeschippe in places wher as yet I have nott be. M. Williams, I trust, hathe certefied your lordeschippe what we have don at Ensham † and Notley, and at the Crowche Fryers at Newberye.‡ And with the farmers of Ensham I have don my best diligens for syr George Darcye,§ and do trust that we shall com to som gudde conclusion. Thys day the late abbott, they, and I shall mete agen for that purpos. Att Delapray besyde Northampton ‖ I have taken thabbesse surrendre. Sche ys a gudde agydd woman, and lately hadde the kinges chartre for the contynuance of herre howse; that notwithstonding, she willingly withowt any refusall renderyd unto the kinges majestie that chartre, wiche with herre and her sisters surrendre I have sent by thys berar, and acording to your commaundment have putt Small, M. Hennage kinsman, in possession of the same. And forasmoche as I founde that late abbesse

---

* On the old custom of giving new year's gifts (étrennes), still preserved in France, see Brand's Popular Antiquities, vol. i. pp. 5—11 (ed. 1841).

† The abbey of Ensham, or Eynsham, in Oxfordshire, was founded by Athelmer earl of Cornwall and Devonshire, at the beginning of the eleventh century. It was a rich house. The last prior was Anthony Dunstan, *alias* Kitchen, who was subsequently (in 1545) made bishop of Landaff.

‡ This was a small priory at Donnington, near Newbury, in Berkshire. See the Monasticon, vi. p. 1562. Henry White was the last prior.

§ Sir George Darcy was the elder brother of Sir Arthur Darcy, mentioned before, and was restored to his father's title of Lord Darcy in the 2nd Edw. VI.

‖ Delapre (*De-la-pré*), a Cluniac nunnery in the parish of Hardingstone, founded in the reign of king Stephen by Simon de St. Liz, earl of Northampton.

so comformable, and the howse in so gudde state, considering dyvers grave chardges sche hathe be att, I dydde assigne unto herre for her comfortt in herre great age the fowrt partt of the schepe, viz. fyve score, a certen of every kynde of grayne, a certen of every sort of the catell, wherof I founde praty store, and lykwise of the stuff and implementes, beseking your lordeschippe to ratefie the same, and to be gudde lorde unto herre and to herre power sisters in ther pensions. I have also receyvide the unwise letters wryten by the monkes of the Chartre House in Coventrye.* Ther and at the priory I schall I trust accomplishe the kinges grace pleasur and yowers. And forasmoche as Colme ys so nye unto Coventry, and thabbott with all hys fryndes at your lordeschips commaundement, as I am pryvie of ther myndes, if it be your lordeschips pleasure I schall be gladde to goo thorow with that howse also. All the sortt of them do lok dulye for ther departing, and therfor they mak ther handes by leesys, salys of wodde, and of ther plate. I suppose thys abbott will leve hys howse and landes lyk an honest man; wherfor, inasmoche the howse hathe many gudly commodities, wherof if any be lett (as in dede som be) and will easily com agen to your lordeschips hondes, I think it best your lordeschipp do tak itt while yt ys at the beste. I am so bolde to desyer M. Thacker to know your lordeschips pleasur in certen other thinges, wiche I schall duly accomplische with the help of God, who with increse of moche honour long preserve your gudde lordeschippe. Oxon., xxviij. Decembris.

I have sent to your lordeschippe also a coote of idolytrie, with iij. frontlettes apperteynyng to the furnyture of the same. I have dyvers other propre thinges, as two heddes of seynt Ursula, wich bycause ther ys no maner of sylver abowt them, I reserve tyll I have another hedd of herse, wich I schall fynd in my waye within thees xiiij. dayes, as I am creadably informyd.

Your most bounden oratour,
JOHAN LONDON.

* The monastery of St. Anne near Coventry, founded by William lord Zouch in 1381, for Carthusian monks.

In the following letter we find Dr. London still on his way to Coventry: it is supplementary to the preceeding.

CXV.

DR. LONDON TO SIR RICHARD RICH (?).

[From MS. Cotton. Cleop. E. iv. fol. 207*.]

Right worschipfull, in my most harty maner I have me commendyd unto yow, in lyk maner thankinge yow for your kynde paynys taken for me, wherby ye have bound me to ow yow the best servys I can do yow, and therof always ye schall be well assured. I besek yow to delyver unto my lord suche surrendors as I have sent uppe. The plate of Notley and Ensham M. Williams being in commission with me ther hath brow3t uppe; and at the Crowche Fryers besyd Newbery wasse no more butt a power chalys. The londes be gudde xxij^{li}. by yere, butt the guddes all were nott worth the mynistre rewardyd vj^{li}.

At Delapray I hadde ij. chalyces and a pyxe, and the howse wasse pratily storyd with catell and corn. Ye schall se me mak yow a praty bank by that tym I com next uppe. I pray yow know my lordes [will], and that I may be acertenyd of the same in thinges folowing.

Imprimis, my lord commandyd me to putt M. Lucy in possession of the Crowch Fryers howse in Thelsford,* and now he wrytithe that I schall putt M. Cheynye in possession of the same. If M. Lucy schall have Thelsford, then if my lord so will that I do go to Nuncotton or Stikkiswold nonryes † in Lincoln schyer, M. Cheyney may be servyd in som of them.

---

* The friary of Thelesford in Warwickshire was founded in the reign of king John. Edward Davy was the last prior.

† The Cistercian nunnery of Stykeswold, or Stixwold, in Lincolnshire, was founded by the widow of Ranulph first earl of Chester, in the reign of Stephen. It had been refounded after the act for the suppression of the smaller monasteries, under which it fell. The last prioress was Mary Missenden.

If my lord will have me do any thing at Colme, then I wolde my lord wold send som oon of hys trusty servantes to me at my being ther, to receyve the howse with all other rekenynges to my lordes use, the guddes indifferently praysed.   He can nott have a more commodiose howse, and the longer he taryeth the warsse every thing will be, as universally they mak ther handes all they can that yet do remayne nott suppressyd.   When I am at Coventry, I am but iij. myles from Colme.   And if my lord percase have syns my being ther sett hys mynde upon any other place, then help M. Gregory or M. Richard may have ytt, ffor yt ys a thynge to be taken.

Your own bounden assuredly,
JOHAN LONDON.

In the next letter we find Dr. London and his fellow commissioners at Gloucester, which had been recently visited by the bishop of Dover, whose letters are given on a former page.

CXVI.

THE COMMISSIONERS OF THE WEST TO CROMWELL.

[From MS. Cotton. Cleop. E. IV. fol. 254*.]

Ower humble dewties observyd unto your gudde lordeschippe, it may lyke the same to be advertysede, that we have taken the surrendre of the late monasterye of Haylys,* wher we founde the father and all hys brothern very honest and conformable persons, and the howse clerly owt of dett.   Over that the father hadde hys

---

* The mitred abbey of Hayles, in Gloucestershire, was founded in the middle of the thirteenth century, by Richard earl of Cornwall.   Stephen Sagar was the last abbot.

howse and groundes so well furnysschede with juellys, plate, stuff, corne, catell, and the wodes also so well savyd, as thoo he hadde lokyde forre no alteration of hys howse. Hys arable londe also wasse in lyk maner husbondyd, no small nombre of acres redy sowen with whete, and the tylthe seasonablie orderyd for barlye; and dydde surrendre hys howse with suche discrete and frank maner, as we have seen no other do better in all ower jorney. The howse clerly dispacchede and commyttede, acording to the kinges majesties lettres, unto the custodye of M. Acton. We have from that howse right honest sortes of juellys, plate, ornamentes, and monye, besyde the garnysschyng of a small schryne, wherin wasse reposyd the counterfett relyke in tymys past,* wiche all we do saflye reserve unto the kinges highnes use, and thow3t it our partes to declare and signifie unto your lordeschipe thys honest manneis behaviour and doinges, to thentent he my3t have at your hondes condinge prayse and thankes for hys trew dealinge, and to humbly desyer your lordeschippe to be gudde lorde unto hym, as hys full trust ys ye will be. We have dispacchyd Haylys and Winchcombe,† and now be at Glocestre, wher we have taken the surrendre, and be dyligently traveling for a new ordre to be sett ther, wherin we fynde the more difficultye, for that as yet the kinges highnes hathe nott determyd hys pleasure upon the master that shall have the governance of thys congregation. From Glocestre we go unto Teuxbery, wher thys weke we trust clerly to mak a fynall conclusion of all our commissions for thys schyer, as we have now don in Hampschyer and Wilshyer, and schall use no

* The following note of the fate of this counterfeit relique, which had been seized some weeks before the date of this letter, is found in Holinshed :—" 1538. The foure and twentith of November, the bishop of Rochester preached at Paules crosse, and there shewed the bloud of Hales, and affirmed the same to be no bloud, but honie clarified, and coloured with saffron, as it had beene evidentlie proved before the king and his counceil."

† The abbey of Winchcombe, or Winchelescombe, in Gloucestershire, was founded by Oswald bishop of Worcester in 985, in the place of a much more ancient nunnery. The last abbot was Richard Ancelme, Anstelme, or Mounslow.

lesse diligens for the next of Worcestre schyer, by the grace of almyghty Godde, who with increse of moche honour longe preserve your gudd lordeschippe.   At Glocestre, iiij°. Januarii.

Your lordschipes most humbly to be comandyd,

ROBERT SOWTHWELL.

EDWARD CARNE.

RI. GWENT.   JOHAN ARNOLD.
JOHAN LONDON.   JOHAN AP RICE.
WILLIAM BERNERS.   RYCHARDE POULET.

Bishop Lee, the writer of the following letter, was lord president of the principality and marches of Wales, the court of government of which was held at Ludlow. The following letter is dated from Wigmore Castle.

CXVII.

BISHOP LEE TO CROMWELL.

[From MS. Cotton. Cleop. E. IV. fol. 256*.]

Right honerabile, my dewte rememberyde unto youer good lordschippe, it may plesse the same to caule unto youer lordschypes rememberans my seute mayd to your lordschipe for the cathedrall churche of Coventre, for the contynewans of the same, that apon alteracion it myght stonde: we moweyd soe to doo, for soe miche it is my principall see and hede churche. Whereunto youer lordschype dyd gyff me levyng answere of comfurthe; and now I am informyd by the letteres herein inclosseyd frome the mayre and aldermen of the citee, that doctor London repareys thether for the suppression of the same.   My good lorde, helpe me and the cite bothe in thys, and that the churche may stonde, wherby I may kepe my name, and the cite have commodite and ease to theyre desyre, wiche schall folew, if by your goodnes it myght be browght to a colege churche, as Liche., and soe that poyre cite schall have a perpetuall comfurthe of the same, as knowyth the holy Trenite, whoo preserve youer lordschyp in honor to youer hartys comfurth. At Wigmere, xij°. Januarii.

Youer lordschypes most bownden,
ROLAND Co. et LICH.

Having thus traced the proceedings of Dr. London, in his progress during the autumn and winter of 1538, we shall return to the summer of that year, to give a few miscellaneous letters relating to different parts of the country, beginning with Essex.

CXVIII.

SIR THOMAS AUDLEY TO CROMWELL.

[From MS. Cotton. Cleop. E. iv. fol. 201.]

After my right herty comendacions to your good lordshipp, I sende to you a true copy of the value of the goodes of Seynt Osies,* and of the particularytees therof, delyvered to me by Myldmay the auditour, oon of the comyssioners, wherby your lordshipp may perceyve the contentes of al the same goodes, with the estymate of leade and belles. I was not at the dissolucion of the howse, nor have eny penyworthe of the goodes, but I thynke the comyssioners have servyd the kynges mageste bothe honestely and truly. The comyssioners were syr John Seynteler, syr William Pirton, Myldmay, and Jobson, whiche be ij of the comyt of the augmentacion, and a master of the chancery with them, to take

---

* The priory of St. Osith's was founded for Austin canons sometime before the year 1118, by Richard de Belmeis, bishop of London. Its site is said to have been occupied, in Saxon times, by a very ancient nunnery. The last prior was John Colchester, *alias* Witherick. The site was granted to Lord Cromwell in the 31 Hen. VIII.

the surrendir. In dede I sent for the abbott afore the dissolucion, and inducyd hym to yelde the howse to the kynges mageste
with his good wyll, and that he shuld exort his covent to conforme them to the same, who by my advise and exortacon con-
formed them selfes as humble subgettes without murmours or
grugge, wherin I trust I have not for my part servyd the kynges
highnes amysse. And now I beseche your good lordshipp to
further my sute. His mageste grantyd al my sute in effect
durynge his graces plesure, and my bil ys for terme of liff. They
be offices and feez that must be gevyn, and I trust to serve his
grace honestely in them. I have no ffee nor office of his highnes
but the chancelourshipp, and althoughe yt be hye and honorabill,
yet it ys cumberous and chargeable. Praying your lordshipp to
knowe his magesteez plesure of this litel sute, to the entent I may
know the end therof, wherby your good lordshipp shal admynyster
to me a right gret plesure and quyetnes. And as towchynge the
archedekenry of Leycettour, I take it that your lordshipp ys at
appoynt for me to have it, and to giff my lord of Hereford lxxx^{li} ; for
your lordshipp ones so advertised me by your lettres ; besechyng
you therfore to help to the resignacion therof, and the kynges lettre
to the byshop of Lincoln for the aleccion. The name of the
person that shuld have it ys William More, clerk, byshopp suffragan of Colchester. Yf the resignacion and lettre be opteyned, my
servant shal discharche the lxxx^{li}. at London to my lord of Here-
fordes use, where your lordshipp wil apoynt hym. I have. wryten
to my ffrend Pope to dispache it for me. I hertely desire your
good lordshipp to putt me to an end and quyetnes in this mater.
And for the travayles your lordshipp takyth in my sutes at this
tyme, I wil accordyng to my last lettre gif you xx^{li} towardes
your paynes, and my poor herty good will duryng my liff. Yt
may lik your lordshipp to understond, that the lord of Seynt
Johanns hath sent to me for comyssion to gather the ffrarys. I have
warrant to make them ye know by the gret boke that the gret
master opteyned at the kynges hand ; neverthelesse I staye in

yt til I may knowe the kynges plesure there. He seyth the kynges mageste hath the xth. of the rates therof in the value of his possessionz. He makyth moche a do for them. I beseche your good lordshipp to move the kynges mageste in yt and to advertise me of his graces plesure therof, besechyng you also to make my most humble recomendacion to his mageste, besechyng our Lord to send his highnes longe and prosperus lyff. And thus ffare your good lordshipp as wel and with as longe liff as I wold my self. Scribelid at Eston, at the erle of Essex howse, the xij. day of August.

Thankes be to our Lord, the contree ys in good order and quyetnes abowt me, and there where I have been, and begyn to fall to good quyetnes without contencons.

Your lordshippes assured to his pour,

THOMAS AUDELEY, chauncelour.

The next letter is also from the chancellor Audley. The priory of Walden was founded in 1136 by the first Geoffrey de Mandeville, earl of Essex. It was changed into an abbey towards the end of the twelfth century. The last abbot was William More, suffragan bishop of Colchester, mentioned in the preceding letter. The site was granted to Sir Thomas Audley, whose descendant, Thomas, earl of Suffolk, in the reign of James I., built on the ruins the noble residence of Audley End, now the seat of Lord Braybrooke.

CXIX.

SIR THOMAS AUDLEY TO CROMWELL.

[From MS. Cotton. Cleop. E. iv. fol. 197.]

Please it your good lordship to understond, that I have serched for the just value of Walden, and send to you the particulariteez therof, assuring you that it ys valued to the most, as al the monesteryes in Essex were, and also it ys treuth that all ys owt in lease by the predecessour of the now comendatery for many yeres. The comendatery at the lest can have no lesse then cc.

markes pencion, viij. monkes prestes every of them viij.^{li}. at the lest, *summa* lxiiij^{li}. The dettes of the howse to the kynges grace and others amountyth to c.^{li}. and above, as I am enformed. I beseche your good lordshipp be my good lord in this my sute, yf it shal plese the kynges mageste to be so good and gracius lord to me, it shal sett forth as moche my pour estymacion as the valu of the thynge. In the besy world I susteyned damage and injory, and this shal restore me to honeste and comodyte. The kynges majeste hath be so good lord to me that I can not of right crave eny thyng, but of his owen goodnes and liberalyte. And where I have promysed you to gyf his highnez v^c. markes redy mony, if ye thynke it to litell, order me as his grace may be best plesid, so that I may have dayes for the rest; ffor, on my fayth, I am in dett; besechyng your good lordshipp to use this my sute as the kynges highnes shal not thynke nor conceyve me to be inportune, ffor I desire more his graces contentacion then eny profight in the world. I have lost by capacyteez liberally and frely granted to relegeous persones of al the howses suppressid, of very ordynary ffeez anexid to my office above a M^{li}., and have it no recompens for it. The charges of the rebellion and the occasion cost me xj^c. markes and above; but that mony was wel bestowed, and ffor my office that the kynges highnes gafe me of exchange, I can take no comodyte by it. I do not repete these thynges but to your lordshipp, not to be declarid to the kynges mageste, as for eny consideracion to restore me, ffor al this and al that I have done and shall do in servyce duryng my life, his highnes hath recompensid with more then I can or may deserve. Remyttyng now all thynge to your lordshippes wisdom to use this my pour sute as to your dyscrecion shal seme best and most convenient, and that whiche I promysed your lordshipp ye shal have, with more, and my hart and good wil duryng my liff; and thus fare your lordshipp hartely well. Wryten this Satirday in the mornyng.

Your assured to his pour,
THOMAS AUDELEY, k. chanceler.

The next letter relates to the abbey of Vale Royal in Cheshire, founded by Edward
I. in 1277. The last abbot was John Harwood, who formally surrendered on the 7th
of September, 30 Hen. VIII.

CXX.

DR. LEGH TO CROMWELL.

[From MS. Harl. No. 604, fol. 56.]

In my most humble manner I commend me unto your good
lordship, ever more thanckyng you of your manyfycency and gret
goodnes at all tymes shewyd unto me, advertising your lordship,
that wheras I have hetherto, accordyng to your commaundement,
visite tharchedaconrye of Coventry, Stafford, Derby, and parte of
Cheshyre, for that I can perceyve accordingly as I heretofore have
wryttyn unto you, ther lackythe nothyng but good and godly
instruction of the rude and poore people, and reformation of the
heddis in thes partyes.   For certen of the knyghtes and gentilmen, and most commonly all, lyvythe so incontinently, havyng
ther concubynes openly in ther howses, with v. or vj. of their
chyldren, putting from them their wyfes, that all the contrey therwith be not a litill offendyd and takithe evyll example of theym.
Wherfor hetherto I have geven and sent commaundement to them,
(forasmoche as I culd not speke with them all, by reason they
war at the assyses) to put from them immediatly suche concubynes as they have hetherto notoriously and manyfestly occupyed
and kept, and to take agen their wyfes, or ellys to appere before
your lordship to shewe a cause whye they shuld not be compellyd.
And iff your lordship wyll commaunde any other thyng to be
doon in the premissis, I shall be redy to accomplyshe the same.
And seing my lord of Norfolke ys cum to the cowrte, I shall most
humbly desire you to have me in remembrans.   And thus Jhesu
preserve you and have you in his moste firme tuytion, with moche
increase of honor, according to the contentation of your lordships

most noble good hartes desyre.   From the monastery of Vale
Royall, the xxij^{ti}. day of August.

Your lordscyps ever att commandment,

THOMAS LEGH.

To the right honerable and his singuler
good lord, my lord prevy seall, this be
delyvered.

In the following letter, which is imperfect at the beginning, the abbot of Vale Royal
refuses to acknowledge the deed of surrender.

CXXI.

THE ABBOT OF VALE ROYAL TO CROMWELL.

[From MS. Harl. No. 604, fol. 62.]

*   *   *   *   *

me and my brothren the kynges most graciouse and drade commyssion, wherein his graciouse plesure was that for the gratuytye
that his grace trusted in me and my brethren, that we wold clere-
lye of our own consentes surrendre into his graciose handes our
monasterye, beying of his most graciouse foundacion, and whereof
your lordship is stuard.   My good lorde, the truthe is, I nor my
said brethern have never consented to surrendre our monasterye,
nor yett doo, nor never will doo by our good willes, onles it shall
please the kynges grace to giff to us commandement so to doo,
whiche I can not perceve in the commyssion of maister Holcroft
so to bee.   And if any informacyon be giffon unto his magestye,
or unto your good lordship, that we shulde consent to surrendre, as is above sayd, I assure your good lordship, apon my
fidelitie and truthe, there was never non suche consent made by
me nor my brethren, nor no person nor persons had auctoritye so

to do in our names. Wherefore I humbly beseche your good lordship, in whome is my single trust under God and the kynges magestye, to be meane for us unto his grace, so that we may contynewe in our sayd monasterye to pray for his most noble grace and your good lordship, whiche we shall dayly doo, accordyng to our bounden duyties, duryng our lyves. I assure your lordshipe I am cumyng upwardes as fast as my sekenes will suffre me, to beseche your lordshipe of charite to be good to our pouer monastery. I sende unto your lordshipe the bill indented made by me and my brethren, whiche in presence of worshipfull men I proffered to M. Holcroft, whiche to take he refused. And thus our Lord God preserve your lordshipe in good helthe. Writen at Lychefyld, the ix. day of Septembre, by your pouer bedeman,

> JOHAN, abbot of Valerayall.

To the ryght honorable sir Thomas
Cromewell, knyght, lord Cromewell,
lord prevye seall, and chieff secretarye to the kynges highenes.

We have next another letter of the chancellor Audley, which relates to the two houses of St. Osith's (mentioned before) and St. John's at Colchester. The latter was founded by Eudo Dapifer at the beginning of the twelfth century. The last abbot was John Beche, who was executed Dec. 1, 1539, for his opposition to the king's commands. His predecessor had suffered the same fate.

CXXII.

SIR THOMAS AUDLEY TO CROMWELL.

[From the State Papers, vol. i. p. 586.]

After my right harty comendations to your good lordship, with my most harty thankes for your last gentill letters, I am required by the erle of Oxford and master chauncelour to desire your good lordshipp, in all our names, to make our moost humble recommendations to the kynges mageste, and to render ouer most harty thankes to his highnes for our licens to visite and see my lord prynces grace,* whom, accordyng to our desires and duteez, we have seen, to our most rejoise and comfort, next the kynges mageste. And I assure your lordshipp I never sawe so goodly a childe of his age, so mery, so plesaunt, so good and lovyng countenans, and so ernest an ye, as it were a sage juggement towardes every person that repayreth to his grace ; and, as it semyth to me, thankes be to our Lord, his grace encresith well in the ayer that he ys in. And albeyt a litell his graces flesche decayeth, yet he shotyth owt in length, and wexith ferme and stiff, and can stedfastly stond, and wold avaunce hymself to move and go, if they wold suffir hym ; but as me semyth they do yet best, consideryng his grace is yet tendir, that he shuld not streyn hymself, as his owen corage wold serve hym, till he cum above a yere of age. I was right glad to understond there that the kynges mageste wil have his grace removyd from Haveryng now ageynst wynter tyme ; for surely it semythe to me that the house wil be a cold howse for wynter, but for somer it ys a good and a goodly ayer. I can not comprehend nor describe the goodly towardly qualiteez that ys in my lord princes grace. He ys sent of almyty Good for al our comfortes. My dayly and contynual prayer ys and shalbe for his good and prosperus preservation, and to make his grace an olde prince, besechyng your good lordeshipp to rendir to the kynges mageste thankes in al our names as ys abovesayd.

Suche brutes hath runne, sythen my last departyng from your good lordshipp, concernyng the dissolution of the abbeys of seynt Johns in Colchester and seynt Osyes, that I am bold to wryte to your good lordshipp after myn old sute for the contynuans of the said 2 places, not, as they bee, religeous, but that it mought plese the kynges mageste of his goodnes to translate them into collegys, after suche sort and ordynaunces as shall seme most

* Prince Edward, son of Queen Jane Seymour, born Oct. 12, 1537, afterwards King Edward VI.

charitable to his highnez; for the whiche, as I seyd to you afore, his grace may have of eythir of them a £1000, that ys for bothe £2000, and the gyft of the deanes and prebendaryes at his owen plesure. The cause I move this ys, fyrst, I consider that seynt Johns stondyth in his graces owen town at Colchester, wherin dwel many pour people, whiche have dayly relefe of the house; another cause, bothe these howses be in the ende of the shire of Essex, where litel hospitality shalbe kept, yf these be dissolved. For as for Seynt Jones lakkyth water, and seynt Osyes stondyth in the mersches, not very holsom, so that fewe of reputation, as I thynke, wil kepe contynual howses in eny of them, oonlez it be a congregation, as ther be nowe. There ys also 20 howses, gret and smal, dissolved, in the shire of Essex, all redy. These, and many other considerationz, movyth me to be a suter for ther traunslationz; and yet I will not nor mynde in eny wise to move or speke in this mater othirwise than shal stond with the kynges plesure; nor, in good fayth, I entend not to have eny particler avauntage for ther standyng. Yt hath plesid the kynges mageste to giff me leve to exchange londes and thynges with eyther of the house, wher with I am satisfyed, and right hertely thanke his highnes for the same. I beseche you, my good lord, if your lord-shipp shal thynke thys sute honest and resonable, to move this mater to the kynges mageste, and to sett it ernestly forward. Your lordshipp knowing bothe the howses, as ye do, can alegge more better considerations then I can imagyn or wryte. And thus I trobill you with my sutes oft tymes, and can not recompens your often gentilnesses and paynes taken for me but with my pour harty good will, whereof your lordeshipp shall be suer duryng my lyff. And besides that, if ye can or may opteyn this sute for the traunslation of these 2 howses, your lordeshipp shal have for your favour therin £200, besechyng you to travayle therin and to advertise me, as sone as ye shal se tyme, of the towardnes or ontowardnes therof. And thus, as a bolde sutour, puttyng your good lordshipp in remembrauns of al myn olde sutes, to use them at your owen leysur, I beseche our Lord to send your lordshipp as good helth, and as wel to fare as I wold myself. Wryten at Berechurch, the 8th day of September.

Your assured, to all his power,

THOMAS AUDELEY, k. chauncelour.

Post scripta. Forasmoche as this day I ryde into Suffolk, to mete the duke of Norfolk at Framyngham, to kyll sum of his bukkes there, I thought good to advertise your lordeshipp therof. His grace desired to have had me to Kenynghale, to his howse there, but I besought hym to pardon me therof, it was so ferre from me; and so, to satisfy his desire, I promysed to mete hym at Framyngham, whiche ys but 24 miles from me; besechyng your lordeshipp to advertise me, by your next letters, of the kynges magestes retourne to London, or nere there abowt, with such other occurrauntes, as your lordshipp maye. And thus fare your good lordshipp hertely well.

The following letter relates to the abbey of Whitby, which has been already mentioned in the present volume.

CXXIII.

THE PRIOR OF GISBURNE AND TRISTRAM TESHE TO CROMWELL.

[From MS. Cotton. Cleop. E. iv. fol. 48.]

Maye it please your good lordeshippe to be advertised, that accordinge to the kinges majestie commaundement we have byne at the monasterie of Whitbye, to have taken thelection of a newe abbott there. Aftre moch comunication hadd with the bretheren of the same howsse, we movid them according to your lordeship pleasure to compromitte the election into our handes, and therupon we to have nominate hym that your lordeshipp commaunded us in your lettres. And yet they nott therwith contentid, we moved them of newe to compromitt their saed election unto your lordeshipp, to thintent that your lordeshipp might have, nominat, and elect any at your pleasure ; and utterly that also they have refused. And that forsomych as your lordeshipp hath send downe the *congie d'eslier* and free election from the kinges majestie, they woll not therfore go to any oodre election, but onlie *per viam scrutinii*. And forsomych as we can not induce them tȯ compromitt their saed election neither to your lordeship nor to us, we have continued the said election tyll we be certified of the kinges and your lordeshipp further pleasure herin. And, that doon, syr Robert Woodhowsse, prior claustrall of the said monasterie, with the counsael of his adherentes which perversly resisted and withstode your lordeshippis pleasure and commaundment, we beyng their present, did departe withowȝt our knowledg, and is commyng towarde your lordeshipp to make (as we doo thinke) sume sinistre and untrewe reporte and enformacion, to whome we humbly besech your lordeshipp geve no creadaunce, unto such tyme as we may ffurther certifie your lordeshippe of his and their demeanors in the premisses, which we shall doo with as moche spede and diligence as we canne. And thus allmyghty God preserve your lordeshipp in honor. At Whitbye, the viijth. day of Octobre, anno Domini 1538.

   Your lordshipps most humble bedman,

     ROBERT SILVESTER, prior of Gysburne.

   Your lordeships moste bounden oratour,

       TRISTRAM TESHE.

The next letter relates to the great abbey of St. Alban's, in Hertfordshire, the abbot of which house also was obstinate in resisting the dissolution. The last abbot of St. Alban's was Richard Boreman, *alias* Stevenage.

CXXIV.

THE COMMISSIONERS TO CROMWELL.

[From MS. Cotton. Cleop. E. iv. fol. 43.]

Please it your lordeship to be advertised, at our commyng to Sainct Albons on Thursedaye last we beganne a visitacion amonges the moonkes, thabbot being than in Londone. And bicause we wolde the more fully knowe the hole state of alle thinges, taried the lenger in thexaminacion of theym. And upon Friedaye last we sent a monicion for the abbot to appere before us, who camme hether on Saturday bifore none, whome we have likewise as fully examined upon alle thinges as we might. And allthoughe as well by the examinacion of the moonkes as by confessioun of thabbot hymself ther doth appere confessed and fully proved juste cause of deprivacion ageinst thabbot, not only for breking of the kinges injunctiouns, but also for manifest dilapidacioun, making of shiftes, negligent administracion, and sundry other causes, yet, by what meanes we knowe not, in alle communications or motions made concernyng any surrendre he sheweth hymself so stiffe, that, as he saith, he wolle rather choyse to begge his bredde alle the dayes of his lif than consent to any surrender. We have everich of us severally and also alle togethers communed with hym and used alle suche motions as we thought might moste further that purpose, but he contynueth allweys one man and waxeth hourely more obstinate and lesse conformable. Whether he so doo upon trust and confidence of any frendeshipp, we knowe not. The premisses we thought our bounden duetie to signifie unto your lordeshippe, moste humbly beseching the same that we maye by Mr. doctour Layton knowe the kinges highnes further pleasure by you, whether we shalle contynewe in this processe of deprivacion ageinst hym and so deprive hym according to thorder of justice without lenger delaye; which doone the house wilbe in suche debt that we thinke no man wille take thoffice of abbot here upon hym, except any doo it only for that purpose to surrender the same to the kinges handes; and by thies meanes we thinke this thing maye most easely and with leste speche be brought to the kinges highnes purpose. Or els whether we shalle staye in owre processe at this tyme, and appoynte some longer daye to here the sentence of deprivacioun, leaving hym in the meane tyme in utter desperacion of any favour; which weye maye also be occasion that he, whan it shalle appere unto hym that he shal be deprived, wille perchaunce sue to have his surrender taken, bicause he wolde be assured of some lyving. The premisses we referre to the kinges highnes pleaser, which knowen by your lordeship, we shalle with alle our possible diligence confourme ourselfes to accomplishe the same, and in the meane tyme travaille with the moonks to knowe howe many of theym maye be induced to this purpose. Thus almighty God have your lordeship in his blessed keping. From Sainct Albons, the xth of December.

Youre lordscyps ever att commandement

THOMAS LEGH.

Your Lordyshippes most bounden servant,

WILLIAM PETRE.

The nunnery of Gracedieu, at Belton in Leicestershire, was founded by Rohesia de Verdon, in the 24th of Hen. III. The last prioress was Agnes Litherland.

CXXV.

JOHN BEAUMONT TO CROMWELL.

[From MS. Cotton. Cleop. E. IV. fol. 216*.]

My dutye unto your ryght honorable lordshype in moste humble fforme remembred, pleyseth hyt the same to be by thes advertysed, that I have caused xx^{li}. to be delyvered unto my ffelowe Thomas Avery to the use of your good lordeshype, humbly besechyng your lordshyppes ffavour and goodnes that as shall stand wyth the kynges plesure I may other purchase or have in fferm the demenez of Gracedewe abbey, whych I am in possessyon of, and my ffelowe Whalley to eethere, by your honorable lettres. Whych seyd abbey the erle of Huntyngdon * doth labour to take ffrom me, whych have no truste but of your lordshyppes goodnes, wythoute whych I am undoyn ; ffor I do ffeyre the seyd erle and hys sonnes do seke my lyffe, and all ffor the truthe sake, ffor I have secret warnyng by one off hys counsell to weyre a prevy cote, whych ys not suffycyent ffor me, hys powere beyng envyron my poore howse. Besechyng God that your lordeshyp wyll take in good parte my inornate colleccyon of the kynges supremyty, wherin ys no thyng apte to be presented unto your lordshyp, but the apparaunce of a trewe herte, with whych I shall contenewally pray and labour to send your lordshyp your moste noble hertes desyre. From Whellesborough, the xxvijth daye of Decembre.

Your humble servaunt,
JOHN BEAMOUNT.†

* This was George Hastings, first earl of Huntingdon of the family which still enjoys the title.

† John Beaumont, Esq. of Thringston, county of Leicester, was appointed Jan. 30, 1534-5, to take the ecclesiastical survey of the county of Leicester. He was appointed Recorder of Leicester in 1550, and in the same year, Dec. 3, was constituted Master of the Rolls. He resigned that office in disgrace May 28, 1552. He was grandfather of Francis Beaumont, the dramatic poet. (See Nichols's History of Leicestershire, vol. iii. pp. 655, 661*, 1125.) His "fellow Whalley" above mentioned was the receiver of Yorkshire.

CHAPTER III.

FINAL SUPPRESSION OF THE MONASTIC HOUSES AND CONFIS-
CATION OF THEIR PROPERTY.

After the searching visitation of the commissioners sent round the country in 1538, only a few of the larger houses, chiefly the mitred abbeys, remained unsuppressed, Some of these latter had been voluntarily surrendered, or confiscated by the attainder of their abbots.   From the Journals of the House of Lords, we find that in the par-liament of 1536, on the seventeenth of July, the following abbots were present (distin-guished by a *p.*) or voted by proxy.

p. Abbas Westm.	p. Abbas de Selby.
p. Abbas sancti Albani.	Abbas Bardeney.
Abbas sancti Augustini Cantor.	p. Abbas de Bello.
p. Abbas Burgi sancti Edmundi.	p. Abbas de Thorney.
Abbas sancte Marie Ebor.	p. Abbas de Wynchecombe.
Abbas Glaston.	p. Abbas de Waltham.
p. Abbas de Abyngdon.	p. Abbas Cirencest.
Abbas Glocestre.	p. Prior de Coventre.
Abbas de Ramesey.	p. Abbas de Tewkesbury.
Abbas de Evesham.	Abbas Salopie.
Abbas Burgi sancti Petri.	Abbas de Hyde.
p. Abbas de Redyng.	Abbas sancti Benedicti.
p. Abbas de Malmesbury.	Abbas Colchestrie.
p. Abbas de Crowlande.	Abbas Tavestok.

In the parliament which was opened on the 28th of April, 1539, they were dimi-nished to the following list, showing those who were present or sent their proxies on that day.

p. Abbas Westm.	p. Abbas de Glocestrie.
p. Abbas sancti Albani.	p. Abbas de Ramsey.
p. Abbas Burgi sancti Edmundi.	p. Abbas de Evesham.
p. Abbas beate Marie Ebor.	p. Abbas Burgi sancti Petri.
Abbas de Glaston.	Abbas sancti Johannis Colcestrie.

p. Abbas de Redyng.   p. Abbas de Wynchcombe.
p. Abbas de Malmesbury.   p. Abbas de Waltham.
p. Abbas de Crowlande.   p. Abbas Cirencestrie.
p. Abbas de Selby.   p. Abbas Tewkysbury.
p. Abbas de Thorney.   Abbas Tavestock.

When this parliament held its second session, beginning on the 12th of April, 1540, all the abbots had disappeared from the house. It was in fact in the session of 1539 that the act was passed giving the monastic estates to the king (Statutes, 31 Hen. VIII. chap. 13). This act, after reciting that a great number of religious houses had been voluntarily surrendered to the king, invests them, as well as all houses afterwards to be surrendered or dissolved, with all their sites, possessions, &c. in the king and his successors. It contains a general saving of rights to present tenants, &c., with a proviso annulling all leases or grants made within a year before the dissolution, which was called for by the eagerness with which the monks endeavoured to make away the property of their houses to enrich themselves before they were driven out, which is frequently alluded to in the foregoing letters.

The Act of Parliament just alluded to did not dissolve the monasteries. It appears to have been the policy of the court to persuade or terrify the occupants into a voluntary surrender, which was successful, except in a very small number of instances. Several of the abbots who were stubborn in refusing surrender, or who thwarted the king's measures or disobeyed his arbitrary commands, were on one charge or other indicted for high treason, and brought to the block or to the gallows, which helped to strike terror into the others. Among these were John Beche, abbot of St. John's at Colchester, Hugh Cook, abbot of Reading, and Richard Whiting, abbot of the ancient and noble abbey of Glastonbury. The following letters relate to the trial and execution of the person last mentioned. The death of abbot Whiting appears to have caused a great sensation and to have been long remembered in the West of England; a Somersetshire peasant, visiting Glastonbury on his way to London, in a song of the seventeenth century,[*] is made to say,—

> " Ice azked whose tooke downe the leads an the beels,
> And thay tould me a doctar that lived about Wels ;
> In the 7th of Jozhua pray bid them goe looke,
> Chill be hanged if thick same chaptar be not out of his booke.
>
> Vor thare you may reade about Achans wedge,
> How thick zame goolden thing did zettz teeth an edge.
> 'Tis an ominous thing how this church is abused,
> Remember how poor abbott Whitting was used."

* A Collection of Pieces in the Dialect of Zummerzet. Edited by James Orchard Halliwell, Esq. (8vo. Lond. 1843.) p. 4.

CXXVI.

THE COMMISSIONERS TO CROMWELL.

[From Burnet's Reform. vol. iii. p. 160, who printed it from MSS. Tanner * at Oxford.]

A Letter of the visitors, sent to examine the Abbot of Glassenbury.

Please hyt your lordship to be advertised, that we came to Glastenbury on Fryday last past, about tenn of the clock in the forenoone : and for that the abbot was then at Sharpham, a place of hys, a myle and somewhat more fro thabbey, we, without any delay, went unto the same place; and there, after communication declaring unto him theffect of our coming, examined him upon certain articles. And for that his answer was not then to our purpose, we advised him to call to his remembrance that which he had as then forgotten, and so declare the truth, and then came with him the same day to the abbey; and there of new proceeded that night to search his study for letters and books : and found in his study secretly laid, as well a written book of arguments against the divorce of his kinges majestie and the lady dowager, which we take to be a great matters, as also divers pardons, copies of bulls, and the counterfit lyfe of Thomas Bequet in print; but we could not find any letter that was materiall. And so we proceeded again to his examination concerning the articles we received from your lordship, in the answers whereof, as we take it, shall appear his cankerd and traiterous heart and mind against the kinges majestie and his succession ; as by the same answers, syned with his hand, and sent to your lordship by this bearer, more plainly shall appear. And so, with as fair words as

* It would have been desirable to have collated this letter with the original ; but, although the Tanner MSS. have been a century in the Bodleian Library, they still remain uncatalogued, and, out of the large number of volumes of letters in that collection, it is almost useless to search for a single document.

we could, we have conveyed him from hence into the tower, being but a very weak man and sickly. And as yet we have neither discharged servant nor monk; but now the abbot being gone, we will, with as much celerity as we may, proceed to the dispatching of them. We have in money 300*l.* and above; but the certainty of plate and other stuffe there as yet we know not, for we have not had opportunity for the same, but shortly we intend (God willing) to proceed to the same; whereof we shall ascertain your lordship so shortly as we may. This is also to advertise your lordship, that we have found a fair chalice of gold, and divers other parcels of plate, which the abbot had hid secretly from all such commissioners as have bine there in times past; and as yet he knoweth not that we have found the same : whereby we think, that he thought to make his hand, by his untruth to his kinges majesty. It may please your lordship to advertise us of the kinges pleasure by this bearer, to whom we shall deliver the custody and keeping of the house, with such stuff as we intend to leave there convenient to the kinges use. We assure your lordship it is the goodliest house of that sort that ever we have seen. We wold that your lordship did know it as we do; then we doubt not but your lordship would judge it a house mete for the kinges majesty, and for no man else : which is to our great comfort; and we trust verily that there shall never come any double hood within that house again. Also this is to advertise your lordship, that there is never a one doctor within that house; but there be three batchelors of divinity, which be but meanly learned, as we can perceive. And thus our Lord preserve your good lordship.

From Glastenbury, the 22 day of September.

Yours to command,

RICHARD POLLARD.
THOMAS MOYLE.
RICHARD LAYTON.

To the ryght honorable and their
syngular good lord, my lord
pryvye seal, thys be delivired.

CXXVII.

THE COMMISSIONERS TO CROMWELL.

[From the State Papers, vol. i. p. 619.]

Pleasithe hytt your lordeshippe to be advertised, that sithen our letters last dyrectide unto yow from Glaston., we have dayly fownde and tryede oute bothe money and plate hyde and muryde up in wallis, vauttis, and other secrette placis as well by thabbott as other of the coventt, and also convaide to diverse placis in the countrye. And in case we shoulde here tarry this fortnigthe, we do suppose daily to increase in plate and other goodis by false knaves convayde. And emonge other petty bryberies, we have founde the twoo thresorers of the churche, monkis, with the 2 clarkis of the vestry, temporall men, in so arraunte and manifeste robery, that we have commyttide the same to the jayle. At our first entree into the threser house, and vestre also, we nether fownde jewellis, plate, nor ornamenttis sufficient to serve a pour parishe churche, wherof we colde not a litell marvill; and therupon ymmediatly made so diligent enquirye and serche, that with vigilante labour we muche improvide the same, and have recoveride agayne into our handes bothe money, plate, and adornamenttis of the churche. How muche plate we knowe not, for we hade no leysure yet to wey the same; but we thinke hit of a greate valewe, and we increase itt more every day, and shall doo, as we suppois, for our tyme here beinge. We assure your lordeshippe that thabbott and the monkis forsaide hade ymbecelyde and stollyne as muche plate and adornamentes as wolde have sufficide to have begone a new abbay; what they mentte therby, we leve itt to your judgmentt. Whether the kyngis pleasur shalbe to execute his lawis upon the saide 4 persones, and to mynister them justice, according to their desertes, or to extende his mercy towardes them, and what his majesties pleasur is, hitt may please your lordeshipp to advertise us therof. The house is greate, goodly, and so pryncely as we have not sene the lyke; with 4 parkes adjoynynge, the furthermoste of them but 4 myles distaunte from the house; a grete mere, whiche ys 5 miles cumpas, being a myle and a halfe distante from the house, well replenished with greate pykis, bremes, perche, and roche; 4 faire manour placis, belonginge to the late abbott, the furthermost but 3 myles distante, beynge goodly mansions; and also one in Dorsettshire, 20 myles distante from the late monastery. We have dispachyde the servauntes, with their halfe-yeres wagies, gevinge humble thankis to the kingis majestie for the same; the monkes also, withe the kingis benevolence and rewarde, and have assigned them pentyons. We fynde them very glade to departe, most humbly thankinge the kyngis majestie of his grete goodnes moste graciously showyde unto them at this tyme, as well for his gracis rewarde as also for their pentyons. Cattell we intende to sell for redy money; and to let owte the pastures and demeynes now from Mighelmas forthe quarterly, untill the kingis pleasure therin be further knowyne, to thentente his grace shall lease no rente, for thabbott had muche pasture grounde in his hande. Other newys we knowe none, but that almighty God have you in his tuytion. From Glaston., this 28 day of September.

Youres to command,

RYCHARD POLLARD.
THOMAS MOYLE.
RIC. LAYTON.

To the right honorable and our
  singuler good lorde, my lorde
  prevy seale.

CXXVIII.

THE COMMISSIONERS TO CROMWELL.

[From the State Papers, vol. i. p. 621.]

Pleasyth hytt youre good lordshyp to be advertysed, that, sythens the dyrection of oure laste letters unto youre lordshypp, we have come to knowlege of dyvers and sundrye treasons commytted and done by the abbot of Glastonbury; the certentye wherof shall appeyre unto youre lordeshyppe in a boke herein inclosyd, and the accusers names put to the same, wych we thyngke to be verye haut and ranke treasons. And thus Jesu preserve youre good lordshypp. Frome Glastonbury, the second daye of Octobre.

Yours to command,

RYCHARD POLLARD.

THOMAS MOYLE.

RIC. LAYTON.

To the ryght honorable and
theare synguler good lord,
my lord pryvye seale, thys
be delivered.

CXXIX.

LORD RUSSELL TO CROMWELL.

[From MS. Cotton. Cleop. E. IV. fol. 99*.]

Right honourable and my verey good lorde, pleaseth youre lordeshipp to be advertysed, that I have receyved youre lettres dated the xij^th. daye of this preasent, and understond by the same youre lordeshipps greate goodnes towardes my friende the abbott off Peterborough, for whome I have ben ofte bolde to wryte unto youre good lordeshipp, moste hartely thankynge your lordeshipp for that and all other youre goodnes that I have founde at youre good lordeshipps handes, even so desiering you, my lorde, longe to contynew in the same.   My lorde, thies shalbe to asserteyne, that on Thursdaye the xiiijth daye of this present moneth the abbott of Glastonburye was arrayned, and the next daye putt to executyon, wyth ij. other of his monkes, for the robbyng of Glastonburye churche, on the Torre Hyll, next unto the towne of Glaston., the seyde abbottes body beyng devyded in fower partes, and heedd stryken off, whereof oone quarter stondythe at Welles, another at Bathe, and at Ylchester and Brigewater the rest, and his hedd uppon the abbey gate at Glaston.   And as concernynge the rape and burglary commytted, those parties are all condempned, and fower of theym putt to executyon at the place of the act don, whiche is called the Were, and there adjudged to hange styll in chaynes to thensample of others.   As for Capon, oone of the seyde offenders condempned, I have repried according to your lordeshipps letters, of whome I shall further shew unto you at my next repayre unto the courte.   And here I do sende your lordeshipp enclosed the names of thenquest that passed on Whytyng the seid abbott, whiche I ensure you, my lorde, is as worsshipfull a jurye as was charged here thies many yeres.   And there was never seene in thies partes so greate apparaunce as were here at this present tyme, and never better wyllyng to serve the kyng.   My lorde, I ensure you there were many bylles put upp ageynst the abbott by hys tenauntes and others, for wronges and injuryes that he hadd donne theym. And I commytt your good lordeshipp to the keapyng of the blessed Trynyte.   From Welles, the xvj. daye of Novembre.

Your owen to commande,

J. RUSSELL.

CXXX.

RICHARD POLLARD TO CROMWELL.

[From MS. Cotton. Cleop. E. iv. fol. 133*.]

Pleasyth it youre lordshyp to be advertysed, that synse my laste letter sent unto youre lordshyp bearyng date the xv. daye of Novembre, the same xv. daye the late abbott of Glastonberye went frome Wellys to Glastonberye, and there was drawyn thorowe the towne apon a hurdyll to the hyll callyd the Torre, wheare he was putto execucion; att wyche tyme he askyd God mercye and the kyng for hys great offensys towardes hys hyghenes, and also desyred my servauntes then beyng there present to se the execucion done, that they wold be meane to my lord presydent and to me thatt we shold desyre the kynges hyghenes of hys mercyfull goodnes and in the waye of charytye to forgyve hym his great offensys by hym commytted and done ageynste hys grace, and thereapon toke hys deathe very pacyently, and hyse hede and body bestowyd in lyke maner as I certyfyed youre lordshyp in my last letter. And lykewyse the other ij. monkys desyred lyke for- gyvenes, and toke there deathe verye pacyently, whose sowllys God pardon. And whereas I att my last beyng wyth youre lord- shyp att Londone movyd youre lordshyp for my brother Paulett, desyryng youre lordshyp to be a meane that he myght have the surveorshype of Glastonbery, wyche I dowt nott but he wyll use and exercyse the sayd offyce to the kynges moyste profytt and advantage, and youre lordshyppes goodnes herein to hym to be showyd he shall recompense to hys lytle powere, I assure your lordshyp he hathe byn very dylygent, and dyvers other by hys meanys, to serve the kynge att thys tyme, accordyng to hys dewtye and ryght. So was Nycholas fytz James, John Sydnam, and Thomas Hornar, youre servantes. Also thys ys to advertyse youre lordshyp that the late abbott of Glastonberye, afore his execution, was examyned apon dyvers articles and interrogatoryes to hym mynystred by me, but he cowld accuse no man but hym selfe of any offense ageynst the kynges hyghnes, nor he wold confesse no more goold nor sylver nor any other thyng more then he dyd afore youre lordshyp in the Towre. My lord Russell takythe hys jorney this present daye from Wellys towardes London. I suppose hytt wylbe nere Crystmas before I shall have surveyd the landes att Glastonberye, and takyn the audyte there. Other newes I knowe none, as knowythe God, who ever preserve youre lordshype. Frome Wellys, the xvj. daye of Novembre.

Your assuryd to command,

RYCHARD POLLARD.

Many projects appear to have been started for the purpose of turning the monastic houses and estates to some public use. We have seen in the foregoing letters different suggestions of this kind, some wishing them to be applied to purposes of education, others praying for their preservation for " the keeping up of hospitality." The advocates of the latter proposition did not understand the great social revolution which was then commencing. The king appears to have entertained a plan of applying them to increase the number of bishopricks. In MS. Cotton. Cleop. E. iv. fol. 182, we find a draught of a proposed act of parliament to embody, in a certain degree, all these purposes, which was drawn up after the suppression of the lesser monasteries, and by which it was proposed " to keep hospitality at the place of the dissolved abbies ; that no bishop have above 1000 marks a year ; that all monks, canons, and nuns be closely confined to their abbeys, and have 40s. a year, besides victuals, and abbots £5 ; that governors be appointed to each house, with a salary of a 1000 marks a year to keep hospitality, if the revenues will answer ; and that the rest of the revenues be applied for the defence of the realm, mending highways, &c." In the same volume we have fragments of another project, drawn up apparently at the time of the dissolution of the greater monasteries, and which certainly originated with the king. The commencement is written, and corrected, in the king's own hand, and runs as follows (MS. Cotton. Cleop. E. iv. fol. 305.) :—

" Forasmuche as it is nott unknowne the slowghful and ungodly lyff whyche hath bene usid amonst all thos sort whyche have borne the name off religius folke, and to the intente that hensforthe meny off them myght be tornyd to better use (as heraffter shall folow), werby Godes worde myght the better be sett forthe, chyldren broght up in lernyng, clerces nuryshyd in the universites, olde servantes decayd to have lyfynges, allmeshousys for pour folke to be sustaynyd in, reders off Grece, Ebrew, and Latyne to have good stypende, dayly almes to be mynystrate, mendyng off hyght wayse, exhybission for mynysters off the chyrche, it is thowght therfore unto the kynges hyghtnes most expedient and necessary that mo bysshopprycys, colegyall and cathedralle chyrchys, shulbe establyshyd in sted of thes forsayd relygyus housys, within the fondasion weroff other tytylles affore rehersyd shalbe stablysyd."

This is followed by a commencement of a preamble of a law written by another hand; and it is accompanied by the following plan for new bishopricks, &c. on a separate sheet of paper, written in the king's hand, but apparently incomplete.

CXXXI.

PROJECT FOR NEW BISHOPS' SEES.

[From MS. Cotton. Cleop. E. iv. fol. 304*.]

Byshopprychys to be new made.

Essex	.— Waltam.
Hertforde	.— Saynt Albonys.
Bedfordshyre and Buckyngham .	Dunstable Nowenham Elnestowe.
Oxford and Barkshyre	Osnay and Tame.
Northhamton and Hontyng.	Peterburrow.
Mydelsex	.— Westm.
Lecestre and Rowttland	Laycester.
Glocester- shyre	Saynt Peters.
Lancaster	Fontayne and archdeconry off Rychemond.
Suffolke	.— Bury.

Stafford and
  Saloppe .   .   .⎫ Shrewsbury.
                      ⎭

Not. and   ⎧ Welbek
  Derby   .   .⎨ Worsop and
                 ⎩ Turgarton.

                  ⎧ Lanceston
Cornewall .   .⎨ Bedmynne
                  ⎩ with another.

*Plasys to be altheryd acordyng to our devyse whyche have sees
in them.*

Cryst chyrche in Cantorbury.
Saynt Swytynnys.
Elye.
Durhame.
Rochester with a part off Lydes.
Worcester.
and all others havyng the same.

Plasys to be alteryd into coleges and scolles wonly.

Burton super Trent.

The project of law last mentioned appears to have shared the same fate as the one preceding; but the king carried into effect a part of his plan of establishing new bishops' sees. Three of those mentioned in the list were created within two years after the dissolution of the houses on the ruins of which they were established. In 1541 John Chambers, last abbot of Peterborough, was made first bishop of Peterborough. At the close of the year 1540, Thomas Thirlby (who had no successor) was appointed bishop of Westminster. In 1541 also, the king appointed Robert Kyng, last abbot of Oseney, bishop of Oxfordshire, making Oseney abbey church his cathedral, but the see was soon afterwards moved to Christ Church, Oxford.* The abbey of Oseney,

-----

* " Upon the erection of the new bishopricks by king Henry the Eighth, in 1542, the abbey of Oseney was changed into a cathedral church of Christ and the blessed

founded in 1129 by Robert de Oily, stood within the suburbs of Oxford. The Cistercian abbey of Thame, or Tame, also in Oxfordshire, was founded in 1137 or 1138; its last abbot also signs himself Robert Kyng, and was perhaps the same person as the last abbot of Oseney. Henry VIII. established two other new bishoprics on monastic sites, those of Bristol and Gloucester; the first bishop of Gloucester, John Wakeman, had been abbot of Tewkesbury.

Many of the monastic estates were retained in the crown several years, but in the sequel they were nearly all sold to secular proprietors, after the moveables and even the materials of the buildings had been disposed of for the use of the king. The following documents, which will help to show the manner in which the moveables of the religious houses were sold, are selected from the papers of the Scudamores of Herefordshire, now in the British Museum. The first contains a part of the accounts of John Scudamore, the king's receiver for several counties on the borders of Wales; it will help to throw a light on the domestic economy of the monks, and may be compared with the survey of the moveable property of the abbey of Peterborough printed in Gunton's History.

Of the houses to which it relates, Bordesley abbey, in Worcestershire, was founded by the empress Matilda in 1136. It was surrendered on the 17th July, 30 Hen. VIII. (A.D. 1538); the last abbot was John Day.

Of the Grey Friars at Stafford very little is known; it stood in the north part of the town. The Austin priory of St. Thomas at Stafford is said to have been founded about 1180 by the bishop of Coventry and Lichfield; the last prior was Robert Wythell.

The Grey Friars of Lichfield is described by Leland as being in the south-west part of the town; but its history is also very obscure.

The Cistercian abbey of Crokesden, or Croxden, in Staffordshire, was founded about 1179 by the Verdons; its last abbot was Thomas Chawner.

Rouceter Abbey, also in Staffordshire, was founded by Richard Bacon for black monks about the year 1146. The last prior was William Grafton.

Very little is known of the abbey of Hilton, or Hulton, in Staffordshire; it was founded by Henry de Audeley, early in the thirteenth century, and its last abbot bore the name of John.

Virgin, wherein were settled a dean, prebendaries, &c. who were to be the chapter of the bishop of Oxfordshire, whose palace was to be at Gloucester Hall: but this establishment continued not above three or four years, when, in 1546, the conventual church of St. Frideswide, then called King Henry the Eighth's College, was made the cathedral, and called Christ Church." (Monasticon.)

CXXXII.

ACCOUNTS OF JOHN SCUDAMORE.

[From MS. Addit. in Mus. Brit. No. 11,041, fol. 86.]

Bordesley.—Sales ther made the xxiijth. day of September, anno regni regis Henrici viij^{vi}. xxx^{mo}., at the survey ther.

sol.	Fyrst, sold to Raffe Sheldon esquyer, and Mr. Markeham, the iron and glasse in the wyndowes of the north-syde of the cloyster . .	xvij^s. viij^d.
sol.	Item, sold to Mr. Markeham the old broken tyle house at the reddyche and a lytle house by the same .	vij^s. vj^d.
sol.	Item, recevyd of Mr. Fowke Grevylle esquyer, for a ffyne for the lytle house by Seynt Stephens chappell, with the close belongyng to the same*	vj^s. viij^d.
sol.	Item, recevyd of the same Mr. Gre-vylle for a lytle table and the pavyng stone ther . .	iij^s. iiij^d.
sol.	Item, sold to Mr. Markeham the pavyng tyle of the northsyde of the cloyster	v^s.
sol.	Item, a lytle belle sold to Raphe Sheldon esquyer . .	xxx^s.
sol.	Item, the pavement of the est syde of the cloyster sold to a servaunt of the busshoppes of Worceter .	v^s.

* This article is erased in the original, as though the bargain had not held good.

sol. { Item, the glasse of the est syde of the cloyster sold to Mr. Morgon . } vij^s. vj^d.

sol. { Item, sold to Thomas Norton a butteras of stone at the est ende of the churche* . . . . } xij^d.

Summa ult. xxx^s. pro campan. } xlvj^s. oneratur.

The Grey ffryers of Staff. surrendryd } The sale of goodes ther made the xxvijth day of September, anno xxx^{mo}. Henrici viij^{vi}., as herafter followyth

Kechyn sol. { Fyrst, sold to the warden of the seyd fryers ij. brasse pottes . . } viij^s.

sol. { Item, ij. brasse pottes sold to Edward Scudamour . . . } iiij^s.

sol. { Item, sold to the towene of Stafford ij. church candelstyckes . . } v^s.

sol. { Item, sold to the seyd Scudamour ij. xij^d vj^d coberds, a cobert, a spytt, and a tryvett . . . . } xviij^d.

sol. Item, sold to the wardene vj. plattes . ij^s.

sol. { iiij^d ij^d Item, a fryeng panne and a peyre of pothangles sold to the seyd Scudamour . . . . } vj^d.

sol. Item, ij pannes sold to . . vj^d.

sol. { Item, sold to the baylyf of Staff. a potthangles . . . . } vij^d.

Summa xxij^s. ij^d.

Butterie sol. { Item, sold to Doryngton a gret basen . . . } xx^d.

Summa patet.

Churche. Item, a cope of tawny damaske . xij^d

* This article also is erased in the original.

sol. { Item, a vestment and ij. tynakles of old prest velvet sold to Johan Savage baylyf . . . } xiij^s. iiij^d.

sol. { Item, sold to Thomas Williams ij. copes of redd tartarne . . . } xij^d.

sol. { Item, a sute of blue sarcenet sold to Thomas Cradock . . . } iij^s. iiij^d.

sol. { Item, a sute of grene branchyd sylk, sold to Mr. Offeley . . } vj^s. viij^d.

sol. { Item, ij. tynakles of dunne sylk, sold to Pereson . . . } xx^d.

sol. { Item, iij. auter clothes, sold to Robert Doryngton . . . } xij^d.

sol. { Item, a cope of lynyn clothe steynyd sold to a fryer . . . } iiij^d.

sol. { Item, ij. table clothes, sold to John a Lee . . . . } vj^d.

sol. { Item, ij. corperas casys, sold to the prior . . . . } iiij^d.

sol. { Item, a corperas, sold to the wardens of the churche . . . } iiij^d.

sol. { Item, sold to William Beutrey a stremer of lynyn clothe . . } iiij^d.

sol. { Item, a vestment of blue fustian and one of whyt diaper, sold to fryere Wood . . . . } vj^d.

sol. { Item, a sute of vestinentes of yolowe say, sold to Edward Rogers . } xij^d.

sol. { Item, sold to John Webbe the tymber worke in the hyegh quyer, and a auter of alablaster in the body of the churche . . . } ix^s. viij^d.

sol. { Item, sold to Rychard Lees all the setes . . . . } vj^d.

sol. { Item, a table of allablaster standyng in the church, sold to Mr. Loveson } ij^s. viij^d.

sol. { Item, in Seynt Fraunces chapelle all the seates sold to Robert Doryngton . . . . } iiij^d.

sol. { Item, a image of Seynt Katerine, sold to Lee . . . } vj^d.

sol. { Item, sold to Robert Doryngton, old bokes and a cofer in the library . } ij^s.

sol. { Item, sold a old peyre of portatyffes organs to Mr. Besum . . } ij^s.

sol. { Item, an old cofer, in the vestry, sold to Jamys Clement . . } ij^s. viij^d.

sol. { Item, old wexe, sold to Robert Doryngton . . . } iiij^d.

sol. { Item, a lampe, sold to Robert Doryngton . . . . } viij^d.

sol. { Item, old bokes in the vestry, sold to the same Robert . . . } viij^d.

sol. { Item, sold to Robert Whytgreve, a missale . . . . } viij^d.

sol. { Item, ij. aulter candelstyckes and a pykes of copper, sold to Mr. Swynnerton . . . } xij^d.

sol. Item, a bere franke, sold to . ij^d.

Summa lv^s. viij^d.

Bruehouse.—Item, sold to the under baylyff and

sol. { to the late warden of the Fryers iij. leads, one to brue in, and ij. to kele in, fates, iiij tubbes, a bultyng hutche, and a knedyng trowghe . } xiiij^s. viij^d.

sol. { Item, ij. peces of tymber lyeng in the bruehouse, sold to Bagnoll . } iiij .

Summa xv^s.

Hall.   { Item, a table on the north syde of   } xvj^d.
sol.   { the hall, sold to Robert Danes   . }

sol.   { Item, sold to the hyeghe baylyff, the } xvj^d.
      { table on the sowthsyde of the hall }

sol.   { Item, sold to Robert Wetwood, the } viij^d.
      { table at the hyeghe deske   . }
           Summa iij^s. iiij^d.

Buyldynges. — Item, sold to Jamys Lusone esquyer
         all the churche and quyer, with all
         edyfyengs and buyldynges within   xxix^{li}. xx^d.
         the precinct of the Fryers Minours   pro qua quidem
         surrendryd, with all the stone, tym-   summa pre-
         ber, tyle, glasse, and iron in the   fatus Jacobus
         same, ledd and belles only exceptyd,   obligat. inter al.
         and also exceptyd and reservyd the   ad solvend. ad
         stone wall next unto the towne of   fest. Pur. beate
         Stafford   .   .   .   .   Marie et Na-
                                                   tivitat. Sancti
                                                   Johannis equal.

sol.   { Item, sold to the towneshyp, the wall }
      { of the Fryers next unto the towne   } iij^s. iiij^d.
           Summa xxix^{li}. v^s.

Sum of all the goodes
and buyldynges of }xxxiiij^{li}. iij^s. x^d.{ R' by Johan } cj^s. ij^d.
the seyd ffryers sold.   Scudamour
                                    esquyer, r.

Item, ij. belles, one a sauncebelle, the other by estimation x^{cth}. in the custodye of Mr. Luson.

Item, in ledd apon the quyer and a chapelle by estimation xlv. fotes brode of bothe sydes and xliij. fotes long, in the custody of baylyffes of Stafford.

The Austen   The sales of the goodes ther made the xxvijth day of
Fryers of } September, anno xxx^{mo}. Regis Henrici viij.
Staff.

Church. sol.	Fyrst, sold to Mr. Whytgreve, a masse boke	xij^d.
sol.	Item, a cope of blake chamlet, sold .	ij^s.
R. B.	Item, a vestment and ij. tynaklez of blake say with albes and amyses, etc. sold to Richard Ward .	iiij^s.
R. B.	Item, a vestment and ij tynakles of tawny sarcenett, sold to	iiij^s.
R. B.	Item, a véstment and ij. tynakles without albes of bawdekyn with images of our lady, sold to Mr. Luson .	xviij^d.
R. B.	Item, ij. tynakles with albes, bawdekyn with bryddes, sold to Affley	iiij^s. iiij^d.
R. B.	Item, a syngle vestment with a albe and a blake orferuns, sold .	xx^d.
R. B.	Item, a vestment of redd fustyan with ij. albes	ij^s. viij^d.
sol.	Item, ij. old copes, one of grene and another of old badkyn parke worke	ij^s.
R. B.	Item, ij. copes grene and yolowe partye colowryd and rewyd, sold to Mr. Luson . . .	xxij^d.
R. B.	Item, iiij. corperas casys . .	viij^d.
R. B.	Item, a peyre of censours, sold to Thomas Browne . . .	iiij^d.
R. B.	Item, a vestment of white bustion, sold to the prior . . .	viij^d.
I. S.	Item, ij. candelstyckes . .	xvj^d.
I. S.	Item, a alter cloth . . .	viij^d.
I. S.	Item, old bokes in the quyer .	vj^d.
R. B.	Item, a pulpytt . . .	iiij^d.
I. S.	Item, ij. ladders . . .	viij^d.

iijs. viijd.   iiijd.

R. B. { Item, a table of alablaster and a dore, sold to Mr. Stamford } iiijs.

R. B. { Item, the hyegh alter, sold to Mr. Stamford } iijs.

R. B. { Item, the bordes of the altar of the northe syde of the church } viijd.

I. S. { Item, ij. grave stones of alablast[er], sold to   Wolrych } xijd.

I. S. Item, the organs, sold to Mr. Offeley   xxvjs. viijd.

Hall. { Item, a table in the old hall with ij.
I. S.   trestylles } iiijd.

R. B. { Item, a table in the inner hall, with ij. trestylles and iij. formes, sold to Robert Doryngton } viijd.

Bruehouse. { Item, a bultyng table, sold to Marga-
R. B.   rett Whytfyld } ijd.

R. B. { Item, a ffurnes of ledd, sold to Mr. Stamford } vjs.

Kechyn. }
I. S.   } Item, a great pot and a lesse   iijs. iiijd.

R. B. Item, iij. pannes of brasse   ijs. viijd.

R. B. { Item, iij. platters, a dysshe, and a sawecere } xijd.
       { Item, a trevett. } iiijd.

Summa lxxixs.

Buyldyngs. —Item, sold to Jamys Leuson esquyre, Thomas Picto, and Richard Warde, all the tyle, shyngle, tymber, stone, glasse and iron, one marble grave stone, the pavementes of the church, quyer, and chapelles, with rode lofte, the pyctures of Cryst, Mary, and Johan, beyng in the church and rec. xl^s.

chauncell of the Austen Fryers, besydes the towne of Stafford, surrendryd with all other superfluos
edyfyes and buyldynges within
the precynct of the seyd Fryers, to
be takyn downe, defacyd, and caryed
away by the seyd Loveson, Picto,
and Ward, at there owne proper
costes and charges, and to pay for
all the premysses to the kyng and
hys heyres, successors and assignes

xxviij^{li}. viij^s.
iiij^d.
Inde sol. pro
Picto xl^s. et
rem.
xxvj^{li}. viij^s. iiij^d.
pro qua quidem
summa Jacobus
Loveson de
Wolverhamp-
ton. ar. obli-
gat. inter al.
ad solvend. ad
fest. Pur.
beatæ Marie
virginis et

Nat. sancti Johannis prox. equal. ut patet obligat. dat.
Sept. anno xxx^{mo} regis Henrici viij. rem. cum J.
Scudamour, ar. rec. partic.

Sum of all the goodes and
edyfyengs forseyd in the
Austen Fryres sold.

xxxij. vj^s. iiij^d.

Rec. per J. S. cxviij^s.
Super. pro edific.
xxvj^{li}. viij^s. iiij^d.

Item, there remaynyth in the custodye
of Robert Burgoyne, audytour, one
playne crosse of copper, with a
lytle image of Cryst sylver apon
hyt, worth by estimation . .

iij^s. iiij^d.

Item, remaynyth in the custodye of
Johan Scudamore esquyer, particuler receivor, etc. one lytle woodden
crosse platyd over verry thyn with
sylver, worth by estimation . .

xij^d.

Item, ther remaynyth in the steple
one belle, by estimation x^{cth}, in the
custodye of Thomas Picto, worth
by estimation . . .

viij^{li}.

Item, one lytle belle$^{\Lambda}$ in the steple,
weyng by estimation di.^{cth}, worth
by estimation . . .

viij^s.

2 N

Prisors $\left\{\begin{array}{l}\text{Robert Ryve,}\\\text{William Colman,}\\\text{Marke Wyrley,}\\\text{Thomas Fanne,}\end{array}\right\}$ jurati.

Grey Fryers } The sales ther made the iiij^th day of October,
of Lychefyld. }   anno xxx° regis Henrici viij^vi.

sol.	ffyrst sold to M^r. Strete all the copes, vestments, and tynakles in gros for	xl^s.
sol.	Item, sold to the seyd M^r. Strete ij. candelstyckes of latten . .	viij^d.
sol.	Item, the pavyng tyle in both the cloysters sold to M^r. Strete . .	xl^s.
sol.	Item, sold to Thomas Bardell, ij. candelstykes	viij .
sol.	Item, sold to sir Thomas Dobsone, a presse, a bedstede, and a dore .	iiij^d.
sol.	Item, the tymber, tyle, and stone of the old hostery and the ffermery, sold to Rychard Rawson . .	iiij^li.
sol.	Item, the tyle and tymber of the lytle cloyster, sold to Johan ap Glm.	xiij^s. iiij^d.
sol.	Item, ij. worte leddes in the bruehouse, sold to Johan Sandelond . .	vj^s. viij^d.
sol.	Item, sold to M^r. Aston, a wynd .	ij^s.
sol.	Item, sold to Thomas Fanne, the bryck wall at the churche ende .	ij^s.
sol.	Item, sold to the master of the Ile, a fate in the bruehouse . .	iiij^d.
sol.	Item, sold to Chapman, a fate .	xij^d.
sol.	Item, sold to Johan Genynges, the tymber, tyle, and stone of the stable buttyng upon the churche ende	iiij^li.

sol. { Item, sold to John Mylward, the tymber, tyle, and stone of the iij. houses joynyng together in the court callyd the Tenys Court . } xl^s.

sol. { Item, sold to Rychard Ballard, the lytle house over the ovyn . . } iij^s. iiij^d.

sol. { Item, sold to M^r. Ryce, mastres Warden, mastres Stonye, vij. leddes for wort . . . . } xviij^s.

sol. { Item, the tymber, tyle, and stone of the kechyn and the bruehouse, sold to Edward Spratte . . } liij^s. iiij^d.

sol. { Item, sold to Johan Laughton, a cofere and a hutche in the buttery . } xij^d.

sol. { Item, the cesterne of ledd, and the stone that hyt standyth in, in the kechyn, sold to John Genynges . } xiij^s. iiij^d.

sol. { Item, the glasse that ys lewse in the newe loggyng, sold to William Colman . . . . } iij^s.

sol. { Item, a lampe, sold to Edmund Bardell . . . . } viij^d.

sol. { Item, the presse in the vestrye, sold to the warden of the gyld . . } xvj^d.

sol. Item, ij hutches, sold to Mr. Warden viij^d.

sol. { Item, a fryers masse boke, solde to Marke Wyrley . . . } iiij^d.

sol. { Item, the stone wall betwene the old ostery and the ffrater, sold to Johan Sadeler . . . . } v^s.

sol. { Item, the pavement of the quyere, sold to M^r. Stretes . . } xiij^s. iiij^d.

sol. { Item, the fryers setes in the quyere, sold to Johan Laughton . . } vj^s. viij^d.

sol. { Item, the cundyt of ledd in the cloyster, sold to the master of the gyld
and his brethern . . . } xxx^s.

sol. { Item, a halywaterstocke, sold to Johan
Howlat . . . . } xx^d.

sol. { Item, all the kechyn stuff, sold to
M^r. warden of the gyld . . } xx^s.

sol. { Item, ij. standert candelstyckes, sold
to the seyd M^r. warden . . } viij^s

sol. { Item, the lytle cundyt standyng at
the revestrye dore, sold to George
Stonyng . . . . } v^s.

sol. { Item, the cesterne of ledd standyng
in the porche at the Tenys Court
ende, sold to M^r. Lytleton . } xx^s.

sol. { Item, a lytle porche standyng by the
dwellyng house, sold to M^r. Lytyl-
ton . . . . } x^s.

recepi
xxj^{li}. iij^s. iiij^d.

Item, the ffrayter and the chambers
stretchyng to the kechyn, with all
the quadrant of the inner cloyster
joynyng to the church and steple,
and the church and quyer, and the
long newe house of the est syde of
the same cloyster, except and reservyd ledd, belles, pavement, and
gravestones within all the seyd
buyldynges, save only the pavement
of the seyd churche, whyche ys
parcell of the seyd bargayne, sold to
Johan Westone of Lichfeld, Johan
Archer, Richard Cotes gent., Hugh
Bowde, Harry Hopwood draper,
Michaell Hylle, Johan Genynges

} xlij^{li}. xiij^s.
iiij^d.

Inde sol. J. S.
xxj^{li}. iij^s. iiij^d.
Et rem. xxj^{li}. x^s.
pro qua quidem
summa Johan-
nes Weston, Jo-
hannes Archer,
Ricardus Cotes,
et Hugo Bowde,
obligat. ad sol.
ad fest. sancti
Michaelis arch-
angeli prox. ut

and Johan Mylward, and hath day to deface the steple, cloyster, and quyer forth, wyth the churche, onles they obteyne lycens otherwyse of the kyng and hys councell, athyssyde the feast of the Purification of our Lady next commyng, and for all the residewe of the buyldynges iij. yeres day to pull downe and carye awey, and to have egresse and regresse for the same .

patet oblig. dat. quinto die Octobr. anno regni regis Henrici viij^{vi}. xxx. rem. cum Johanne Scudamour, ar. r. partic. etc.

Crokesden.—The salez ther made the xv^{th} day of October, anno xxx° regis Henrici viij^{vi}. as herafter followyth:

sol.	Item, a lytle gatehouse on the northsyde of the comyn wey, sold to M^r. Bassett . . .	xiij^s. iiij^d.
sol.	Item, sold to M^r. Basset, the loft under the organs . . .	x^s.
sol.	Item, sold to M^r. Bassett, the lytle smythes forge . . .	iiij^s. viij^d.
sol.	Item, the bott of an asshe sold .	xx^d.
sol.	Item, the roffe of the churche, sold to sir Thomas Gylbert and Edmund Wetheryns of Chekeley parysshe .	vj^{li}.
r. xxxiij^s. iiij^d.	Item, the roffe of the dorter, sold to M^r. Bassett . . .	xxxiij^s. iiij^d.
sol.	Item, sold to Johan Ferne, all the old tymber in the cloyster . .	vj^s. viij^d.

Summa, ix^{li}. ix^s. viij^d. oneratur.

Rouceter.—The sales there made, the xvj^{th} day of October, anno xxx°. regis Henrici viij.

sol.	Item, the glasse and iron in the wyndowes of seynt Michaelles chapell, sold to Johan Forman . .	iij^s iiij^d.

sol. { Item, the tymber of the seyd chapell, sold to William Loghtonhouse . } vij^s. vj^d.

sol. { Item, the shyngle of the same chapell, sold to William Bagnall . . } viij^d.

Summa, xj^s. vj^d. oneratur.

Hylton.—The salez ther made, the xxjth day of October, anno xxx^o regis Henrici viij^{vi}.

rec. iiij^{li}.
oneratur iiij^{li}.

Item, sold to Stephen Bagott, gent. three belles, a grett   , for the somme of nynetene poundes syxtene shyllynges, after the rate of xviij^s. the hundredd ——————

} xix^{li}. xvj^s.
inde sol. J. S.
ar. iiij^{li}. Et
rem. xv^{li}. xvj^s.
pro qua quidem
summa prefatus
Stephanus ob-

lig. solvend. ad festum sancti Michaelis archangeli prox. ut patet oblig. gerent. dat. xxj^o die Octobr. anno xxx^o regis Henrici viij. cum Johanne Scudamour ar. rec. rem.

————————

The priory of Wenlock was founded as a nunnery as early as the seventh century; but was refounded as a convent of Cluniac monks, and made dependant on the house of La Charité sur Loire, by Roger de Montgomery, in 1080. It is still remarkable for its interesting ruins. The last prior was John Bayly (or Baylis), *alias* Cressage.

CXXXIII.

SIR RICHARD RICHE TO JOHN SCUDAMORE.

[From MS. Addit. No. 11,041, fol. 18.]

Mr. Sckidmore, this shalbe after my right hertie commendacions to requyre you to assingne and apoynct unto my ffrende James Lewson, the five bellis remaynyng at the late monasterie of Wenlocke, he givyng unto you unto the kinges highenes use lyke waight of belle mettell for the same, or elis for the performance therof he to pay after xx^s. the hundreth waight therof, praying you to accomplyshe the same accordinglie as I trust you. And this shalbe your discharge in that behalff. From London, this xxiiij[th] of Aprill, anno xxxij[do] H. viiij[vi].

Your lovyng ffrende,

RYCHARD RYCHE.

To my right loving ffrende Mr. Skidmore,
receivour generall unto the kinges majestie of
the dissolvid possessions in the countie of
Salopp.

The two next letters relate to Bordesley abbey; the second gives some curious illustrations of the process of salt-making at that time.

CXXXIV.

SIR RICHARD RICHE TO JOHN SCUDAMORE.

[From MS. Add. No. 11,041, fol. 26.]

Forasmoche as I am creadiblie advertised that the late monastery of Bordesley is defacid and pluckid downe, and the substance therof solde to dyverse persons without proffitt or lucre paide or aunswerid to the kinges majestes use for the same, thiese shalbe to requyre you, in the kinges hyghenes behalff, as convenyent oportunytie may serve you, as welle to enquyre of theym that so hath defacid the said howse, and of their auctoritie in that behalff, as also of those persons that have bought or have hadd given any of the same, and what somes have ben paide therfor, and to whose use, not omytting to charge all and every of the said persons whiche heryn shalbe touched to apere personally at this next terme following before me at London, as they will aunswer at their perills, there to make aunswere to suche mattier as shalbe by me objectid agenst theym; eftsones praying yow for my sake to graunte unto sir George Throgmerton, knight, the preferment of all suche stone, glasse, and iron as is at the said late monastery lefte to be sold, he giving therfor as any other will, not faylyng herof as I may doo you pleasure. Thus fare ye well. From London, the last of Julie.

Your lovyng ffrende,
RYCHARD RYCHE.

To my loving ffrendes, Mr. Sckidmore and Mr. Burgoyn, the kinges highenes offycers of the dissolvid possessions in the countie of Worcestre, and to every of theym.

CXXXV.

ROGER BEDULL TO SCUDAMORE AND BURGOYN.

[From MS. Addit. No. 11,041, fol. 48.]

Right worshypple masters, my dewty rememberyd, I have me commendyd unto yow, sertyfying yow that your servanttes hathe demawndyd of me serten salte that the abbye of Bordysley hade yerly, for the whiche sawlte that was laste made I have payd to Mr. Thomas Evans, liijs. iiijd. Consytheryng the chargys therto belongyng, I thynke hyt be all payd, soo ther ys no more dewe to be payd as yet; for Bordysley salte ys wont to be made alweys betwene Estur and Pentycoste. Also I have recevyd your rente-rowle, and getheryd up the rent, and fownde more then ys there, as hytt aperythe by a rent-rowle that your clarke made owte of myne, as knowythe God, who ever kepe yow.

From Droytewyche, the iijde day of Decembre.

By yours, ROGER BEDULL.

The chargys that belongythe to the salte makyng.

Item, for the salte makyng . . . xs.
Item, for the cuttyng of the wod . . . ijs.

Item, for the beryng of the bryne . . xvj^d.

Item, for the drawyng of the bryne . . v^d.

Item, for the reparacyon of the fates . . xvj^d.

Also, for the getheryng of the rent and the makyng of the salte, my ffee is yerly a lyverye cote and . . . . . vj^s. viij^d.

To the ryght worshypple Mr.
Scuddamore aud Mr. Burgoenye
thys be delyvered with sped, dd.

The places mentioned in the following letter are all in Shropshire. Caynham is a village in the neighbourhood of Ludlow, which was a manor of the abbey of Wigmore. There was a house of Austin friars at Woodhouse near Cleobury; it was one of the earliest establishments of this order in England, said to have been founded not long after 1250 by a member of the family of the Turbervilles. At Bridgnorth there was a convent of grey friars, founded by John Talbot earl of Shrewsbury in the time of Henry VI. Wigmore abbey, founded by the Mortimers in the twelfth century, was one of the most important religious houses on the borders of Wales.

CXXXVI.

ROBERT BURGOYN TO JOHN SCUDAMORE.

[From MS. Addit. No. 11,041, fol. 31.]

Right worshippfull sir, after most hartie recommendations, with lyke thankes for your gentill lettres, and ffor your sedulious paynes and labours taken aboute the survey off Cayneham, and certen ffryre houses, off the whiche I have receyved parte off the surveys, and wher you entend to survey the ffrire houses in Herefford, and ferther that you will send Mr. William Scudamore, your sone, and my clarke, to surveye the ffryers at Wodhouse and Bridgenorth, I thynk my selff muche bounde unto you that yt will please you off your goodnesse so to fforder me in my greate and intollerable busynesse; but, sir, because I cannott convenyently, nor before thys tyme I have not used, to certefie but by hoole shires, yt myght therfore please you to

2 o

appoynt your seid sone, together with my servaunte Palmer, to survey ffully alle ffrire houses within your and my circuite, and they to do no more but onlye to survey the houses and landes, and make estate off the scytuacion off the houses, and to prayes all and every house within the precyncte of eny suche house, and to note which off them be moste meteste for a tenaunte, and to make no manner off sale, but suffre suche as be nowe in possession of every suche house to occupie the same *quousque*, etc., and to charge them with the sauffe kepyng theroff, and to mesure the ledes and take the contentes, etc. and to mesure the belles, and to certefie the c^{thes} by estimacion, and ferther to take a note off all the ffrires names, off the order, religion, and dioces, and off whose ffoundacion, etc. And as you write unto me, we maye sell no housyng unto suche tyme we have furste certefied, save only the churches, cloysters, and dorters. Howbeyt, Mr. Giffard and I have sold in some ffrire houses all the buyldynges, the cause was for that they werre so spoyled and torne by suche as sold the goodes, that in manner they werre downe, and yff they shuld nott have ben sold, the kyng shuld have hadd nothyng theroff. Ferder, sir, they muste surveye the wodes belongyng to the seid ffryre houses, etc. Besides this, Mr. Bradeshawe, who hath the demeans off Wigmore, hath wrytten unto me to requyre you to be so good to survey the demeans theroff, and such thynges as he shuld have in fferme, and my servaunte Palmer shall wayte apon you. I beseche you do so muche for hym, for my good lord precedentes sake; * and what you do theryn I am right well contented therwith, etc. Sir, I have sente you by your servaunte a buk; such as he ys, I pray you take yt in good parte. And ther had ben eny better that I could have gotten, you shuld have hadd yt. Good Mr. Giffard kylled yt for you yesterdaye, and I begged yt; I wold yt werre a stage. I pray you have me hartely recommended to my good mistres your

* The lord president of the Marches and Principality of Wales, which office was at this time held by bishop Lee.

wyffe, and to Mr. Monyngton and Mr. Dansey, your sones in lawe, with ther good wyffes. And thus I am always bolde off you, as off one whome I wold shuld commaunde me. From Thellesferd, the vjth daye off Julii.

The kynges majestie will take his journey this yere into Sussex, and so be the coste, and to Wodstoke and Grafton, and so returne.

> Your owne, to the uttermoste off his little power,
>
> ROBERT BURGOYN.

To the right worshippffull Johan
Scudeamore esquyer, one off
the kynges receyvoures, geve
thies.

The next letter relates to the destruction of the abbey of Evesham, and the sale of the stones.

CXXXVII.

PHILIP HOBY TO JOHN SCUDAMORE.

[From MS. Addit. No. 11,041, fol. 57.]

After my right hartty commendacions hadd, where at my last communycacion hadd with yow I desyred yow that I myght have hadd some partt off the stone that shuld be solde at Evisham ffor my money, the princypall and best whereoff, as I am informed, ys sold, yett fforasmoche as my necessyte which shall shorttely happen in buyldyng wyll requyre a grett partt off that stone that ys unsold there, this shalbe, therefore, right harttely to desyre and praye yow that ye wyll sell me resydew that there remaynyth, and I wyll paye thereffore yeven as ye shall thynke reasonable. And iff ye shuld nott shew me this pleasure, I were lyke in tyme of my necessyte to be very destitute. And as consernyng the spoyle or waste that ye wrate to me off that hath be done there,

I assure yow both I and myne be gyltles thereoff, besydes that hit did cost me money to persons ffor a long tyme nyghtly to weche and to take hede lest any thyng shuld to be mysordered there. I trust alsoo that att your there beyng and others the kynges highnes commyssyoners, ye remember that there was no lytell spoyle made, and I promyse yow sythens then your departure therehence there hath byn nothyng mynyshed to my knowlege ; and iff it bee, I wold the offenders were ponysshed to the example of other. Thus I wyll leve to wrytt unto yow any more at this tyme, trustyng that we shall mete shorttely and talke thereoff more largely, commyttyng yow to Goddes tuycion, who preserve yow with as good health as I wold to my selff, desyryng to use me as ye know ffor your assuryd to my power. Wrytten at the courtt, the last off October :

Your lovyng ffrend,
PHELYP HOBY.

To the right worshipfull
and my especyall good
ffrend, master Johan
Scudamore esquyer,
this be delyvered.

The priory of Worcester, attached to the cathedral, was founded in 971. Henry Holbech is said in the Monasticon to have been the last prior, More having been his predecessor. The manor of Batenhall was one of the possessions of the priory.

CXXXVIII.

ROBERT BURGOYN TO JOHN SCUDAMORE.

[From MS. Addit. No. 11,041, fol. 37.]

Right worshippffull, I commend me unto you and to good mistres Scudamore, etc. Sir, thies shall be to advertise you that I have sold as much off the stuffe off the late priorie off Worcester

as remayned in the custodye off the deane there, by inventorie, as
is appoynted by Mr. chauncelloures note made in the seid inventorie
to be sold, and have receyved money for all the same, savyng
xiij^s. ij^d., for such parcelles as your servaunte Baston hath taken
for you, which be such as he wold chuse; he hath a bill off the
parcells theroff. The council bord in the greate chamber was
bought and taken upp or he cam to Worcester; you have another
in manner as good as that. Sir, there be dyvers parcelles off
stuffe remaynyng at Battenhall, which Mr. Borne hath in fferme,
which be praysed at lviij^s. x^d., and olde Borne hath desiered daye
tyll candelmasse to knowe whether his sonne will have them or
no. He is bounde to paye ffor them then, or elles to bryng a discharge. There be dyvers other parcelles which Mr. More *quondam*
prior off Worcester hath in his custodye, wheroff you shall receyve a bill off parcelles with ther pryses by your servaunte berer
hereoff. He is at no poynt with me for them; his chapleyn was
with me, and have promised to give me an aunswere off the thynges
this daye at Glessam; he claymyth them by his pattent; neverthelesse I shewed his chapleyn that one off his beste beds with one
off the lyke coverlettes werre sold, and I mente them for you. I
entend to cause hym to come to you to take an order for the
same. Ferder I have receyved to the kyngs use cxliiij. oz. off
plate, which I do carry with me; and where ben reserved to the
kynges use x. copes off grene velvett, a coope off nedle worke
wrought with gold, and a coope priest dean and subdean off rede
velvett embrodered, which I assure you be but corse and base
thynges, the seid deane hath requyred me to have the delyvery
off them to Mr. chauncellour hym selff, consyderyng that wher they
lake ornamentes to ffurnysshe the churche, and the thynges off
them selff but course, he trustyth to obteyne them at Mr. chauncelloures hand agen to the use off the churche. I have a remembraunce off his hand for them, that he hath the custodye off them
to the kynges use; and he standeth bounden other to delyver them
to the seid Mr. chauncellour betwene this and the purification off

our ladye next commyng, or elles to bryng a discharge for them from the seid Mr. chauncellour by that daye; and to all such parcelles as ben appoynted in the seid inventorie to the church, to the deane, and to the bodye off the house, the deane standyth charged with thes parcelles styll by the seid inventorie delivered hym at the surrender off the seid late priorie, unto such tyme as the ffull establyshement off the college shall be forth, and commissioners appoynted to sett the same in an order, etc. And nowe, sir, to Lorrymers dowghteris mattier: Mr. Packingtons opynion is that she shall nott clayme yn by her graundefather, to whom she is off hole bludd, because off the ffeoffement; and she can nott be heyre to her syster Mergerie, because off the halff blodd; and seyth fferder that in his opynyon yff ther be none off the hole blodd to inherrytt that, then yt shall exchete to the lord and not goo to eny off the halff blodd. Mr. Packyngton and his wyffe have them hartely recommended unto you, and wold verry ffayne have sene you in ther house. Mistres Packyngton ys hungry, but she can not be fede: she hadd provyded a ffatt swane for you. And thus I committ you to God, as my selff. My lord suffragan hath hym hartely commended unto you. Written in haste, this presente Wendesdaye, at my departyng ffrom Worcester.

Your oune assuered,

ROBERT BURGOYN.

To the right worshippffull
Johan Scudeamore esquyer,
one off the kynges receyvours
off his courte off augmentations
be thies delyvered.

———————

The following letter also relates to the priory of Worcester.

CXXXIX.

ROBERT BURGOYNE TO JOHN SCUDAMORE.

[From MS. Addit. No. 11,041, fol. 35.]

Right worshippffull, I commend me hartely unto you, and I pray you that I may be the same to my good mistres your wyffe, assertenynge you that I have perused the copie off the councelles lettres which you sente unto me, wheruppon I have sente you an abstracte off such arrerages as have growne in the laste audite for such rentes and ffermes as werre dewe betwene Michaelmas anno xxxij^{do} H. viij^{vi}. and Michaelmas anno xxxiij^{tio} *ejusdem regis,* that ys to wytt such as I thynk to be good and trewe debtes, requyryng you accordyng unto your lettres to use some diligence in thaccomplisshyng off the councelles lettres theryn, as yt shall beste seme your wysdome. And as to the kynges lede lyeng in the kynges castell at Worcester, yff the walles theroff be close, then I thynk the same well enough, and yff not, I thynk yt myght be layed verrey well into the great belfrey within the newe college in Worcester, where I suppose yt might lye verrey sauffe. I thank you right hartely for my ij. baked salmons, which werre verrey well carried and well baked, and lykewyse seasoned, and came to me in verrey good tyme. And, sir, as for the table at Worcester, which I thought to have hadd home to me, I am right well contented that my mistres your wyffe shall have the same; neverthelesse I thynk I shall not bye soche anothere for money; at my commyng to London I shall so; neverthelesse, I wold yt werre so good as I cowlde fynd in my harte yt werre for her. I muste pray you to take no displeasur with your servaunte for his long tarryeng; his horse dyed at Dunstable, and I tarryed hym tyll Mundaye after the xijth. daye for the makyng off the seid abstracte off arrerages, etc. You muste send to Mr. Brougham my lettre herwith sente, when you send for the seid table; as knoweth God, who send us merye metynge. From Watton at Stone, the ix[th]. daye off Januarie.

Yours assured to his power,

ROBERT BURGOYN.

To the right worshipfull Johan
Scudamore esquyer, be this delivered.

The next letter relates to the abbey of Augustine Canons at Lilleshull, in Shropshire. This house was founded by Richard de Belmeis in 1145. The last abbot was Robert Watson.

CXL.

WILLIAM CHORLTON TO JOHN SCUDAMORE.

[From MS. Addit. No. 11,041, fol. 51.]

Jhesus.

Right wourshipfull Mr. Scudamor, in my hartiest maner I commend me unto you, ever more thankyng you for your kyndnes shewid unto me, trystyng to God that ye be amendyt of your fever, wiche shuld be gret comforthe unto me and many other, and so long to contenew to Godes pleasure. Sir, where hit pleased you to wryt your letter to Bostok and to Byst, that they shuld pay suche money as was in ther handes for the payment of the late abbott of Lilleshull and the brether ther for ther penciouns unto my handes, and farther your pleasure was that I shuld pay them, hit was so that Bostoke promysed to come unto me, but truthe hit ys that sythe the tyme of his promyse makyng he ys to London abowt besenes of his maysters, and he hathe recevid part of the rent and other part dothe remayne styll in the tennance handes ungedrede; and also as yet he ys not come home, nor no knolage ys to be had wat tyme he wyll come home. Moreover William Byst saythe that at his beyng with your mastership he payd all that he had to pay by your appoyntment, and hathe no more in his hands for to pay. In consideracion wherof, that hit may please your mastershipe to be so good master unto the late abbott and brether to pay them ther pensions, and rather at this my request by thes bereres, they ar moche bownden to pray for you. And so to retayne in your handes the fee wiche the late abbot hathe with goode will granted you, and the brether, as ye shall of your goodnes thynke convenyent at your pleasure. Sir, the late abbot hathe set to his seale to the acquittance, and other of the brether with ther names subscribed; and for the rest of the acquit-ance the bereres herof ar put in tryst in lyke maner. No more, but Jhesu have you in his blessed kepyng. At Wombrige, by yours ever to his litle power,

per me WYLLYM CHORLTON.

To the right worshipfull
Mr. Johan Scudamour, esquier,
theis be delivered.

CXLI.

JOHN FREMAN TO CROMWELL.

[From MS. Cotton. Titus, B. i. fol. 394.]

Yt may ples your good lordshipe to understond, that in the makynge of this half yeres resaite in Lincolnshier, I well parsayve of the gyvyn owte of late, not only there but also throwghowte the realme, thies superfluus ffees gyven by the late surrenderd howses. Whiche ffees be gyven in three sortes. The ffurst to bailles, ho hath for smale somes resayving large ffees, and where they have made a dosen, one war sufficient. Secondlye, they have gyven to generall resayvors greater ffees, whiche sorte shall never resayve no money; for the particuler bailles doth gather the rentes and so brynges it to the kinges resayvor, who stondes charged with the same. And the thirde sorte haith their ffees to be accounseill with the howse, and yet the greatest nomber of theym hath no lernynge. Inded they gave counsel to thabbott to gyve theym a covent seale to robe the kinge of part of his revenues. Wherfore me thinke they might lawfully at this parliament be called in agane, and the kinges highnes shuld resayve therbye within his realme iij. or four thowsand markes by the least yerly. And further as consarnynge the kinges leade within his realme, yf it wold ples his grace to make sales therof it shuld turne hym to a great proffite. Their be merchantes within his realme, I thinke a great sorte, wold gyve him iiij^{li}. for a foder, and fynd his grace suerties sufficient to be pad yerly one porcion therof, whiche I thinke wold be no less than xx.M^{li}., a yere for the space of foure yeres, whiche war a goodlye payment; and yet or the foure yeres war expired their wold every foder be worthe to the kinge xx. nobles, considering the costome in and owte. And further I thinke that c.M^{l}. of his pore sugetes shuld be benefite takers of their retorns, whither it war in money or in ware. And also the yeres beynge expired, it wold qwyken well agane one of the commodities of his realme that nowe is ded, whiche is the myndes of his leade. Yt may ples yow to consider that, and yf other owtward prynces wold take apon theym to redres their idell fayned religiouse howses, as the kinges highnes hath done, as I mystrust not but and their powers war accordinge as the kinges was and is they wolde so do, and than shall they have suche abundance of lead of suche like howses that they woll than sett litell by ours. Beschinge your lordship for my follyshe oppynyon so boldlye to you to write of, that ye wold take with me no displeasure. And thus I remayn your pore man. From Lowthe, the xth. day of May.

Yours,

JOHN FREMAN.

To the right honorable and his singuler
good lord my lord prevy seale be this yeven.

It appears that many of the accounts of the sales, &c. of the religious houses remained long unsettled. The following letter was written in the reign of Philip and Mary.

Several of the places enumerated in the following letter have been previously mentioned. At Ludlow in Shropshire there were houses of Austin and White friars, and a hospital of St. John the Baptist, of the history of which very little is known. The abbey of Dieulacres in Staffordshire was founded by Randulph earl of Chester in 1214; its last abbot was Thomas Whitney. The Benedictine priory of Tutbury in Staffordshire was founded by Henry de Ferrers, about the year 1080; the last prior was Arthur Meverell *alias* Throwley. The præmonstratensian abbey of Halesowen, of which the ruins are still interesting, was founded by king John; the last abbot was William Taylor. Dudley priory, in Worcestershire, was founded about the middle of the twelfth century by Gervase Paganell or Painel, who placed in it a party of Cluniac monks from Wenlock, of which house it was considered as a cell; the last prior was John Webley. At Westwood, in Worcestershire, there was an alien nunnery, dependent on the abbey of Fontevrault, but its history is obscure.

CXLII.

LETTER TO JOHN SCUDAMORE.

[From MS. Addit. No. 11,041, fol. 78.]

After our harty comendacyons, theise maye be to advertyse you that we have perused the indentures made bytwyxte Mr. Sheldon and you, and accordynge to the tenure of the same have charged the sayed master Sheldon with all the leade, bell metalle, and redy money mencyoned and conteigned in the sayed indenture, which beynge deducted oute of youer charge, yett there dothe remayne to be aunsweryd by you bothe leade and bell metalle as ffollowythe, that ys to saye, for leade att Bristoll, iij. ff. iiij^c. quarter, x.lb.; Wygmore, liij. ff. j. quarter ff. de. cxxij. lb.; Ludlowe, v. ff. iij. quarter, ff. ccciij. quarter c^{ne}.; at Severne, in the custodye of Thomas Irelonde, j. ff.; Rocestre, vj. ff.; Croxden, xiiij. ff. de.; Delacres, iiij. ff.; Tuttberye, vj. ff. j. quarter; *nuper prioratus canonicorum de* Stafford, xliiij. ff.; Lylleshull, v. ff.; Halesowen, x. ff.; the late monestarye of Shrewsborye, lxvij. ff. de. ccc. lb.; the celle of Dudley, iiij. ff.; and ffor belle metalle att Westwoode in the county of Worcestre, cccc. lb.; ffor the aunswere whereof we requyer you, by the vertue of the kynge and quenes majesties comyssyon to us dyrected, that withe as convenyente spede as you may after the receyte hereof you sende unto us youre suffycyente deputie to accoumpte byfore us for the same, so as hereuppon their majesties may be satisfyed by you of the dett that shall faul out uppon the same.   And bycause we be moche callyd uppon to reporte youer estate and dett herein, we therefore are constrayned the more ernestly to calle uppon you, whome we dought not wylle have suche regarde hereunto as bothe their majesties expectacyon herein may be served (as ys mete), as also for the full ende of this charge towardes youer selfe, with which as before the ende ys troblesome and comberous unto you, so will the ende thereof be to youer quyetnes and comforte.   Whereof, for that you are ouer oulde ffrende and of oulde acquayntaunce, we thought to advyse you the rather, for that commyssyon ys nowe oute for the ende of those causys, of which you nowe may be dyscharged yf the faulte be not in youer selfe.   We also advertysse you that Mr. Sheldone wylbe no further charged concernynge the leade and belles within youer late circuyte there thenne ys conteyned in the indentures bytwyxte you and hym; and therefore you muste aunswere the reste youer selfe, whereunto we dought not but you wyll have suche respecte as we may receyve youer aunswere withe expedy-cyon.   And so we bydde you hartely ffare well.   From Westminster, laste of February, 1555.

Youer very lovynge ffrendes,

WILLIAM BERNERS.
THO. MILDMAY.
JOHAN WYSEMAN.

To the worshippfull Johan
Skudemore, esquyer, in haste.

INDEX.